Hate in the
Homeland

homeland noun

home·land | \ ˈhōm-ˌland *also* -lənd \

Definition of *homeland*

1. native land : FATHERLAND
2. a state or area set aside to be a state for a people of a particular national, cultural, or racial origin

—*Merriam-Webster.com*

Hate in the Homeland

The New Global Far Right

Cynthia Miller-Idriss

Princeton University Press

Princeton and Oxford

This book is dedicated to
all victims of hate and their families,
along with the broader communities who
suffer with and support them

Contents

Preface and Acknowledgments

Academic scholars are notoriously slow creatures. Most of us take years to plan, conduct, and analyze research, and then need years more to write up the data, go through academic peer-review processes, and finally publish the results—often in journals or other outlets that primarily target peers within our own academic fields and communities rather than those outside of academia. And because academic careers are rewarded for this kind of scholarship, it can be particularly challenging to develop and share expertise in ways that broader publics find both relevant and responsive. I am no exception to this dilemma. Each of my previous books took approximately a decade to research and write. Until quite recently, most of my writing and speaking has been directed toward other academics, rather than to broader publics.

This book is different. It is a book written to and for the public—for educators, policy makers, parents, coaches, and anyone who interacts with people who are at risk for radicalization to hate. It came out of the learning that took place as I was rapidly thrust into a new, more public world while I was writing my previous book, *The Extreme Gone Mainstream*. Seemingly overnight, my previously niche, subcultural research in a foreign country, had mainstream relevance at home, in ways I never could have anticipated. I was suddenly privy to more generalist and policy-related conversations about the underlying problems and grievances fueling rising extremist violence, about the drivers and organizational tactics of terrorist and violent extremist groups, and about what might work to stem rising hate and extremism. Journalists, policy makers, friends, colleagues, and random people on trains asked me to explain the global dimensions of far-right extremism, how mainstreaming happens, and how far-right youth culture and the tactics and strategies of far-right groups and movements are evolving. These conversations took place in the media, in a variety of government agencies and offices, and in broader circles of interventionists, educators, funders, and policy makers. My learning curve was necessarily swift as I worked to distill what I had learned from twenty years of empirical work on the ground with youth in and around far-right scenes—and school-based efforts to combat extremism—into broader discussions and frames.

The urgency around the current state of far-right and white-supremacist extremism globally changed the way I write. From the time that this book was first conceived, in a conversation with an editor in winter 2019, to its actual publication in fall 2020, only about eighteen months passed, including the entire production process. The pace of writing forced me out of my quiet office with its dual screens and ergonomic keyboard to whatever spaces and places I was in, whenever I could squeeze out time to write. I wrote this book on my laptop in doctors' and dentists' office waiting rooms, on trains and planes, and even in the passenger seat of a car on two ten-hour summer drives. I wrote in the early dawn hours, before I had even brushed my teeth. I wrote in the middle of the night, when I woke up and could not fall back asleep.

Taking advantage of all the possible moments to write was one reason I could pull this book together with relative speed. But the other major reason is that I already had been encouraged to write quite a lot about this topic before I realized it would become a book. I am immensely grateful to the many editors and hosts who nudged me toward exploration of the ideas I develop here. Since I finished my previous book, I've given more than fifty invited talks, keynotes, plenary speeches, conference papers, and visiting lectures, across the United States and in ten other countries. Each of these talks was crucial for allowing me to explore the ideas that made their way into these pages. In invited discussions and briefings for policy makers, governmental agencies, embassy representatives, intelligence analysts, law enforcement, and other public authorities in the United States and abroad, I was not only forced to hone these arguments but also had the opportunity to learn from scholars, practitioners, and policy makers through shared presentations, discussions, and roundtables. Scores of extremism and terrorism experts and researchers, from think tanks, government agencies, nongovernmental organizations, research institutes and centers, and advocacy groups, contributed immensely to my learning in a wide variety of focused research conversations and discussions. My September 2019 written and oral congressional testimony before the US House of Representatives Committee on Foreign Affairs' Subcommittee on the Middle East, North Africa, and International Terrorism and the Committee on Homeland Security's Subcommittee on Intelligence and Counterterrorism helped further clarify and articulate my arguments about how we should understand white-supremacist and far-right extremism, how to assess the threat, and what should be done about it.

In over two dozen op-eds and short essays during the same period, I articulated early arguments that would later develop into the chapters of this book. These essays were key to my thinking processes and decision to write this book.[1] Feedback from readers, listeners, viewers, and editors helped refine my thinking. I am equally indebted to the dozens of journalists, students, and colleagues whose insightful and sometimes challenging questions in media interviews, classrooms, and hallway conversations forced me to better articulate the logic of my arguments in a variety of places. The out-of-the-box thinking and innovative ideas constantly batted about by my colleagues in our newly launched Polarization and Extremism Research and Innovation Lab (PERIL) in American University's Center for University Excellence (CUE) were essential to the conceptual development of my arguments as well as my specific thinking about intervention and prevention.

There are several individuals whose support, coauthorship, editorial advice, or keen eyes have helped shape my thinking in ways that show up in this book in big and small ways that deserve mention. In particular, I owe a tremendous intellectual debt to Akiko, Archie, Audra, Brian, Brian, Caleb, Cas, Daniel, Eviane, Fabian, Graham, Heidi, Hilary, John, Kathy, Larry, Mabel, Matthew, Maureen, Meagan, Oren, Pete, Scott, Shannon, Tamir, and Will. For research assistance and other support essential to this book's production, I am grateful to David, Emily, Jackie, James, La'Nita, Laurie, Kathryn, and Maia. Several colleagues read early versions of chapters or the entire draft manuscript and provided feedback, and for this I am especially indebted to Brian, Caleb, Cas, Daisy, Daniel, Emily, Erin, Gary, John, Jon, Kai, Kathleen, Liz, and Ryan, along with three anonymous Princeton University Press reviewers. My immediate and extended family, along with Jan, Julie, Andrew, Sarah, Ryan, and their families, deserve incredible thanks for putting up with me, especially while I wrote this book. I owe them everything.

Abbreviations

ADL   Anti-Defamation League
AfD   Alternative für Deutschland (Alternative for Germany)
AIM   American Identity Movement
AmRen   *American Renaissance*
C-REX   Center for Research on Extremism
CUE   Center for University Excellence
DHS   Department of Homeland Security
DOE   Department of Education
DVKE   German Association of Martial Arts Schools against Violent Extremism
FHU   Foundation for Human Understanding
GIRDS   German Institute for Radicalization and Deradicalization Studies
ISSEP   Institute for Social Sciences, Economics and Politics
KKK   Ku Klux Klan
LGBTQ+   lesbian, gay, bisexual, transgender, queer, and others
MMA   mixed martial arts
NAFTA   North American Free Trade Agreement
NATO   North Atlantic Treaty Organization
NGO   nongovernmental organization
NPI   National Policy Institute
NPR   National Public Radio
NSDAP   Nationalsozialistische Deutsche Arbeiterpartei
PC   politically correct
PERIL   Polarization and Extremism Research and Innovation Lab
RAM   Rise Above Movement
RAN   Radicalisation Awareness Network
SPLC   Southern Poverty Law Center
TRF   Testing Research Fund
TP   Terza Posizione
TPUSA   Turning Point USA
TTPs   tactics, techniques, and procedures
UCL   University College London
UFC   Ultimate Fighting Championship

Hate in the
Homeland

Introduction

The Where and When of Radicalization

On August 3, 2019, Americans went to bed grieving a white-supremacist mass shooting that killed twenty-two people in El Paso, Texas. The next day, we awoke to the news of another mass shooting in Dayton, Ohio, which left ten dead. Although the ideological motive for the Dayton shooting would turn out to be muddled, its timing—so quickly on the heels of El Paso—helped boost the global far right anyway. Within hours of the shootings, extremists were celebrating on social media with phrases like "it's happening!" and "the fire rises!"[1]

These shootings came nearly two years after the world was stunned by scenes from the University of Virginia showing scores of white men in polo shirts marching across campus, bearing flaming tiki torches and chanting "white lives matter" and "Jews will not replace us." The following afternoon, the governor of Virginia declared a state of emergency in response to the violence at the Unite the Right rally, downtown. Shortly thereafter, a twenty-two-year-old neo-Nazi drove his car into a crowd of counterprotesters, injuring at least nineteen people and killing thirty-two-year-old Heather Heyer.[2] All of this came on the heels of an increase in violent hate crimes. Dylann Roof had recently received a death penalty sentence for murdering nine African American worshippers in a South Carolina church, amid a wave of hate incidents in schools, college campuses, and public places across the country. In short, the events at Charlottesville catapulted the modern far right into the public eye and helped cement a growing realization: white-supremacist and far-right movements were unquestionably on the rise in the United States.

In the months that followed, a steady stream of hate confirmed that Charlottesville was not an exception. In 2018, the number of hate groups in the United States reached an all-time high, with white-nationalist groups alone experiencing a nearly 50 percent increase.[3] That same year, right-wing extremists killed at least fifty people in the United States, outnumbering all other terrorist- and extremist-related deaths.[4] Meanwhile, hate incidents have surged in local communities nationwide, with thousands of incidents of swastikas, nooses, white-supremacist fliers, and hate crimes reported across the country, from synagogue shootings in Pittsburgh and Poway, California, to arson attacks on Black churches in the south. In spring 2019, a private militia self-deployed to the US-Mexican border and—under no authority from the US government—began illegally holding migrants and turning them over to US immigration authorities.[5] Combined with global developments like the March 2019 right-wing terror attack on two mosques in New Zealand, which killed fifty-one worshippers, these trends have spurred an increase in attention to the far right. Ordinary Americans along with journalists, policy makers, and scholars alike have scrambled to answer several key questions: What is driving growth in the contemporary far right? Why do people join far-right movements? How should communities respond when far-right propaganda or violence occurs?

Most attempts to answer these questions have focused on two broad categories of explanation, examining either far-right groups or the individuals who join those groups. We might think of these as "top–down" and "bottom–up" approaches. Top–down approaches generally focus on groups, organizations, and broad social structural issues like economic changes, globalization, demographic shifts, and the impact of new media technologies. Scholarship on groups and organizations, for example, looks at the strategies and tactics of formal extremist organizations in their messaging, recruitment techniques, and radicalization efforts. Researchers have studied the varied ways that groups communicate extremist messages and ideology; how they recruit, radicalize, and plan violence; and whether and how banning groups from social media or financial platforms can constrain their growth or impact. Sometimes these are referred to as the "supply-side" aspects of extremism: how top–down messaging and structural or organizational dynamics among extremist groups shape patterns of radicalization and terrorist violence.

Studies of individuals, on the other hand, focus from the "bottom up"—on ways that individuals can be drawn into extremist groups and movements. This is referred to as the "demand-side" aspect of radicalization toward extremist violence. Research on individuals usually focuses on vulnerabilities that might make people more receptive to extreme ideas, including individual psychological and personality traits, personal and early childhood trauma, exposure to violence, and a variety of cognitive aspects of radicalization—in other words, what is happening inside people's heads. This includes research on the emotional and intellectual aspects of radicalization, such as the role of individual grievances related to perceived marginalization, disenfranchisement, or relative inequality; a sense of betrayal, anger, and shame; exposure to violence; or the desire for belonging, meaning, purpose, and engagement. Scholarship on individual vulnerabilities has been key to helping understand both what drives individuals to the far right as well as what kinds of de-radicalization interventions might work to draw them away.

This book takes a different approach. In addition to focusing on the *why* and *how* of far-right radicalization and growth, I suggest we should be asking *where* and *when* radicalization happens. Where do people encounter extremist messages in their day-to-day lives? What are the new spaces and places of contemporary far-right extremism? Answering these questions requires looking closely at the physical and virtual scenes, the imagined territories and sacred geographies, and the cultural spaces where hate is cultivated. By asking where and when radicalization happens, we shift the lens to people's ordinary and everyday encounters with radicalization messages—or what I call new gateways where people can be radicalized toward far-right ideologies and actions. This includes, for example, cultural spaces like far-right coffee shops, pop and country music, clothing brands, fight and fitness clubs and the mixed martial arts (MMA) scene, schools and college campuses, social media and online spaces, clubs and soccer stadiums, and spaces and places specific to microcommunities that overlap with far-right-extremist groups, from evangelical churches to doomsday prepper communities and gun shows. It also includes imagined or symbolic spaces like the "American heartland" and national homelands—geographic ideas reconceived in racist and exclusionary ways by the far right, as white spaces that need to be protected from incursions, invasions, and being overrun.

By de-emphasizing formal social and political movements and far-right individuals and focusing instead on where extremism is concentrated, *Hate in the Homeland* offers a new lens with which to examine individuals' experiences with extremism. It focuses on the kinds of places where young people in particular may encounter extremist messages and ideas in their ordinary lives—perhaps long before they have made an ideological commitment to the far right—and the role that these new, mainstream gateways may play in shaping extremist engagement. Before we can even begin to address these questions, though, it is important to be clear about just what the "far right" means, and how it should be understood in its modern form.

What Is the Far Right?

In order to fully understand the far right, we have to look at four separate but overlapping categories: antigovernment and antidemocratic practices and ideals, exclusionary beliefs, existential threats and conspiracies, and apocalyptic fantasies.

Antigovernment and Antidemocratic Practices and Ideals

Far-right ideas run fundamentally counter to the norms, values, and beliefs that underpin democratic practice across the globe, threatening hallmarks like free and fair elections; systems of checks and balances; the protection of individual freedom; the rule of law; and freedoms of the press, religion, speech, and assembly.[6] Far-right movements pose a challenge because they seek to undermine one or more of these key features, challenging how rulers are elected (by promoting authoritarianism, for example) or seeking to loosen the limits placed on rulers once in office—and thereby reducing the protections guaranteed to the people against unjust rule.[7]

Some far-right groups and movements seek to undermine democracy globally, through extreme actions that include disinformation campaigns, election interference, attacks on freedom of the press, violating the constitutional protection of minority rights, or using violence and terrorism to achieve political goals. Others engage in radical actions that promote authoritarianism, seek to undermine the free movement of people, advocate for restrictions on rights, challenge principles of equality and egalitarian liberty, and interfere with the functioning and rule of democratic states. The goals of the extreme far right lead to nondemocratic ends, typically around the establishment of white ethno-states, the re-migration and deportation of nonwhites or non-Europeans, and the reduction of rights for ethnic minorities.

Historically, the far right has worked actively against mainstream governments, but in recent years, there has been a tactical shift toward trying to undermine governance from within. In the United States, where the political system does not allow for smaller or third parties to engage seriously in mainstream politics, far-right groups have encouraged members to run on Republican platforms and have worked to get far-right anti-immigration platforms onto mainstream political agendas.[8] In Europe, far-right movements have taken a different approach, running for office and winning parliamentary seats in nearly every European country. More importantly, as mainstreaming strategies and tactics have become more effective all around the globe, they have forced issues and ideals of the far right into the mainstream. For their part, established conservative political parties have fought to retain the voters to whom far-right arguments and policies appeal. This has made it harder and more confusing for the public to distinguish between groups that once reflected the extreme fringe from those who are in the mainstream conservative right. Some far-right groups are explicitly antigovernment, antiauthority, or intentionally separate from mainstream society, organizing themselves into patriot militias, sovereign citizen groups, paramilitaries, and doomsday prepper groups. But the election of Donald Trump shows how a candidate running on a mainstream political platform can be successful by capitalizing on the appeal of anti-elite and antigovernment arguments, most clearly expressed in his promise to "drain the swamp" of the current government.

In sum, the far right is a fluid spectrum of groups and individuals who represent more extreme and less extreme versions of the antidemocratic and illiberal ideals, practices, and beliefs described above. Some far-right ideas have bled into the mainstream, and mainstream politicians, pundits, and media platforms also reinforce, validate, and legitimize far-right ideas. This is clearest in the adoption of exclusionary and dehumanizing language, which is at the core of far-right ideology.

Exclusionary and Dehumanizing Ideologies

Far-right ideologies are hierarchical and exclusionary. They establish clear lines of superiority and inferiority according to race, ethnicity, nationality, gender, religion, and sexuality. This includes a range of racist, anti-immigrant, nativist, nationalist, white-supremacist, anti-Islam, anti-Semitic, and anti-LGBTQ+ (lesbian, gay, bisexual, transgender, queer, and others) beliefs. At their extreme, these are ideologies that dehumanize groups of people who are deemed to be inferior, in ways that have justified generations of violence in such forms as white supremacy, patriarchy, Christian supremacy, and compulsory heterosexuality. These kinds of ideologies have imbued individuals from the dominant groups with a sense of perceived superiority over others: slaves, nonwhites, women, non-Christians, or the LGBTQ+ community.

Dehumanization refers to language and beliefs that position entire groups of people as subhuman or less than human. It rests on the unconscious belief that while some groups of beings appear fully human, "beneath the surface, where it really counts, they aren't human at all."[9] Such beliefs are what allow individuals to imagine other people as subhuman animals who "have the essence of creatures that elicit negative responses, such as disgust, fear, hatred, and contempt, and are usually thought of as predators, unclean animals, or prey."[10] Sometimes this belief is expressed explicitly, such as the Nazi labeling of Jews as *Untermenschen* (subhumans), but often it is evoked through the use of metaphors like rats, wolves, cockroaches, vermin, and snakes, or with language that evokes those animals—such as references to immigrant infestations, invasions, swarms, "shithole" countries, or being overrun. It also comes across in language that equates immigrants from particular regions or countries as rapists or criminals, or positions Muslims or Islam as an existential threat to European or Western civilization.

While dehumanization is often cited as a foundational aspect of exclusionary far-right ideologies, it is also important to acknowledge the counterargument made by philosopher Kate Manne in her analysis of misogyny. Manne argues that dehumanization cannot entirely account for the kinds of brutal mistreatment that human beings are capable of enacting toward one another. Instead, she suggests, "the mistreatment of historically subordinated people who are perceived as threatening the status quo often needs no special psychological story, such as dehumanization, to account for it." Rather, "people may know full well that those they treat in brutally degrading and inhumane ways are fellow human beings," despite the horrific violence they may perpetrate against them. Manne argues that the notion of aggrieved entitlement holds more explanatory value—the idea that dominant groups are being surpassed by individuals from groups they deem beneath them in social status, taking jobs or positions to which they believe they are entitled.[11]

Whether rooted in dehumanization or aggrieved entitlement, white supremacism in the United States has been the primary—although not the only—form of exclusionary ideology, and is therefore especially key to understanding the American far right. Racist ideas coalesced into a fully fledged ideology sometime around the 1830s, initially oriented around the defense of slavery but eventually fixated on opposition to equality for African Americans.[12] Uniquely American variations on white supremacy emerged over time, including Christian-identity groups who believe whites are God's chosen people, white-supremacist prison gangs like the Aryan Brotherhood, and groups inspired by overseas ideologies, including neo-Nazis and racist skinheads. The so-called "alt right" and "alt lite" that emerged in the 2010s are the latest American innovation in the white-supremacist scene.[13]

At their core, then, all far-right ideological beliefs share exclusionary, hierarchical, and dehumanizing ideals that prioritize and seek to preserve the superiority and dominance of some groups over others. Modern far-right groups will often use suggestive or coded language that implies exclusionary beliefs rather than espousing them directly. The rapidly growing Identitarian movement, for example, uses euphemisms like "European heritage" or "European descent" to talk about whiteness. Racist and white-supremacist ideas are not the only entry point to the far right. Far-right groups focused on other themes—like antiabortion extremists—can also become gateways to white-supremacist extremism, in part because of the considerable overlap among groups in online spaces. For example, incel (involuntary celibate) and men's rights groups—often referred to in online spaces as the "manosphere"—espouse misogynistic beliefs that sometimes overlap with white-supremacist and racist ideologies. In fall 2019, for example, the neo-Nazi Andrew Anglin referred to himself as the "self-appointed spiritual successor to Elliot Rodger" in a caption under a photo of the female founder of the Institute for Research on Male Supremacism.[14] Rodger is the name of a 2014 Isla Vista, California, shooter who murdered six people after becoming radicalized as an incel. He was initially labeled a "misfit" whose mental health and personality problems led him to lash out in anger at women for rejecting him and at men who were more successful at dating.[15] But after a 2018 Toronto van attack inspired in part by Rodger killed ten people, along with other incel-inspired mass violence such as a shooting in a Florida yoga studio, closer analysis of Rodger's manifesto revealed that his misogynistic views were strongly laced with racist and white-supremacist beliefs as well. The fact that Rodger has now been lauded by a neo-Nazi on his prominent far-right website is just one more illustration of the overlaps among misogynistic incel movements and the far right. This also confirms the potential for groups in one part of the far-right spectrum—such as incels—to act as gateways for other parts of the spectrum.

A common focal point for exclusionary ideologies is the issue of immigration and demographic change. In Europe and the United States, native and white populations are aging out of the majority, while nonwhite and immigrant-origin populations are growing. In the United States, the country is projected to be minority white by the year 2045.[16] These trends are used by far-right groups to mobilize followers around themes of white identity and the need for its protection and defense. The clearest example, of course, is in the conspirational narrative about a great replacement.

Existential Demographic Threats and Dystopian Conspiracy Theories

The extreme far right not only expresses exclusionary and dehumanizing ideologies, but also embeds those ideologies within a framework of existential threat to the dominant group—such as white people, men, Europeans, Americans, or Christians. In its suggestive form, this sense of existential threat appears in language about the need to defend or protect the country, the homeland, or the dominant people from immigration or demographic change. In its most extreme iterations, far-right extremists rely on three overlapping dystopian fantasy theories: the "great replacement" (used globally), white genocide (used predominantly in the United States), and "Eurabia" (used primarily in Europe). They are dystopian because they imagine a frightening future of decline, degradation, or chaos. All three theories emphasize the need to preserve and defend whiteness against an invasion of immigrants, Muslims, or Jews who will eradicate or replace white nationals, Christians, Americans, or Europeans. These fantasies rely on a sense of white victimhood and are frequently tied to emotional appeals to protect, defend, and take heroic action to restore sacred national space, territory, and homelands.

The "great replacement" is currently the leading far-right conspiracy theory of demographic change. It argues that there is an intentional, global plan orchestrated by national and global elites to replace white, Christian, European populations with nonwhite, non-Christian ones.[17] The term was coined by French scholar Renaud Camus in 2011 and was quickly taken up globally by white supremacists, for whom the theory now provides a single, overarching framework for ideas that had already been percolating for years in more disparate ways. Decades before Camus wrote *Le Grand Remplacement*, the American neo-Nazi David Lane had already popularized the idea of "white genocide," arguing that white populations were dying out demographically due to immigration, abortion, and violence against whites. Lane's famous "14 Words"—"We must secure the existence of our people and a future for white children"—is a call to defend whites against genocide,[18] and the term, or even just the number fourteen, became a global mantra for white supremacists and pan-Aryans, frequently paired with the number eighty-eight (for the eighth letter of the alphabet, "H," making "HH," or Heil Hitler). In the American case, the idea of a "great replacement" is underlaid with anti-Semitism and linked to a broader conspiracy theory that suggests that an organized international group of Jewish elites is deliberately funding or otherwise supporting migration in an intentional effort to create multicultural societies.

While Lane was busy peddling anti-Semitic conspiracy theories about white genocide in the United States, a parallel theory of demographic replacement emerged in Europe. Coined by the British author Bat Ye'or and published in 2005 in a book of the same name, the concept of "Eurabia" suggests that Muslims are deliberately working to replace white Europeans through immigration and high birthrates in order to broaden the territory of the Caliphate. Ye'or argues that this will create a territorial space in which white Europeans are subject to Sharia law and Islamic rule, forced to convert to Islam or surrender into subservient roles.[19] The end result, described as Eurabia, is a Europe that has been converted from a white, Christian civilization to an Islamic one.[20] Eurabia is clearly a motivating concept for violent extremists, most notably discussed in the manifesto of the Norwegian terrorist who murdered seventy-seven people—mostly children—in Oslo in 2011. But Eurabia was also invoked in a 2019 advertising campaign for Germany's Alternative for Germany (Alternative für Deutschland, AfD) party, which used Jean-Léon Gérôme's 1866 *The Slave Market* painting, depicting a naked white women having her teeth and mouth probed by a turban-clad Arab man. In a billboard-size poster, *The Slave Market* image is overlaid with text urging voters to learn from history and vote for the AfD "so that Europe does not become Eurabia."[21]

Together, the great replacement, Eurabia, and white-genocide theories have helped to inspire a sense of shared mission among the global far right, who see themselves as facing a common demographic threat. But what has changed in recent years is that we are closer to the demographic changes that underpin replacement and genocide conspiracy theories. It is well documented that whites in the United States will be an ethnic plurality—the largest group in a nation with no ethnic majority—in a couple of decades. National political leaders regularly frame this demographic reality as a threat and a problem, which reinforces and legitimizes white supremacists' fears and sense of urgency. The neo-Nazi Matthew Heimbach summed this up in a recent conversation with journalist Vegas Tenold:

> The majority of births in this country aren't European American. There's no way to stop this thing, even if you were to ban all immigration. Whites will be the minority in twenty-five years, and people are beginning to see it now, but more importantly they are starting to feel it. Nobody wants to be a minority. Being a minority fucking sucks. Look at how we've treated black people. Don't for a second think that they'll treat us any better, which is why people are starting to realize that we need to think racially.[22]

Conspiracies like the great replacement and mottos like "14 Words" are used to inspire anger, resentment, and hate, coupled with fear of existential danger and a sense of betrayal and backlash against those elites who are deemed responsible. But existential threats and dystopian fantasies can also be used to call for cohesion, shared purpose, and meaning. They can offer a sense of belonging, brotherhood, and the opportunity to engage in what is seen as heroic action to save one's people from an imminent threat. They rely on a sense of nostalgia (or faux nostalgia, based on a past that never was) and utopian desires for a better future, the restoration of a beloved homeland, and a righteous call for justice. This combination of both negative and positive emotions—not only anger and resentment but also the desire for belonging, meaning, and purpose—is proving to be a deadly formula for recruitment and radicalization to far-right extremism.

These three overlapping fantasies—the great replacement, white genocide, and Eurabia—create a sense of urgency and call whites to action. Each has already inspired mass terrorist violence by far-right extremists.[23] The terrorist responsible for killing seventy-seven people in Norway in 2011 wrote a manifesto heavily referencing the concept of Eurabia.[24] The shooter who allegedly gunned down fifty-one Muslim worshippers at two Christchurch mosques in 2019 justified his actions based on the great replacement theory. Before he allegedly murdered twenty-two people in an El Paso Walmart, a Texas man posted a document online that explicitly referenced the Christchurch shooting and referred to a "Hispanic invasion of Texas."[25] The terrorist who allegedly murdered thirteen people in a Pittsburgh synagogue in 2018 was motivated by white-genocide theories suggesting Jews were orchestrating the resettlement of refugees in order to create a multicultural society that would eventually eradicate whites. Together, white genocide, Eurabia, and now the overarching theory of the great replacement have helped foster transnational inspiration and a sense of shared mission among the global far right.

These conspiracy theories represent ideas that have been core to white-supremacist beliefs for decades. They place blame on ethnic and racial minorities or immigrants for the degradation of society, coupled with global elite manipulation and intentional orchestration.[26] But the past several years has seen one of the most significant shifts in the history of global white supremacy. The far right has increasingly moved from the realm of fantasy to one of reality. Conspiracies today are not mere stories to frame far-right ideas. They are motivating violent action. After I testified before the US Congress on white-nationalist terrorism in September 2019, someone wrote to me from an anonymous account to tell me that "White genocide is not a theory," noting that I am "complicit" in the US state sponsorship of "genocide against the White population of America and those European descent worldwide [sic]." For growing numbers of individuals like this, white genocide is no longer just a fantasy or a theory. It is a deeply held belief. What were once frequently written off as fringe conspiracy theories and doomsday cult fantasies about demographic replacement are now beliefs that forge global connections across the far right and inspire individuals to engage in violent terrorist acts. This happens in part through a specific principle that motivates extreme violence—far-right acceleration.

Acceleration, Destabilization, and Apocalyptic Fantasies

As the previous sections have established, the far right relies on a set of dehumanizing and exclusionary ideologies that establish hierarchies of racial and ethnic difference and then position whites as facing an existential threat from demographic change. The inevitable result, according to this logic, will be the replacement of Western civilizations with Islamic ones, the implementation of Sharia law, and the ultimate genocide of white populations by nonwhite or non-Christian immigrants. On the extreme fringe, the far right believes that the only way to prevent this process is through an apocalyptic race war, which will result in the rebirth of a new world order and a restored white civilization.[27] This is an exceptionally similar ideology to the Islamist extremist effort to restore the Caliphate—in this sense, Islamist and far-right extremists share a similar apocalyptic vision and use the same kinds of violent terrorist strategies in an effort to accelerate the process toward the end times. This becomes particularly relevant for what is known as reciprocal radicalization or cumulative extremism—acts of terror that develop out of revenge or in response to terrorist acts from the "other side."[28] The 2019 Islamist extremist Easter attacks in Sri Lankan churches, for example, were a direct response to the Christchurch mosque attacks a few weeks prior.

At the most-extreme fringe, far-right extremists not only believe that a violent apocalypse is coming, but also argue that the best and fastest way to reach the phase of rebirth is to accelerate the path to the apocalypse and eventual new world order by speeding up polarization and societal discord as a way of undermining social stability overall.[29]

Violence is foundational to this approach, because violent acts create immediate societal panic, inspire copycat actors, and encourage reciprocal or revenge terror attacks from affected groups. For this reason, each violent act of terror is viewed as heroic, celebrated in the name of the global cause, and is understood to bring white supremacists one step closer to the end-times collapse and subsequent restoration of a new white civilization. This principle—acceleration—is a key aspect motivating terrorist violence from the far right.

Acceleration is not unique to the far right. A variety of fringe groups and philosophies across the political spectrum can be characterized as "accelerationist" for the ways they aim to hasten the demise of current economic and political systems and create a new one. What unites accelerationists is a sense that global economic, technological, political, environmental, and demographic changes are happening faster than anyone can control, with disastrous effects on human well-being. Since those changes—so it is argued—can't be effectively directed, a more strategic path is to accelerate the inevitable collapse of political and economic systems and start anew.[30] The apocalyptic fantasy component of white-supremacist extremist ideology and accelerationism also overlaps significantly with the beliefs of survivalist and extreme prepper groups, along with doomsday cults and Islamist-motivated extremism.

Although accelerationism isn't unique to the far right, violent far-right extremists' adoption of it as a strategy is recent and reflects a major shift from the realm of apocalyptic fantasies into direct action. In Germany, eight members of the group Revolution Chemnitz have been on trial since fall 2019, charged with forming a right-wing terrorist organization.[31] The group had plans to launch a "civil-war-like rebellion" in Berlin on October 2, 2018, and five of the defendants allegedly led a "test run" in September 2018 in Chemnitz, using glass bottles, weighted knuckle gloves, and an electroshock appliance to attack several foreign residents.[32] Similar approaches are evident in the neo-Nazi terrorist group Atomwaffen, active in the United States since 2015 and responsible for five recent murders.[33] Atomwaffen follows a set of strategies laid out in neo-Nazi James Mason's book *Siege*, which calls for leaderless terrorist cells and guerrilla war against "the System." The group openly calls for violence as the primary strategy to achieve white revolutionary goals.[34] Similar themes are evident in the plans of the white-supremacist group the Base to lead a "violent insurgency" against nonwhites and the US government; several members of the group were arrested in January 2020, just prior to a gun-rights rally in Richmond, Virginia, where "credible intelligence" of extremist violence led Governor Ralph Shearer Northam to declare a state of emergency.[35]

In sum, white-supremacist extremism is a global ideology based on extreme and violent ideological beliefs that rely on violence—as a solution and an imperative response—to a perceived existential threat to white civilization posed by demographic change and immigration. Individuals do not need to believe in the full theory of an apocalyptic solution in order to be drawn to the vision of rebirth and renewal. Indeed, the language of restoration and renewal is key to a range of populist nationalist and far-right movements, through both a sense of nostalgia for a traditional past and utopian fantasies about the future. In the United States, the language of a coming civil war—evoked periodically by conservatives and the far right alike—evokes the same kinds of emotions and a sense of end times. These kinds of stories are what J. M. Berger calls violence-inducing "crisis narratives"—descriptions of threatening developments in the world that require solutions through violent, hostile action against enemies to protect one's group and identity. Importantly, crisis narratives don't come only from the extreme fringe—they also originate in the mainstream, as illustrated today in the "constant stream of crisis narratives" from elected politicians and media pundits.[36] In this way, extreme ideas can be reinforced and normalized by the mainstream.

Contested Labels

Although there is broad agreement about the range of ideas, beliefs, and practices the far-right spectrum represents, there has been no agreement to date among policy makers, scholars, or the media on which term best reflects the phenomenon. No single term currently in use captures the broad range of ideologies, frameworks, and actions espoused by the far right in one phrase. Terms currently in use in the United States to refer to parts or all of the far-right spectrum include the extreme right, right wing, radical right, right-wing radicalism, right-wing extremism, right-wing terrorism, white power, white nationalism, white supremacism, white separatism, neo-Nazism, counter-jihadism, Identitarianism, racially and ethnically motivated extremism, alt right, and alt lite. Some parts of the far right also include antigovernment, antiauthoritarian, sovereign citizen, patriot militia, and paramilitary movements. There is overlap with groups such as conspiracy theorists, doomsday preppers, and apocalyptic cults, along with "single-issue" extremist groups like incels (involuntary celibates), antiabortion extremists, anti-Muslim extremists, and anti-immigration extremists.[37]

The FBI has controversially proposed the designation "racially motivated violent extremism" to encompass both white-supremacist groups as well as what they previously—in a highly criticized move—labeled "black identity extremists."[38] The term has been critiqued for drawing a false equivalency between the extremist fringe of black-separatist and white-supremacist groups. Many scholars argue that the better equivalency is between Islamist and white-supremacist extremists, who both work toward an apocalyptic end times, prioritize the restoration of sacred geographies (the Caliphate, a white ethno-state), and believe in mass-scale violent attacks as an imperative to accelerate societal chaos and lead toward an eventual world collapse and rebirth into a restored (Islamic or white) civilization and new world order.[39] This is further complicated by a distinction that the US federal government draws between international and domestic terrorism. The category of international terrorism includes a category of "homegrown violent extremists" inside the United States who are understood to be radicalized by a global ideology. But there is currently no such category for domestic terrorism, which is understood as comprising individuals who are motivated by ideology that comes from "domestic influences, such as racial bias and anti-government sentiment."[40] This distinction is unfortunate because it can lead individuals to overlook the many ways that far-right extremism, especially today, is globally networked and intertwined. White-supremacist extremists are inspired to act not only

because of domestic issues, but also through a global and intercon-
nected ideology of a great replacement and the need to accelerate violent acts to bring about the collapse of current society and the rebirth
of a new white civilization.[41]

The term "white nationalism" is problematic for similar reasons, inadvertently softening the extreme nature of white-supremacist ideas
with the more neutral term "nationalism," and simultaneously obscuring the global interconnectedness of the far right, making it seem as if
movements are only domestically oriented instead of collaborating with
and learning from one another.[42] The definitional challenges are global
as well. Other countries have distinctive ways of depicting the far right
that contribute to the difficulty in defining a common set of terms cross-
nationally. In Germany, for example, there are legal distinctions between categories like right-wing extremism (acts that are against the
German constitution) and right-wing radicalism (acts that may be trou-
bling but are technically within constitutional bounds). There are also
several countries in Europe where far-right and even neo-Nazi parties—
such as Greece's Golden Dawn—have been democratically elected into
office. These global developments tend to complicate the kinds of terminology that US government agencies use, particularly in cross-
national conversations.

Blurriness and Contestation
across the Far-Right Spectrum

In the face of the wide range of definitional complications, I find the
term "far right" to be the broadest and most practical term to refer to
the broad spectrum of exclusionary ideologies and groups described
above. I often refer to "far right" as the "best bad term" we have available,
and acknowledge that not everyone will agree on the terminology.[43]
Throughout this book, I use the term "far right" unless referring to specific categories used by other scholars, policy makers, or law enforcement. I also use terms like "white supremacist" or "antigovernment"
when I am referring to specific groups or elements within the overall
far-right spectrum. In referring to the specific subset of the far right

responsible for the Charlottesville or Christchurch violence, for example, I will use the terms "white supremacist" and "white-supremacist extremist." Where it is helpful or necessary, I occasionally use the term "alt right" to refer to the specific form of the modern far right in the United States that is distinct from previous far-right groups as well as from groups abroad. However, because the term "alt right" came from within the far-right spectrum as part of a rebranding effort, using it can make journalists or scholars inadvertently complicit in helping soften extremist ideas. For this reason, I use quotation marks around the phrase to signal its contested nature.[44]

Far-right ideologies, individuals, and groups espouse beliefs that are antidemocratic, antiegalitarian, white supremacist, and embedded in solutions like authoritarianism, ethnic cleansing or ethnic migration, and the establishment of separate ethno-states or enclaves along racial and ethnic lines.[45] The entire far-right spectrum does not share belief in all of these elements equally. In fact, there is sometimes significant contestation across groups within the spectrum on particular points of this broader set of frames. The term "far right" must always be used and understood as representing a spectrum of beliefs and approaches. To add confusion to the mix, some groups that fall within the far-right spectrum officially espouse nonviolence, promote positions on some issues that counter some part of these three key domains, or work to deliberately disrupt the optics of traditional white-supremacist movements. For example, while traditional far-right groups have typically been opposed to same-sex marriage and LGBTQ+ people, some far-right parties and groups in Europe promote women's and LGBTQ+ rights as part of Western values, in order to position those values as under threat from increasing Muslim populations or immigration from Muslim countries.[46] In other cases, far-right groups promote violent ideas— like "re-migration" to countries of origin for ethnic minorities—while officially espousing nonviolence as an operating principle.

Viewing the far right as a spectrum or as a cluster of overlapping ideologies and practices is essential for understanding the potential motivation of violent actors. This also matters for public legislative and private regulatory efforts to monitor, surveil, and shut down far-right extremism on social-media sites or elsewhere. For example, although incel groups are now considered part of the far-right spectrum, this was not always the case.[47] Such understandings are crucial for helping understand how the range of exclusionary and dehumanizing far-right ideologies can mutually reinforce and amplify one another.[48]

How Big Is the Threat?

White-supremacist extremism is currently the most lethal form of extremism in the United States. The vast majority (81 percent) of the forty-two extremist-related murders in 2019 were attributed to white-supremacist extremists, with another 9 percent committed by other right-wing extremists, such as antigovernment extremists. The 2019 figures come on the heels of high numbers in 2018 as well.[49] Far-right extremists were responsible for at least fifty US deaths in 2018—the fourth-deadliest year since 1970 in terms of domestic extremist deaths—with the majority of those deaths linked to white supremacy specifically.[50] There have been over one hundred deaths in the United States and Canada at the hands of white-supremacist extremists since 2014.[51] The number of hate groups in the United States, which had more than doubled to over 1,000 after the presidential election of Barack Obama but then declined by 2014 to 784, rose to a record high of 1,020 in 2018. White-nationalist groups alone increased by nearly 50 percent in 2018, from 100 to 148.[52]

The pace of far-right attacks is also rapidly increasing. In the four weeks after the El Paso shooting that killed twenty-two people, forty individuals were arrested for plotting mass shootings, a dozen of which were linked to far-right ideology.[53] Even before El Paso, domestic terrorism incidents were outpacing the numbers from previous years. FBI director Christopher Wray testified in July 2019 that his agency had made about one hundred arrests related to domestic terrorism in the first three-quarters of the 2019 fiscal year, noting that a majority of those arrests were related to white supremacy.[54] The United States has also seen a significant rise in far-right propaganda, recruiting, and activism. The Anti-Defamation League (ADL) reported that white-supremacist propaganda hit an all-time high in 2019, with 2,713 incidents, more than doubling the 2018 numbers, along with a steady rise in propaganda tactics and increasing hate crimes.[55] This comes on the heels of a 182 percent increase in white-supremacist propaganda incidents from 2017 to 2018.[56] Propaganda is often linked to recruitment through fliers, banners, and other actions that express white-supremacist statements and may include a website link for more information. Moreover, the propaganda is not limited to any single group. The hundreds of instances of far-right propaganda documented in 2018 came from at least ten separate national "alt-right," white-supremacist, and neo-Nazi groups.[57]

But while growth in the far right is well documented, the potential for future violence is harder to assess, in part because the federal government has put the clear majority of terrorism-related resources into tracking and combatting Islamist extremism, neglecting the threat of white-supremacist extremism. In recent congressional testimony, FBI officials noted that 80 percent of their counterterrorism field agents focus on international terrorism cases and 20 percent on domestic terrorism. The imbalance in resources is consequential. Between 9/11 and the end of 2017, two-thirds (67 percent) of violent Islamist plots in the United States were interrupted in the planning phase, but this was the case for less than one-third (26 percent) of violent far-right plots.[58]

The best estimate—looking across all groups and organizations—is that there are currently 75,000 to 100,000 people affiliated with white-supremacist extremist groups in the United States, not including individuals who engage occasionally from the peripheries of far-right scenes or who are ideologically supportive but unengaged either online or offline.[59] Data from countries with more comprehensive monitoring and surveillance of extremism are more precise. The German intelligence services, for example, estimate that in 2018, Germany had 24,100 right-wing extremists, of whom over half were not members of formal groups or organizations. Of those 24,100, an estimated 12,700 are considered potentially violent.[60]

One important aspect of threat assessment has to do with how well connected white supremacists are transnationally, and whether these connections rise to the level of a global movement. There are indications that the global interconnectedness of white-supremacist extremist groups is growing in at least five areas.[61] Far-right groups and individuals are increasingly crowdsourcing funds online, enabling more fundraising and growing financial interconnections, along with the use of internet-based currencies like Bitcoin and other cryptocurrencies like Monero.[62] There is clear evidence of increased sharing of tactics, techniques, and procedures (TTPs) for attacks, as well as other support activities, potentially contributing to more attacks, greater lethality, and more extensive propaganda. Experts have documented increased cross-national recruitment for combat. For example, former FBI agent Ali Soufan testified before the House Committee on Homeland Security in September 2019 that over 17,000 fighters from Western countries—including many from the United States—have traveled to Ukraine to fight, mostly for white-supremacist groups.[63] The internet has facilitated increased sharing of manifestos and livestreamed attacks, driving more inspiration from terrorist attacks globally. And finally, there is clear evidence of increased global gateways to extremist youth scenes in cultural realms like music festivals and combat sports tournaments, which contribute to more networked relationships.

Social media and online modes of communication are key to supporting all five of these global strategies. Online spaces offer training, advice, how-to guides, ideological materials, and places where violent attacks are livestreamed, downloaded, circulated, and celebrated.[64] Importantly, while online spaces and modes of communication facilitate these cooperative engagements and have significantly reduced burdens to transnational collaboration, they are not the root cause of the collaboration—rather, those collaborations are motivated by shared, global ideologies based in common understandings about a threat to "white civilization" from immigration and demographic change. And online spaces work in tandem with in-person gatherings that also enhance global interconnections, such as transnational music festivals, conferences, MMA tournaments, and festivals associated with or linked to white-supremacist scenes.

No single estimate of the numbers of far-right individuals in a given country can help us understand the potential for any one of those individuals to become violent. Despite decades of research on violent extremism, we still do not have a very good understanding of what makes one individual turn toward violence while another remains ideologically supportive but nonviolent. For this reason, the trends I describe above—which clearly document an escalation in murders, violent attacks, and hate crimes; increases in the number of arrests and thwarted attacks; rising propaganda and increased recruiting from far-right and white-supremacist groups; and show evidence of multiple strategies enhancing cross-national collaboration and transnational terrorist inspiration—provide the best indication of the rising threat of far-right and white-supremacist extremism in the United States and globally.

Serious attention on the part of government and law enforcement began to shift in the wake of the spring 2019 Christchurch shootings, with particular urgency emerging following the El Paso shootings that left twenty-two dead. Six separate congressional hearings related to white-supremacist extremism and white-nationalist terrorism were held over the spring and early fall of 2019. And in September 2019, the Department of Homeland Security (DHS) announced a new strategic framework for countering terrorism and targeted violence, which notably includes a new major focus on white-supremacist violent extremism and an acknowledgment of the threat posed by it.[65] The impact of any of these efforts is still to be determined. What is clear, however, is that in important ways the United States and many of its allies overseas are only scratching the surface of understanding the dynamics of rising far-right extremism and the strategies that might work to combat it.

Youth Spaces, Youth Places

This book makes frequent reference to "youth," "young people," and "youth culture" in discussions of radicalization to and engagement in extremist violence. Extremism is not the exclusive domain of youth, of course.[66] In fact, among the most violent offenders—those who have killed someone—extremists are almost as likely to be older men as they are younger ones.[67] Older people are key to far-right-movement

leadership and to the development and mainstreaming of far-right ideologies and conspiracy theories consumed in traditional media outlets.
But young people are disproportionately engaged in or affected by extremist violence, including violent extremist plots as well as murders,
assaults, hate crimes, and other related forms of youth violence like bul-
lying.[68] Youth also have a higher risk of terrorist recidivism and reengagement after release from detention.[69] From the issue of violence
prevention alone, there are good reasons to focus on young people.

Youth are also particularly vulnerable to recruitment and radicalization. Adolescence and early adulthood are key phases of identity forma-
tion and transition, as youth become more independent, meet new
people and friends, and navigate complex sets of expectations from the
cultural worlds of their peers, families, and the broader society. Young
people are more likely to be impulsive, seek risk, or engage in experimentation in ways that aim to break norms or rebel against adult expectations.[70] These are all factors that put youth at greater risk for engaging
with extremist ideas and movements as they try on new identities and
life philosophies. The kinds of emotional needs already known to be key
to extremist radicalization—such as the desire to provoke or to rebel
against authorities, and the need to fit in and belong to a community—
are particularly strong among youth. This makes them especially vulnerable to extremist recruiters' attempts to weaponize existing grievances
and feelings of exclusion, rejection, and anger. And because adolescence
and early adulthood is the primary period in which political attitudes
develop and solidify—in ways that tend to persist across the life
course—engagement with extremist ideas is potentially more consequential during this phase of life.[71]

In this light, the efforts of organized far-right groups to engage with
young people in the spaces and places described in this book—combat
sports and MMA clubs, music scenes, YouTube cooking channels, college campuses, and a variety of youth-oriented online spaces like gaming chatrooms or social-media platforms—are especially important.
Far-right groups have always worked to recruit young people to their
movements and politicize youth spaces like concerts, festivals, youth-
oriented events, and music lyrics.[72] These are sometimes referred to as

youth "scenes"—a word that reflects a less hierarchical and more disorganized structure than traditional social movements. Today there exists a broader range of spaces, places, and scenes to engage young people in the far right. Older leaders in far-right movements rely on college students for speaking invitations and campus activism. They recruit young people to join boxing gyms and compete in combat sports tournaments. Propaganda videos featuring fit, young men in training camps and shooting ranges use music and imagery clearly oriented toward younger recruits.

Young people are also the drivers of the cultural changes in online modes of communication—like meme sharing—in ways that have been tremendously consequential for the growth of the modern far right. Youth and young adults were essential architects of the kinds of online trolling and harassment that predated the emergence of the "alt right" through phenomena like Gamergate—a 2014 online movement that launched a torrent of misogynistic abuse and harassment of women in the gaming industry. Milo Yiannopoulos, for example, rose to prominence as a journalist at Breitbart by championing Gamergate and its narratives about "social justice warriors," "snowflakes," and an overreaching liberal left that was trying to indoctrinate youth. Gamergate channeled a peculiar form of young men's disaffection and alienation into narratives about culture wars and male entitlement in ways that quickly intersected with broader far-right and white-supremacist themes.[73] The contemporary far right is unimaginable without the influence of these youth-driven developments.

It's not only youth who drive most of the violence on the far right, of course. Mostly, it's youth who are men. There is much to say about masculinity and toxic masculinity as drivers of far-right violence in both online and off-line contexts, through online harassment and trolling as well as physical violence against others. It's also important to note that we have seen and are still seeing increasing participation of women in the far right, including in violent fringe and terrorist groups. Women also enable the far right in important ways, whether through YouTube cooking videos that create a softer entry or by playing more supportive roles in extremist movements as mothers, partners, and wives who help to reproduce white nations.

There is no dedicated chapter related to gender in this book, in part because I see issues of gender and misogyny as central to all of them.[74] Each chapter takes up questions of gender in specific ways. I explore how women are called on to produce white babies and nurture them with wholesome, organic food, and how men are marketed to by clothing brands selling a particular kind of far-right manhood, through messages about brotherhood, loyalty, and togetherness, as well as language around being a warrior, soldier, defender, or protector or taking heroic action. I look at how far-right recruiting through combat sports and MMA infuses messaging about physical fitness and male bodies with ideas about preparedness for national defense, street battles, and the coming race war. I note how a subculture of young men engaged in trolling, misogynistic sexual harassment, and antifeminist ideologies emerged from Gamergate and helped fuel the growth of the far right. In each of the new, mainstream spaces and places where the far right is recruiting and radicalizing young people today, gender, misogyny, and masculinity play a foundational role.

This book takes a deep dive into the new spatial domains of far-right extremism in the United States, looking at where and when youth engage in these kinds of spaces. Focusing on the spaces and places where far-right extremism is thriving today builds on and extends prior work on violent white-supremacist movements in the United States, but situates modern movements within the changing ecosystem of far-right radicalization. As this book shows, today's far right is characterized by more diverse entry points, fragmented scenes, and newer groups and associations, some of which deliberately target domains not previously known to be particularly key to far-right and white-supremacist groups. Far-right youth today might initially encounter extremist narratives through chance encounters in mainstream spaces like the MMA, a campus auditorium, a podcast, or a YouTube video. Each of those mainstream spaces, however, can act as a channel, opening the door to dedicated far-right MMA festivals, alt-tech platforms and encrypted communication platforms, and dedicated YouTube subscriptions that mix mainstream interest in cooking or music with far-right ideology. Understanding these new spaces and places—the geography of hate— is key to comprehending the far right in its modern form.[75]

The movement of far-right ideology into mainstream spaces is particularly important because growth in far-right extremism in the United States and globally is driven in no small part by growing numbers of youth who are on the periphery of the far right rather than at its core. Because they are prone to experimentation and exploration, youth are more likely to be moving in and out of the kinds of places and spaces where they might encounter extremist messages. Young people on the periphery of extremism are particularly consequential for how extremist rhetoric, ideology, beliefs, and conspiracy theories are channeled from the core to the mainstream as these youth interact with others in non-extremist spaces. Placing space and place at the center of our analysis makes this clear. Focusing on space and place requires us to consider hate groups and far-right extremism not only as static, organized movements but also as flows of people who move in and out of the periphery and interstitial spaces of far-right scenes. This dynamic is understudied and underanalyzed in scholarship on the far right more broadly.

This approach is an extension of studies of far-right extremism that focus on youth or adults at the hard core of far-right-extremist movements. For many—perhaps even most—modern far-right youth, I argue, extremist engagement is characterized by a process of moving in and out of far-right scenes throughout their adolescence and adulthood in ways that scholars and policy makers have yet to understand. Extremist radicalization processes are fluid and staggered, and may well reverse course, veer off into new trajectories, or intensify in unanticipated ways. We need better ways of understanding where and when youth on the margins of far-right scenes are mobilized through quotidian, flexible engagements in mainstream-style physical and virtual spaces, especially ones that the far right has actively targeted for this purpose. This approach to far-right extremism and radicalization significantly broadens what we know about the far right, and how and when people engage with it. It also offers a new way of thinking about how to study and engage with the fragmentation and broadening of the scenes and spaces where far-right youth and adults gather today.

Overview of the Book

Hate in the Homeland focuses on the mainstreaming of far-right extremism in the United States over the past decade, with reference to global events related to the rise of the far right where relevant.[76] The first part of the book has two overall goals, both aimed at providing readers with foundational knowledge about the kind of far-right content youth encounter when they enter the kinds of spaces and places discussed later in the book. In this introduction and in chapters 1 and 2, I define terms, lay the groundwork for understanding the role of space and place in mobilizing extremism, and examine three simultaneous developments that have characterized the rise of the US far right: the mainstreaming of far-right political rhetoric, the mainstreaming of far-right conspiracy theories, and transformations in far-right aesthetics and communication styles, particularly for youth. This lays the groundwork for understanding the changing nature of far-right content that youth encounter when they engage with the far right in the kinds of mainstream spaces and places discussed in depth in the remaining chapters.

In chapters 3 to 6, I turn to the question of where and when radicalization happens, focusing on young people's ordinary and everyday encounters with radicalization messages in mainstream spaces and places. In these chapters, I trace new gateways where youth are radicalized toward far-right ideologies and actions: cultural spaces related to food and fashion; fight clubs and the MMA scene; educational settings and college campuses; and social media/online spaces. In the conclusion, I address the implications of a focus on space and place for how we respond to rising far-right extremism, and suggest what better interventions might look like.

I chose these four cases for their power to illustrate some of the unexpected places where violent hate groups are recruiting young people today. As I will argue, new, mainstream spaces are helping mobilize financial capital, cultural markets, physical capacity, and intellectual foundations that support the far right's growth, along with a broad ecosystem of new media technologies to communicate about it all. But it is important to remember that these are not the only places where the growth of extremist rhetoric and ideas is taking place. My hope is that the examples I highlight will inspire analysis of other ways that everyday encounters with extremism in mainstream places matter, challenging readers to pay attention not only to how radicalization happens, but also where it takes place.

Chapter 1

Space, Place, and the Power of Homelands

Long before John Denver sang about country roads bringing him to the place where he belongs, human beings formed deep emotional attachments to particular places and spaces. The far right is no different. In rhetoric, narratives, propaganda, and messaging, far-right groups and individuals constantly invoke spaces of belonging, nationalist geographies, and white territory. These include references to fifteenth-century pogroms, ancient homelands, white ethno-states, and the need to build border walls, along with language about national defense, incursions, and invasions. The centrality of space and territory in historical far-right movements was clear in the very metaphors used by the Nazi party, such as "blood and soil," and the need for ever-more living space (*Lebensraum*) for the *Volk*.[1] Space and place are constant backdrops to contemporary far-right fears of a "great replacement" and conspiracies about Europe turning into Eurabia. For the far right, in short, issues of territory, belonging, exclusion, race, and national geographies are foundational for imagining collective pasts as well as anticipated futures.

Decades of scholarship have traced the connections between nationalism, territory, and identity. Perhaps most notably, Benedict Anderson's work on "imagined communities" showed how national identities and territories are created across communities of people who have never met (and likely never will) but still share some sense of affinity and belonging to one another. Imagined national communities command such a strong emotional pull, Anderson argues, that people are even willing to die in their name by enlisting in armies and fighting in wars with other nations.[2] For the far right, though, such national communities are imagined in racially defined ways, with clear guidelines for who belongs and who does not. White ethno-states and exclusionary ideas

29

about the homeland are deeply linked to ideas about rootedness, ownership, space, and place in ways that many analyses of the contemporary
far right have overlooked. For the far right, a sacred and eternal bond
ties geographic space to racial, ethnic, and cultural groups. Those who
claim ownership of that space are therefore entitled to it, at the expense
of other racial and ethnic groups.[3]

Space and Place

Scores of social scientists have attended to questions of space and place,
particularly in fields like geography and anthropology, demonstrating
how places and spaces are fundamental to a sense of belonging and
identity and are imbued with emotional attachment and meaning.[4] Indeed, we cannot fully understand the social dynamics of human beings'
lives and actions without understanding their engagements in place and
space.[5] From neighborhoods to nations, the places where we live and
spend time matter for how we develop, express ourselves, and identify
with others around us.[6]

This is no less true for extremists' engagements in and attachments
to place. Pathways to extremist beliefs and violent actions themselves
are rooted in geographic settings.[7] But with some exceptions, most work
on the far right has not seriously considered space and place, focusing
instead on far-right groups' organizational strategies and tactics or psychological approaches to individuals' cognitive radicalization. These are
critically important domains, of course. But extremist engagements take
place *in* particular places and spaces—at protests, marches, political rallies, festivals, tournaments, concerts, campaign meetings, and more.
This is true even when extremist engagement takes place online—
because even online engagements are rooted in particular physical
spaces somewhere, on laptops or mobile devices in dorm rooms and
coffee shops, in living rooms and classrooms.[8] Online engagements may
well lead to off-line engagements, working in tandem to shape far-right
youth engagement. This challenges the prevailing tendency to separate
the study of physical from virtual places in discussions of terrorism and
extremism. At a moment of rising far-right extremism, it is imperative

to rethink the relationship between space, place, identity, and action as it applies to the far right.

One place to start is with the very experts who spend their time focusing on space and place—especially in the field of geography. This book cannot do justice to the extensive and rich interrogations of space and place, but a few key interventions are especially germane. Yi-Fu Tuan's 1977 *Space and Place* challenged geographers' scientific reliance on topographical maps and field studies, arguing that space is imbued with meaning in ways that cannot always be studied through a field survey or a map. Space is sensual and emotional, Tuan showed, reliant on the senses—through sounds, smells, and tactile touch—to evoke deep feelings about belonging, rootedness, and home.[9] In the decades that followed, geographers and other scholars focusing on space and place came to understand places—the local contexts of people's everyday experiences—as deeply intertwined with personal, social, and symbolic meanings.[10] Places are the settings where individuals "face, evaluate, and attempt to resolve problems and agendas on a daily basis."[11] Place both reflects individuals' identities and social actions and helps shape and direct them. Thus local contexts like a coal-mine closure or an opioid epidemic may deeply influence individuals' vulnerabilities to antigovernment and anti-elite rhetoric or to hate directed toward others and outsiders deemed responsible for local problems.[12] This is true for national belonging, too, which is linked not only to an imagined sense of identity with other people in the national community, but also with native flora and fauna, national landmarks, parks, habitats, and landscapes.[13]

People also encounter ideas in particular places, even as they may be mobilized to move beyond them.[14] Individuals' encounters with extremists in physical places like prisons or radical houses of worship have launched radicalization pathways. Specific places become key parts of collective grievances about government surveillance and suppression in ways that have mobilized extremist action.[15] Place can also be meaningful as a way of framing nostalgia for a past era and fantasies about restoration of a utopian future one.[16] This, of course, is the very premise of the white ethno-state and far-right claims about geographic entitlement, belonging, and exclusion. Of all the ways that place and space may be constitutive for the far right, the call to protect physical territory and defend the homeland—whether that is a nation-state like the United States or the white or Aryan nation more specifically—is one of the most consequential.

Homelands and Heartlands

The emotions and ideologies that underpin far-right and white-supremacist extremism are deeply rooted in a sense of territorial belonging, possession, and ownership. White-supremacist fantasies and myths about sacred, racialized territory underpinned historical far-right ideas about the mystical link between "blood and soil" in Nazi Germany. Today they underpin the anti-immigrant, anti-Islam, anti-Semitic, and racist sentiments that inspire policies like border closure, segregation, forced relocation, re-migration, and the establishment of separate racial enclaves or ethno-states.[17] The El Paso shooter railed against "Mexican invaders," while a terrorist in Oslo justified the murder of dozens of children with the fear that Europe was becoming overrun by Muslims. The very language of the "great replacement" and white-genocide theories clearly invokes geographic space, as immigrants and nonwhites will purportedly take over space, expelling or eradicating whites from their native lands. These fears and fantasies rely on a conception of personal and community belonging that ties individual identity and racial groups to specific geographies, and that marks "home" as inseparable from "land."

The concept of homelands is central to ideals of territorial belonging in ways that extend well beyond the far right. "The profound attachment to the homeland appears to be a worldwide phenomenon," the geographer Yi-Fu Tuan wrote, explaining that place provides a sense of reassuring permanence in the face of constant change.[18] Some may find it hard to reconcile the importance of local homelands with rising globalization and deterritorialization. A common complaint about globalization is that it erases unique local places and cultures in ways that can leave one place feeling much like the next. At the same time, in some ways, local places have become ever more irrelevant to ordinary people's lives, as remote work, internet shopping, video conferencing, and on-line education programs supplant the spaces and places that once de-fined school, work, and even everyday errands in myriad ways.

But if individuals' attachments to local and national spaces are declin-ing in favor of more rootless, cosmopolitan flows and increased global mobility, the effect is uneven.[19] For some people, globalization's impact on local cultures and economies creates a backlash, leading to deeper desires for identity and meaning and more intense attachments to local places.[20] This is what the British journalist David Goodhart describes as the distinction between people who are "Somewheres"—rooted in particular places and nostalgic for the past, typically more conservative—and "Anywheres"—geographically mobile, more liberal, and less at-tached to local and national spaces.[21] The Somewhere/Anywhere di-vide suggests that place simply matters more for some people. Where livelihoods are tied to what the natural environment offers—in farming, mining, or fishing industries, for example—attachments to land and regional identity take on particular import, connected to family histo-ries and local economies alike. From the silk and steel mills in Pennsyl-vania to the beer industry in central Europe, local places have a lasting influence on regional identities and belonging—helped along by dia-lects, place-specific cuisine, and local myths and legends.[22] This is true even when the relationship is "co-dependent and often abusive," such as with coal mines that led to early deaths from blackened lungs and accidents. Importantly, when those mines failed in Appalachia, locals did not blame the coal industry itself. Instead, they turned their anger toward Washington and the "coastal elites" who referred to them as "fly-over country."[23] Anti-elite sentiment, for many rural Americans loyal to the US heartland, is directly linked to perceived disrespect for local re-gions and their people.[24] Those local regions, in turn, command loyalty but also offer a deep sense of belonging.

Homelands are thus clearly linked to concepts of rootedness and be-longing to local regions. But they are also racialized in ways that are critical to interrogate. The geographies of white supremacy are deeply intertwined with global and national histories of imperialism,

colonialism, white property accumulation, residential and school segregation, the establishment of reservations for native peoples, and systems of apartheid.[25] These intersect with gendered geographies, since
"the protection of white womanhood" was a key rationale for a wide
range of disenfranchising white-supremacist practices, including segregation laws, discriminatory lending practices, and other policies that
created and perpetuated "white propertied power."[26] White women are
key to the domestic realms that helped sustain white supremacy, from
birthing and raising white babies to fighting school integration, making
attention to "home and the spaces of everyday life, to care and community work and to the role of white women in nurturing and producing the white nation" a critical aspect of the relationship between space,
place, and the far right.[27]

Homelands are biological and ecological concepts, linking a sense of
belonging to the body—through the related term "heartland"—and the
home. Indeed, it's not for nothing that so many metaphors linked to the
idea of national belonging are tied to ecological ideas like roots and soil,
or to ideas of kinship and home: homelands, motherland, fatherland.
After all, such metaphors "are thought to denote something to which
one is naturally tied."[28] At the same time, the United States has a second
set of connections related to the frontier, westward expansion, and associated ideals of liberation, adventure, ruggedness, and masculinity.[29]
With such deep emotional links to natural spheres of belonging, it is
perhaps less surprising that the vulnerabilities that emerge from the loss
of local livelihoods help shape a sense of loss and of a particular way of
life "slipping away." This, in turn, lends appeal to political rhetoric and
nationalist or far-right symbols that depict or evoke a sense of nostalgia
for sacred lands and geographies and promise to restore the nation and
its local communities. Combined with language that asserts ownership
over space and suggests there is a limited amount of it, these kinds of
strategic tactics help define and reinforce ideas about who belongs in
specific territorial and political spaces and who does not.[30] This is geographic "othering"—using real or imagined borders to evoke an origin
story, create justifications for exclusionary policies and practices, and
designate enemies who threaten those geographic spaces.

Such sacred geographies need not be actual places (although they sometimes are). They can also be fantastical, relying on national myths and legends to help imagine a nation that never existed but is nonetheless aspired to.[31] Thus the "alt right" can logically look to the paradigm of Wakanda, a fictional African diasporic homeland conceived in Hollywood, as well as to the mythic Chicano homeland Aztlán, imagined as a "recovered and thoroughly decolonized Southwest," as models.[32] These kinds of mythic or fantasy places harken back to an imagined, prior form of the collective but also draw real or symbolic boundaries around the contemporary and future nation. They establish ideals that link specific territories to racial destinies, where whites can reproduce and thrive, as far-right Counter-Currents editor Greg Johnson advocates in an essay about white homelands called "The Slow Cleanse."[33] For the far-right fringe, these geographic yearnings about "white territorialism" are critical foundations for later violence.[34]

Historical episodes linking extreme violence and defense of territory are especially powerful, through reference to Christian Crusades and pogroms like *Reconquista*, as well as through comparisons to Indigenous genocides. At least since the Nazi era, the European far right has drawn on the Native American experience, warning that Europeans would end up "on reservations," restricted to limited territories within their own native countries.[35] The 2011 terrorist in Oslo who killed seventy-seven people—mostly children—also referenced Indigenous struggles, defending his and other far-right extremists' actions as no different from Native American leaders' fight against an imperialist invasion.[36] The theme appears periodically in European far-right political speeches, advertisements, and slogans, often as a way of evoking the conspiracy of white genocide without stating it outright. A 2014 tweet from a regional office of the AfD party depicted a Native American chief with the words "Indians couldn't stop immigration. Today they live on reservations."[37] After the German town of Nuremberg named a young woman of mixed-ethnic background to be the 2019 "Christ child" who opens the Christmas market, the local AfD district branch commented on the choice on Facebook, noting that Germans would "go the way of the Indians."[38]

Europeans aren't the only ones making the analogy. The El Paso shooter pointed specifically to the Native American experience in his manifesto, describing the "nearly complete ethnic and cultural destruction brought to the Native Americans by our European ancestors" and warning that because "the natives didn't take the invasion of Europeans seriously," their communities are "just a shadow of what was."[39] In a 2019 video, the white supremacist Jared Taylor argues that the Native American story is "one of the strongest possible arguments for tight borders," suggesting that whites should be allowed to fight for their land just as the "Indians" did.[40] The rhetorical usage of Indigenous experiences allows the far right to "create a myth of survival" among a heroic people fighting for their homeland.[41]

Myths and legends about homelands are key parts of far-right sacred geographies, linking contemporary lives to nostalgic pasts and utopian futures.[42] Such myths become intertwined with individual identity, in part because they are perceived as authentic stories that connect people with places. For people who identify intensely with local, regional, or national geographies, such myths are seen as being "as real as the rocks and waterholes" people can see and touch. The land holds "the ancient story of the lives and deeds" of revered ancestors, making the countryside itself the individual's "family tree."[43] In Germany, where far-right nationalists see modern-day Germans as the descendants of Nordic tribes whose origins were supposedly Aryan,[44] Nordic symbols like the swastika, along with Norse legends, weaponry, mythology, and Nordic gods, all help shape this nationalist imaginary. This fantasy also enables an expression of national whiteness, evoking a sense of racial superiority without being overtly racist, and contributing to collective unconscious assumptions about the nature of German-ness and who belongs in the nation. The Nordic region, for German far-right extremists, thus becomes sacred space that helps mediate the collective past, by providing fantasy origin narratives, stories, principles, and aspirational traits for "good" nationalists, like loyalty and heroism. The region's stories and myths help filter and reconstruct cultural memory and invoke nostalgia for a fantastical past while helping people imagine a shared, idealized future nation.[45]

White supremacists outside of Germany also rely on a wide variety of Nordic and other historical legends and symbols, either because they are simply copying Nazi symbols and aesthetics or because they are also valorizing a myth of Nordic origins of the Aryans. Globally, the far right uses references to Greek and Roman history, pogroms in the Middle Ages like Reconquista, and Norse gods and goddesses to help demarcate the lines between "us" and "them" and signal a desired return to a previous exclusionary world. Charlottesville marchers carried Deus vult crosses in 2017, while in 2018, far-right activists in Rostock, Germany, waved a Templar flag.[46] Fans of one clothing brand that is well-known for its use of far-right symbols could connect with other brand fans and learn about in-person meet-ups on a now-defunct Tumblr blog. In 2016, this included an announcement of a one-week trip to the "lands of Hyperborea—a mythical pre-historic motherland of our race"—in the region of the Karelia and Kola Peninsula in northwest Russia. Hyperborea was also the name of a prior clothing product line for the German brand Ansgar Aryan, which featured website and catalog text that explained the importance of Hyperborea and described its epic battle between the people of the "light" and the "dark men."[47]

Sacred national space is key to the far right because it promises an alternative, noble existence that transcends the purportedly immoral, declining, or decrepit contemporary nation. That same sacred space is used to mobilize the most extreme fringe, whose desire for restoration of white civilization motivates extreme violence intended to bring about an apocalyptic societal collapse and subsequent rebirth into a new world order. These sacred spaces are easily called upon as part of the "imagined geographies of white demise" referenced in the kinds of fears, uncertainty, and sense of threat embedded in language about a "great replacement" or white genocide.[48] In this way, national myths and geographies work to mediate not only the imagined past but also white fears and hopes about uncertain futures whose end results are either apocalyptic demise or aspirational future glory.[49] In more ordinary terms, political and media rhetoric referencing the notion of replacement, or using the language of invasion, incursion, and being overrun, grounds these fantasy expressions in very real political dynamics of immigration and demographic change. Racialized territory—or idealized white geography—is used to simultaneously activate a sense of belonging and of imminent threat.

The emergence of eco-fascism as a motivating force for far-right violence has to be understood in this context.[50] Both the Christchurch and the El Paso terrorists cited environmental motivations as part of their broader ideologies. This is the "greening of hate"—justifying immigration restrictions by pointing out that ongoing climate change and environmental degradation require preserving and protecting national space for national citizens and reducing migration.[51] Eco-fascism, along with far-right affinities with paganism and deep ecology, is linked to ideals about racialized territory and sacred national space. The idea of white ethno-states thus helps "consecrate the relationship between European man and nature," connecting nature-loving worship of the land with preservation efforts that present immigration and overpopulation as a threat not only to white people but also to their homelands.[52] But this very sense of threat could exist only in a context in which whites consciously or unconsciously hold a sense of "possessive geography" over the land.[53] This is the mystical bond that connects "blood" with "soil" in the Nazi imaginary, making ownership and entitlement to national space an assumed racial inheritance, regardless of what citizenship laws say on paper.

Exerting control over the physical territory of the United States—including its borders as well as spaces and places within it—is thus foundational to the "exclusionary visions and practices" of the far right.[54] These visions are enacted through far-right rhetoric and marketing campaigns that use the language of defense and employ words like "invasion," "incursion," "flood," "overrun," "fortress," or "ruin," along with calls to defend, protect, or fight back against those threats. Such language can inspire fringe actors to enact violence in the name of their people and their national space. "I can't sit by and watch my people get slaughtered," the Pittsburgh synagogue shooter declared, based on conspirational thinking about the purported invasion of his national space. "Screw your optics, I'm going in."[55] The shooter clearly saw his action as heroic, directing his words not only to the general public but also to the faction of the far right that advocates for nonviolent solutions and argues that the optics of violence are bad for the movement overall. These kinds of terrorist actions rely on a territorial fantasy about particular racial groups belonging to specific and separate geographic spaces, even when, such as in the case of the United States, some of those groups arrived in that space only through immigration.[56]

Geographic territory is important to the far right in spaces smaller than entire nations, too. The white-supremacist obsession with establishing a separate white ethno-state or white enclave along with separate geographic territories for Blacks, Latinos, and other ethnic minorities is perhaps the clearest example.[57]

The Fantasy of a White Ethno-state

The desire to establish a separate white territory or to restore a white homeland is at the root of far-right and white-supremacist extremists' calls to end immigration, re-migrate ethnic minorities, and accelerate a race war in order to achieve rebirth and restoration of white civilization. Far-right extremists and racist groups have a clear "geography of racial activism," as the scholar Kathleen Blee describes, based on a shared "commitment to territorial and social separation between the races."[58] This vision is at the heart of groups within the broader far-right spectrum who claim they are white separatists rather than white supremacists. White separatists argue that whites should stick to white enclaves, as the neo-Nazi Matthew Heimbach explained in a documentary in VICE, while the "black community" should have "their own homelands" in the South or in urban areas like Detroit.[59] Far-right groups use this logic to claim that they are the "true multiculturalists," because they are the ones who will protect and preserve racial groups as unique and separate. In contrast, they argue, "global elites" aim to eradicate the white race by increasing immigration and migration and "replacing" whites through demographic change, with the goal of creating blended, multicultural societies. Separate ethno-states thus become "hallowed destination[s]" that promise to "protect and fortify whiteness."[60] Using this logic, far-right groups who espouse white separatism argue that they are not establishing hierarchies of racial groups and do not espouse white supremacy—instead, their interest is in separating and preserving racial uniqueness and promoting white civil rights.

But it is critical to be clear that white separatism—especially when followed all the way to its end goal of separate racial ethno-states—is necessarily white supremacist. The imagined ideal of the white ethno-state necessitates violent ethnic cleansing and separation practices like forced deportations, along with policies that would revoke birthright citizenship and annul naturalization for selected groups and individuals.[61] Policies like re-migration of ethnic minorities could be enacted only with force and violence, including forced removal from homes, seizure of private property, and separation of individuals from lands where their families have lived for generations. The founder of the far-right Counter-Currents website, Greg Johnson, argues that "all races and ethnicities, including various white ethnicities, should have their own homelands."[62] But his description of the strategies and policies that would be required in order to achieve that goal illustrates exactly why white separatism cannot be distinguished from white supremacy. Johnson advocates for giving African American citizens in the United States a homeland of their own in the South and "decoloniz[ing]" the rest of the country through a "well-planned, orderly, and humane process of ethnic cleansing," which he admits may entail "morally justified" violence.[63] The ethnic homelands that would result from such a plan, of course, would also be necessarily inegalitarian. Existing proposals for white homelands, for example, establish hierarchies of rights that allow some nonwhites to live in white ethno-states, but with only "partial or minimal citizenship" that prohibits leadership positions or rights like owning firearms and requires higher tax rates.[64]

White ethno-states are not mere fantasies of fringe groups—they represent real policy aims and proposals that groups have tried and continue to try to enact. In the 1990s, the white-supremacist group Aryan Nations tried to build a white-separatist enclave in Idaho, followed by broader efforts to create a five-state white homeland through the "Northwest Imperative."[65] These efforts built upon historical white-supremacist legacies in the Pacific Northwest that date to the nineteenth century, when the region's "foundational laws criminalized African-American residency in the newly established region."[66] The idea of a separate white territory or ethno-state remains a key mobilizing narrative for white separatists across the United States. And, of course, the virtual space of the internet now facilitates and underpins efforts to create or restore such physical homelands.[67]

White enclaves and separate spaces are not limited to homelands and ethno-states, and American far-right groups aren't the only ones linking geographic territory to white-supremacist political goals. The German far-right effort to create "national liberated zones"—independent political and economic territories outside of the state's control—is a case in point.

National Liberated Zones

Far-right extremists' efforts to build far-right "national liberated zones" (*national befreite Zonen*) in Germany in the 1990s and 2000s received so much attention from state authorities and the media alike that a group of German linguists declared the term the "unword" of the year in 2000.[68] National liberated zones referred to the creation of economically independent far-right areas within a local state or region where the state would lose its monopoly on power, essentially ceding control to far-right authority.[69] The tactic called for establishing a network of independent printing presses, travel agents, advertising agents, bookshops, pubs, restaurants, craftspeople, cooperatives, agricultural communities, and media distributors that would create an alternative, separate society and counterculture, coexisting with the mainstream.[70] The concept first appeared as a strategy discussed among far-right groups in the early 1990s.[71] Space was foundational to the idea, both in geographic and symbolic terms. National liberated zones were imagined as places where far-right extremists would have physical control of the streets and the ability to gather and move about in undisturbed ways, but would also achieve the cultural, intellectual, and cognitive liberation that was seen as a necessary precursor to economically liberated zones and self-governance.[72]

The strategy was never realized, but it still served important goals that shaped how far-right groups engaged with one another and with local communities in Germany. For example, although national liberated zones were designed as spaces of exclusion, the strategy also called for specific outreach to local communities through everyday acts of kindness. National liberated zones would be anchored in local communities, according to the proposals, if far-right extremists acted as helpful, courageous alternatives to the "anonymous system"—helping the elderly with shopping, babysitting children, cleaning up neighborhoods and playgrounds, or singing national hymns in retirement homes.[73] In so doing, far-right extremists would gain the support, solidarity, and loyalty of the local people within their broader geographic regions. This would not only build broader acceptance of far-right political goals, but also undermine the state's ability to suppress the far right, and would therefore weaken the state itself.[74] The plan also called for regular outreach to "gray zones" of organizations on the periphery of the far-right core, including fraternities, military reserves, sport clubs, volunteer firefighters, and unions.[75]

The idea of national liberated zones wasn't unique to Germany. Similar efforts to build economically and politically independent territories for the far right took place in Italy, Spain, Portugal, and France. In Italy, for example, the group Terza Posizione (TP) succeeded in creating independent shops and schools, radio programs, printing presses, and more in the 1970s and 1980s.[76] The German far right was also clearly influenced by far-left approaches to creating autonomous communities with networks of bookstores and cultural or social institutions.[77] A 2000 article in a far-right political publication praised leftist efforts in this regard and pointed to the need for similar far-right infrastructure.[78] Wherever they appeared, national liberated zones shared a goal of not only establishing independent geographic territory for the far right but also cultivating alternative economic and cultural systems that would grow far-right movements so they could ultimately undermine the authority and legitimacy of the state.[79]

National liberated zones were linked to two related spatial concepts that emerged in Europe around the same time, called "zones of fear"

(*Angstzonen*) or "no-go areas." These were places purportedly dominated by right-wing extremists, where outsiders were not safe.[80] The
concept referred to whole neighborhoods or regions as well as to public
or semipublic spaces in neighborhoods, parks, youth centers, clubs, and
train stations. While the economic and political aspects of national liberated zones were never fully realized, "zones of fear"—places dominated by right-wing extremists—did meet with some success in parts
of Germany, creating places where foreigners, leftists, or people of color
were not welcome or were met with violence. These were generally tem-
porary spaces, where the far right was dominant for a summer or a season or on specific days of the week, in places like discos or youth clubs
or a town square. These kinds of physically controlled spaces play
important roles in building far-right youth identity and establishing
boundaries that exclude others in threatening or violent ways. They help
the far right demarcate "us" from "them" and establish who is allowed
to be present in particular physical places and who is not. Far-right-
dominated spaces also act as important gathering places to exchange
and share information and build integration and belonging within the
group.[81]

There are plenty of other examples of white-supremacist spaces and
their importance for shaping extremist movements. White supremacists
have established summer camps for children in Germany and Ukraine
(echoing similar US camps from the early twentieth century).[82] An annual summer camp for far-right Identitarians in France aims to "train
future militants," focusing on those twenty to twenty-five years old and
combining physical-fitness training with history classes and simulated
street riots.[83] Pete Simi and Robert Futrell's work on the white-power
movement's "hidden spaces of hate" details a variety of "Aryan free
spaces" where white supremacists meet, including house parties and
backyard barbeques, Bible study meetings, and camping excursions.[84]
And, of course, there is a long history of paramilitary training camps for
the far right, dating to the end of the Vietnam War and including recent
reports about camps operating in Washington State and in Virginia. But
the concept of white homelands—separate, sacred geographic communities for whites only—underpins it all.

Space, Place, and Extremist Radicalization

National homelands and white ethno-states aren't the only ways that space and place matter to the far right. The targeting of college campuses for propaganda campaigns, the use of MMA and music festivals to recruit and radicalize, the creation of dedicated far-right-clothing online shops and physical stores to sell commercial products, and the wide variety of online spaces used by the far right are all key to its growth. In new and changing ways, people are having encounters in mainstream spaces with far-right ideological messages about immigrants, globalization, and elites, as well as conspiracies about Jewish orchestration or Muslim efforts to turn Europe into Eurabia. It's not only that encounters with such messages are more frequent. The very appearance of extremist messages in otherwise mainstream spaces and places can help normalize them, as extremism moves from the periphery to the core.[85] In chapter 2, I turn to three examples that illustrate how extremist ideologies and narratives are becoming normalized in mainstream spaces and places: through the mainstreaming of extremist political rhetoric, conspiracy theories, and aesthetics and communication styles.

Chapter 2

Mainstreaming the Message

When a conservative think-tank executive named Joseph Overton created a brochure in the mid-1990s with a sliding cardboard feature to show potential donors how policy solutions could be moved from the fringes into what he called the "window of political possibility," he had no way of knowing he had created a metaphor that would become widely used, a quarter of a century later, to explain the mainstreaming of extremism in American politics.[1] The "Overton window" describes the range of political ideas and policy solutions considered acceptable by the public at any given time. It is rare for politicians to act on ideas outside the window because they are beholden to the constituents who elected them and are therefore reluctant to support policies or legislation that fall outside the range of what most voters deem acceptable.[2] Movement into the window of politically possible ideas is typically gradual, occurring through the slow evolution of mainstream norms, values, and beliefs over time. This can happen either organically or as a result of the strategic efforts of think tanks, lobbyists, and grassroots activists who work to intentionally shift the Overton window, moving ideas out of the fringes and into mainstream acceptability.[3] But sometimes, shifts in the Overton window happen quickly, reflecting a more rapid mainstreaming and normalization of political ideas and policy solutions that most people would have once considered too extreme.[4] This can happen from both sides of the political spectrum, allowing politicians to take advantage of rapid shifts in the Overton window to implement public policy from previously fringe ideas that became possibilities as they became more widely accepted by the mainstream public.

The normalization of far-right and white-supremacist ideas is one such example. Ideological beliefs once thought of as extreme have—with relative speed—become more widely accepted by the general public. This is what people refer to as the mainstreaming of extremism—the process through which previously extreme ideas become normalized as part of the acceptable spectrum of beliefs within democratic societies. Extreme ideas have been mainstreamed in contexts as varied as political speeches, the media, and a variety of online and youth-culture settings, such as memes, T-shirts, and video games. Mainstreaming is critical to the growth of far-right movements globally, because it helps them recruit, radicalize, and mobilize individuals toward violence, while reducing the likelihood that the public will raise the alarm about their efforts. The normalization of extreme ideas reduces barriers to entry to far-right extremist groups and broadens the base of sympathizers as extremist beliefs become less shocking and seem more acceptable to a broader range of people. Mainstreaming extreme ideas also helps the far right achieve political goals related to border closures, restrictions on immigration, and deportations by smuggling previously extreme ideas and views into mainstream political parties' platforms—effectively shifting the Overton window of what is considered acceptable public policy or political discourse.

One consequence of the mainstreaming and normalization of far-right extremism is that ordinary people more frequently encounter extreme ideas in their everyday lives, making engagements with the far right more fluid and frequent. Mainstreamed extremism moves far-right ideas out of the domain of backwoods militias and prison gangs. These ideas are no longer found only in destinations that must be intentionally sought out. Instead, people might simply encounter white-supremacist ideology while shopping online, listening to a podcast, turning on the evening news, or walking past a bulletin board on their college campus. Space and place are central parts of this process. People don't just stumble across hate in abstract ways—they encounter it in particular physical and virtual places. Geography is therefore a part of the story of how ideas make their way from the far right into the mainstream.[5]

Mainstreaming helps expose new people to hate and recruit them to extremist ideologies, but it also softens extremist beliefs through coded terms that obscure their violent underpinnings. In this way, mainstreaming and normalization help further radicalize individuals who are drawn to far-right-extremist ideas. Thus, relabeling concepts like the forced deportation and ethnic cleansing of immigrants as "re-migration" can make hateful expressions seem more acceptable to a broader range of ordinary individuals. Racist expressions may appear more acceptable when they come from elected officials in mainstream political parties, helping legitimize and spread ideas that used to be considered fringe. For example, a sitting president tells four congresswomen of color— three of whom were born in the United States—to go back to the countries they came from, and crowds of people start chanting "send them back" at his political rallies.[6]

But how does mainstreaming happen? What are the mechanisms that help previously extreme ideas move into the realm of acceptable discourse, or that bring about shifts in the Overton window? I suggest there are at least three simultaneous developments that have helped move extremist ideas and content into the mainstream. The rise of populist parties has helped mainstream extreme ideas through campaign rhetoric and political speech. The spread of disinformation and conspiracy theories introduces and reinforces extreme ideas while simultaneously undermining the idea of truth. And finally, the weaponization of youth culture—especially the use of humor and memes, along with a new, mainstream far-right aesthetic—makes extreme ideas seem less dangerous than they really are.

Each of these three areas—political speech, conspiracy theories, and the mainstreaming of extremist aesthetics and communication styles— helps to introduce and elaborate on extreme ideas in new ways. They are essential components of the changing nature of far-right content that people encounter today in a radically altered set of mainstream spaces and places that are far beyond the traditional domains of the far right. The modern far right relies on these strategies to mainstream and normalize extreme ideas.

Extreme Ideas in Political Speech

Extremist ideas are normalized when they are explicitly adopted or implicitly suggested in the speeches or communication of mainstream politicians. I focus here on two specific and related ways in which this happens. First, we see the embedding of anti-immigrant language in antiglobalization frames, and second, support for white-supremacist framings of demographic change. In both examples, far-right ideological positions and philosophies have been deliberately "seeded" by far-right and white-supremacist intellectuals who have intentionally worked to disseminate far-right "metapolitical"—or pre-political—ideas in ways that can help inform the political positions of electable politicians. Chapter 5 explains this strategy in greater detail, but I mention it here because it is critical to understand the long-term intentionality that underpins the mainstreaming of extremist ideas.

In both topical areas—anti-immigrant sentiments and the notion of an existential threat from demographic change—the far right relies on broader frames copied from successful populist political strategies positioning the pure, ordinary people against a nefarious elite.[7] I will explain this populist framing first, and then elaborate on how extremist ideologies are embedded in this framing by mainstream politicians as they use dehumanizing language to talk about immigrants and hint at a future white genocide.

Valorizing the Pure People

Populism is a rhetorical strategy used across the political spectrum by politicians who argue that their own party or platform is a better and more authentic channel for the voice of the people, in contrast to current political leaders, who are deemed elite, out of touch, untrustworthy, and unethical.[8] Populist strategies have been used not only in the Trump campaign's promise to "drain the swamp" but also in the anti-elite language of campaign speeches from Bernie Sanders and Elizabeth Warren. In its extreme iterations, those who oppose the proposed platform are positioned as enemies of the people or traitors to the nation.[9]

Populist parties have used this strategy to great effect across the globe, as the well-documented rise of such parties across Europe, in Brazil and India, and in the United States shows clearly. These successes have helped anti-elite discourse become much more mainstream.[10] But nationalist and far-right parties have been especially successful with the "pure people–corrupt elite" frame, meaning that frame has also helped carry far-right-extreme ideas into the mainstream. In other words, the broad success of populism as a rhetorical strategy helps mainstream the political ideologies of the far right.

This happens in part by broadening both the understanding of the "pure people" and the nature of the threat facing them. Far-right populists try to mobilize voters by arguing that the nation's people are threatened by demographic change, immigration, ethnic-minority birthrates, or religious changes, and that those changes are happening because current political elites are out of touch with what the ordinary people need. In these cases, the people are deemed pure not only in contrast to "corrupt" elites, but also to impure or threatening migrants or ethnic and religious others. In such iterations, populist rhetoric is not only pro-people but also xenophobic and exclusionary. Restoring the purity of the people requires or relies on policies like ethnic re-migration and restricted immigration.

This is what the scholar Jan Kubik calls a "thick" form of populism, elaborating on Cas Mudde's seminal 2004 definition of populism as having a thin ideology. In thick populism, the pure people are not only positioned against the bad elite but also against bad others.[11] Such boundaries divide not only elites and ordinary people but also those people and others, resulting in what we see as rising polarization across groups.[12] And because populist parties and candidates work to channel citizens' real or imagined grievances related to social and demographic changes into resentment toward both elites and ethnic and racial minorities, populist polarization contributes to rising hate and white supremacy as well.[13]

Importantly, populist nationalists do not only pit local interests against national policies—they also position national interests against the global, arguing for restricted trade, refusing to participate in international treaties or climate accords, and lobbying for reduced power for transnational groups and policies like the North American Free Trade Agreement (NAFTA) or the North Atlantic Treaty Organization (NATO). But these antiglobalization frames also embed anti-immigrant language in ways that help normalize extremist ideas about migration and threat. In this way, globalization itself becomes a catchword for threats to national citizens' cultural identity, democratic practices, and economic security, primarily due to immigration. Antiglobalization language becomes a kind of Trojan horse, carrying anti-immigrant, anti-Semitic, and anti-Muslim ideologies into the mainstream and normalizing them—along with calls to defend the pure, ordinary, national people against these threats. The following sections elaborate.

Embedding Anti-immigrant Messages in Antiglobalization Frames

Far-right-extreme ideologies become mainstreamed in political discourse when antiglobalization framing normalizes far-right positions on immigrants and migration. The far right's opposition to globalization is oriented around both economic and cultural impacts, brought about by loss of local power and increasing immigration.[14] The primary target—especially for the far right—is elites, who are blamed for orchestrating both threats. And antiglobalization acts as an ideal channel for both anti-elite and anti-immigrant sentiment.

Antiglobalization language pits ordinary people who feel economically marginal or precarious or who experience relative deprivation against "global" forces they can blame. Those forces are then defined as national or cosmopolitan elites who "sell out" their country, facilitate power transfer to global entities, and let jobs go to foreign countries.[15] This tension—not only between the global and the local/national but also, by extension, between urban elites and nonurban, ordinary citizens—creates an opportunity for the far right to link globalization and elites. A common frame is to point to globalization as the source of local and national woes, and simultaneously blame elites for globalization's growth and for being out of touch with the common people.

In the ordinary lingo of the extreme far right, this is most commonly expressed with a simple frame: "they" are out to get us. "They are killing us, literally killing us," the neo-Nazi Matthew Heimbach told journalist Vegas Tenold on the morning of the 2016 US presidential election, referring to Washington elites and especially the Democrats.[16] This trope is as useful for political fodder as it is for conspiracy thinking, as "they" are responsible not only for labeling white people racist and ignoring the needs of poor white communities but also for putting chemicals in meat to make "men more feminine," as the white nationalist Tom Pierce stated at a 2015 rally in support of the Confederate flag. "I heard that too," another man confirmed. "They put some kind of stuff in there." They, it turns out, can be blamed for quite a lot.[17]

In this way, global financial and political elites became a bogeyman for the far right, who argue that elites are working against the interests of the common, national people and their natural, pure condition. Anti-elite discourse acts as a channel, laying the blame for the pure, national people's suffering at the feet of liberal migration policies forged by cosmopolitan and progressive elites. This allows the far right to frame anti-globalization and antimigration sentiments as logically pro-nation and anti-elite at one and the same time.[18] Global, multiculturalist elites are faulted not only for embracing diversity and welcoming immigration, but also for making those issues "litmus tests" for moral responsibility and respectability, passing judgment, and "labeling" those who don't adhere to these cosmopolitan values as racist.[19]

This is where populist and anti-elite rhetoric opens the door to extreme anti-immigration positions. The argument goes like this: supranational trade deals result in an unnatural pace of development in the global South, driving millions of economic refugees and migrants north in ways said to threaten Western civilization.[20] Nations will be forced to adopt more liberal immigration policies and privilege multiculturalism over nationalism.[21] Immigration itself is a threat to jobs and the welfare state, bringing crime and terrorism and eradicating local and national cultural identities. But multiculturalism itself is bad for all pure peoples, not just the nationalists at home, because it strips immigrants and host countries of their own distinct cultures and identities in favor of blended worlds where no one is distinct.[22] This frame allows the far right to present its ideas as protectionist rather than exclusionary.

National citizens can thus blame liberal elites and their lenient immigration laws for a wide variety of ills brought about by globalization—economic precarity, the loss of local identity, and the downfall of Western culture itself.[23] Only a stronger state can counteract these trends, the argument goes, promising stronger trade barriers and more domestic protection from global markets so that the organic civil society and economy can thrive nationally. Far-right movements and parties thus promise to protect the "everyday" and "ordinary" citizen and the pure people from the destructive forces of globalization and economic liberalization.[24] This logic has underpinned much of the rhetorical framing of the Brexit vote and widespread Euroscepticism among populist nationalist parties across Europe, as well as anti-immigrant rhetoric from the Trump administration.[25]

This approach strategically intertwines anti-elite, pro-nationalist, and anti-immigrant discourse all at once. This means that antiglobal language has carried far-right ideas into the mainstream, by using antiglobalization discourse to introduce and strengthen anti-immigration sentiments. Immigration itself—and cultural or racial diversity more broadly—is posed as a threat to the nation and its pure people. This threat is even posed in existential terms, through metaphors about the nation's healthy body and the threat posed by the "degenerate" left, diseased immigrants, criminal rapists, or pests like rats and cockroaches who threaten the vitality of the nation and its pure people.[26] When mainstream politicians use terms like "vermin" and "infestation," they help channel the far right's dehumanizing and hierarchical ways of thinking into the mainstream—as President Trump did in July 2019 when he described the city of Baltimore as a "rat and rodent-infested mess" where "no human being" would want to live.[27] This is where the second way that far-right ideologies are normalized through mainstream political discourse becomes particularly evident, by framing immigration as an existential threat.

Immigration as Existential Threat: Normalizing the Rhetoric of White Genocide

The far right has long suggested that a white genocide is under way, based both on demographic change and the paranoid belief in an orchestrated invasion of immigrants, Muslims, or Jews who will eradicate or replace whites. But in recent years this conspiracy theory has made its way from the far-right fringes into the mainstream spotlight, helped both by political speeches and media commentators, who regularly use the language of replacement, invasion, infestation, and a flood of illegals. *Fox News's* Tucker Carlson has warned that Democrats want "demographic replacement" through a "flood of illegals" in order to increase their voter base, while Laura Ingraham has warned viewers that "the Democrats want to replace many of you," suggesting there is an "invasion of the country" and referring to Texas as a state that is "completely overrun" by an illegal invasion.[28]

Political discourse and campaign advertisements, rally speeches, and election rhetoric that dehumanize immigrants and suggest an existential threat to the nation help normalize extreme ideas about immigration. Consider the examples we have heard just in the past few years from politicians who depict Mexicans as rapists or use language that implies that people of color, migrants, refugees, Jews, or Muslims are not human or live in places where "no human being" would want to live. The media plays a role too, publishing cartoons that replace human beings with rats or other animals, or articles that use metaphors about disease and infestation. Such dehumanization stokes fears and identifies immigrants as the source of "threats" to the healthy nation and its pure people.[29] In Poland, for example, the far right has used metaphors about Ebola, along with language of contagion, viruses, and disease, to suggest that the European Union's policies threaten the healthy Polish nation in potentially fatal ways.[30] Language that positions white women or children as especially in need of protection or defense has proven to be highly effective at mobilizing far-right violence and action, as illustrated by the 2017 case of a gunman storming a Washington, DC, pizza shop to save children he believed were being held in a basement by a pedophile ring run by Democratic operatives.[31] Similar calls urge whites to defend white territory and fight against "criminal migrants."

Sometimes this existential threat is linked to broader conspiracies about Jews in ways that help introduce, reinforce, and mainstream anti-Semitism. For example, references to "globalists"—a term that acts as coded speech for Jews—as responsible for the economic precariousness of local populations simultaneously communicate anti-elite and anti-Semitic ideas. This can help mainstream and normalize exclusionary and anti-Semitic ideas to broader populations. The neo-Nazi Matthew Heimbach did this explicitly in efforts to promote white-supremacist solutions to local problems, as the journalist Vegas Tenold has documented. Heimbach framed local struggles to secure jobs, health care, and clean water in Appalachia in "the context of an international fight against globalism and its perceived task masters: the Jews."[32] The only solution, for extremists like Heimbach, is to emphasize the importance of racial and ethnic bonds, which they argue are stronger than national ties and will therefore be more effective at interrupting globalists' efforts. The logical outcome is thus to split the country into autonomous ethno-states.[33]

A related way that extreme ideas are mainstreamed in political rhetoric is when far-right ideology is blended with ideas and stances that have traditionally belonged to the left. For example, far-right groups have linked the notion of freedom fighters to far-right causes. Some groups appropriate the language of diversity by claiming that white supremacists are the true multiculturalists, because they seek to separate and preserve all cultures, as opposed to those who would promote "race mixing," which reduces heterogeneity across cultures and ethnic groups. Others have promoted progressive stances on gender and sexuality instead of the far right's traditional stance on women's roles as wives, mothers, and homemakers.[34] In this approach, far-right groups explicitly position women's or LGBTQ+ rights as "Western" rights in order to make arguments against Islam and Muslim immigration and suggest that these "Western" rights are threatened by Islamic rule or Sharia law. Examples like these illustrate how the far right co-opts some of the left's language around feminism or minority rights in order to make arguments about the supposed threat to the West or to Western women and sexual minorities from immigration. These strategies have helped the far right successfully mainstream ideas that previously would have been regarded as extreme or fringe.

Finally, as other scholars have documented in greater depth, the media play a critical role in communicating extreme political rhetoric in mainstream outlets—both in traditional formats and in rapidly evolving social-media channels. Various media outlets, from the *New York Times* to NBC's *Today Show*, have been critiqued for being too sympathetic, or for hosting far-right provocateurs and white supremacists on radio and television programs. And the rapid evolution of online communication and news sharing on social media has changed people's ability to evaluate and sort reliable sources of information from fake news or ideological propaganda.[35] This is where it becomes especially clear that political rhetoric that hints at a white genocide is only part of a much broader challenge. New and old conspiracy theories, along with systematic disinformation campaigns, are also helping mainstream extremist ideologies and violence.

Disinformation and Conspiracy Theories

New ecosystems of online communication allow the far right to create and quickly spread conspiracies, which are powerful tools for destabilizing people's sense of truth. Conspiracy theories introduce new ideological frames that seem to explain people's social worlds. Such theories position a clear line between "us" and "them" and allow a wide variety of grievances to be explained by the orchestrated efforts of an elite few, offering a way of making sense of perceived injustice and making uncertain times feel clearer and more stable.[36] And perhaps most notably in terms of the recent spate of white-supremacist violence globally, conspiracy theories help to mobilize action by creating moral claims about right and wrong that make it seem immoral not to act. Several recent violent far-right and white-supremacist extremists have engaged in terrorist or violent acts out of a sense of moral obligation, trying to save children from a supposed pedophile ring or white populations from an immigrant invasion.[37] "Once you see the truth," journalist Anna Merlan explains, "once the light has penetrated the life you previously led and the lies you previously believed—who could do otherwise?" Conspiracism, she argues, creates a "legible moral map of the universe" that can spur the extreme fringe to violent action.[38]

Conspiracy theories are an effective tool for mainstreaming far-right ideas because even when the conspiracy itself is not adopted by large parts of the mainstream, certain far-right elements of it do take hold—through, for example, the language of invasion, disease, and the idea of Jewish global funding. Individuals may not believe that there is a global "cabal" of Jews orchestrating migration and demographic change. But they can still absorb anti-Semitic messages or be left with a sense of suspicion or bias in ways they may not be fully aware of. Even when well-intentioned individuals are trying to refute them, the repetition of conspiracy theories in the act of refutation can "embed them in receptive minds"—making for very challenging territory for journalists and scholars who speak to the public about them.[39] And because conspirational thinking allows even established facts to be interpreted as "further evidence of the conspiracy and its efforts to hide the 'truth,'" logical or fact-based arguments don't work to refute conspiracies.[40] This is most evident in the case of the "migrant caravan" conspiracy theory, which I examine in depth below—but there are numerous other recent examples illustrating how conspiracy theories affect the mainstream, particularly when fringe actors are motivated by the theory to engage in real-life violence.[41]

From Pizzagate to the Migrant Caravan: Conspiracy Theories and the Far Right

Americans love a good conspiracy theory. From the earliest postrevolutionary warnings about the "Illuminati's plans to destroy the republic," to beliefs about the orchestrated assassinations of John F. Kennedy and Martin Luther King Jr., and Trump's claims that President Obama was not born in the United States, conspiracies have long been part and parcel of Americans' belief systems.[42] But there has been a shift in recent years, enabled by social media, the easy spread of fake news, and the adoption of conspiracy theorizing by mainstream politicians. As Merlan explains, "while conspiracy theories are as old as the country itself, there *is* something new at work: people who peddle lies and half-truths have come to prominence, fame and power as never before."[43] And the new conspiracies are different in nature from the ones that came before. They are a "new conspiracism," as the scholars Russell Muirhead and Nancy Rosenblum describe it: conspiracy without the theory.

Classic conspiracism helps ordinary people make sense of a "disorderly and complicated world" by taking events that seem to defy explanation (like the 9/11 attacks or John F. Kennedy's assassination) and framing them as the organized work of a group of powerful people.[44] But the new conspiracism "dispenses with the burden of explanation," relying on innuendo, suggestion, and repetition—with legitimation of conspiracies and accusations built through retweets, forwards, reposting, and *social* validation.[45] Language is also key to the mainstreaming of conspiracy theories. Using words like "skeptic" or "dissident" instead of "denier" in relation to climate change, human immunodeficiency virus, or vaccinations can make conspiracists' positions seem more positive.[46] This combination of more-positive terms and frequent repetition is a key driver of the normalization of extreme ideologies. Familiarity reinforces messaging around themes like surveillance or elite control, while softer terminology conveys a positive stance rather than a negative one, potentially making people more receptive to the ideas.[47]

Over half of Americans endorse at least one conspirational narrative about a current political phenomenon or event.[48] Half of self-identified Republicans in the United States believe American elections are "massively rigged."[49] Even when mainstream politicians do not actively circulate conspiracy theories, they can help validate them by failing to denounce them. Politicians also actively legitimize conspiracies by alleging that they might be true. Regarding the claim that Democrats had deliberately manufactured the Charlottesville violence, Idaho Republican state representative Bryan Zollinger said, "I am not saying it is true, but I am suggesting that it is completely plausible."[50] By alleging that the claim is "true enough" or that there is "something there" or that "every-body is saying" something happened, mainstream politicians and members of the general public have helped legitimize conspiracy theories through innuendo—helping contribute to delegitimation, political disorientation, and weakened democratic institutions.[51]

Conspiracy theories aren't limited to the far right, of course. But the use of conspiracy theories is especially appealing among hate groups globally. The far right's "terrified, wild conjectures" about Jews, Sharia law, the government, and even attempts to emasculate them with soy products, are well documented.[52] There are even conspiracies about whether white supremacism exists at all, as evidenced when *Fox News* host Tucker Carlson claimed on air after the El Paso shooting that white supremacy was a "hoax" and a conspiracy theory deliberately introduced to help those in power retain it.[53] When I gave an interview to the *Washington Post*'s Jennifer Rubin a few weeks later, the comments section of the newspaper's social-media share of the article drew plenty of conspirational comments. One reader wrote that "white supremacy is a political slogan invented for the purpose of dividing, confusing," while another commenter noted that "The only ones keeping White Supremacy alive is the left." The media were also blamed, as another reader noted, complaining that "it's just another lie by the media, who has nothing on Trump so they play the race card."[54]

The uptick in far-right conspiracy theories online wasn't an organic development. They were promoted through content producers—like Alex Jones of Infowars—who used podcasts, viral memes, and publicity stunts to take ideas and propel them "from the fringes of the internet into the mainstream."[55] The lack of significant efforts by social-media companies to regulate, remove, or counter conspirational content—along with a lack of government regulation of those companies—means there are few options available for interrupting its spread.[56] These developments are consequential. In May 2019, the FBI's Phoenix field office issued an intelligence bulletin noting that conspiracy theories are very likely inspiring domestic terrorists, suggesting that "certain conspiracy theory narratives tacitly support or legitimize violent action." It also notes that it anticipates this phenomenon to evolve and grow owing to the ease of communications on internet platforms and as the 2020 election cycle ramps up.[57]

To illustrate the way that conspiracy theories underpin the modern far right and help far-right ideas enter the mainstream, consider the far-right conspiracy that liberal financier and philanthropist George Soros is a funder of migrant caravans to the southern US border. Soros has long been vilified by organized far-right extremists, who use anti-Semitic rhetoric casting him as a left-wing radical financier and master-mind of a group of elite globalists working to dismantle white, Christian nations through immigration.[58] The goal, so the conspiracy goes, is to create multiethnic, multicultural communities that all look the same everywhere. Importantly, while Soros is painted as the lead architect, the conspiracy theory has grown well beyond wealthy and powerful individuals like Soros. The increasing circulation of these kinds of conspiracy theories has also taken place alongside rising everyday anti-Semitism across the United States.[59]

The Trump administration has repeatedly drawn attention to migrant caravans—groups of thousands of migrants who make their way to the southern border together. But in the fall of 2018, the conspiracy theory that George Soros was funding a migrant caravan gained steam. At a Montana campaign rally in October 2018, Trump told the crowd that "A lot of money has been passing to people to come up and try to get to the border. . . . there are those that say that caravan didn't just happen. It didn't just happen. A lot of reasons that caravan, 4,000 people." The day before, Republican representative Matt Gaetz had tweeted supposed footage of a migrant caravan and wrote, "Soros? US-backed NGOs? Time to investigate the source!" Three *Fox News* hosts had also suggested that a group of migrants was being funded by Soros or other groups.[60] Less than two weeks after that October Montana rally, a shooter killed eleven people at a Pittsburgh synagogue because he believed they were funding migrant invaders.[61]

Once a fringe conspiracy, the Soros-migrant-caravan theory made its way into mainstream populist nationalist discourse in two ways. First, it became intertwined with a larger far-right narrative pitting "globalists" (meaning Jews, in far-right code) against nationalists. Thus, when the

French far-right leader Marine Le Pen noted that "the division is no longer right-left (but) patriot-globalist," such rhetoric not only signals that the nation stands against global forces, but also sends anti-Semitic, racist, and exclusionary dog whistles, harkening the nation back to a fantasy period of purity and homogeneity, now threatened by some nefarious, elite, global force.[62] Whether or not intentional, politicians who use the term "globalist" send signals that reinforce this conspiracy theory.

The other way the Soros caravan conspiracy was mainstreamed is when it moved from fringe right-wing news and social-media sites like Gab and Breitbart into major media platforms like *Fox News* and the statements of mainstream politicians, including President Trump and Congressman Gaetz.[63] Frequent mention of the "migrant caravan" in these spaces, along with language like "invasion" and "flood" and reference to Soros funding, reinforced and helped legitimize the conspiracy. Importantly, Trump's legitimation of the Soros conspiracy relied on the same innuendo-laden strategies that Muirhead and Rosenblum articulate in their book. When asked by a reporter, Trump said he "wouldn't be surprised" if someone was funding the caravan, and when the reporter then prompted with, "George Soros?" Trump replied, "I don't know who, but I wouldn't be surprised. A lot of people say yes."[64]

The Soros-migrant-caravan case illustrates how conspiracy theories themselves have become powerful tools for the far right. I suggest there are at least four impacts of far-right conspiracy theories on the mainstream: undermining democratic institutions and expertise, identifying key enemies, linking racialized territory to national security, and mobilizing violence by fringe actors.

First, conspiracy theories undermine democratic institutions and the sources of knowledge that have historically supported them. Accusations of fake news, Democratic-organized violence, and manufactured activism undermine the public's understanding of the line between fact and fiction. Calling the gun-control activism of David Hogg and other high school survivors of a Florida school shooting—or the parents of murdered Sandy Hook schoolchildren—"crisis actors" working on behalf of adult anti-gun advocacy groups is just one horrific example. Conspiracy theories from the far right have the effect of reducing trust and creating uncertainty within the mainstream. What is real and what is not? In a world already unsettled by knowledge of foreign governments' election meddling—or bots manufacturing Twitter outrage to polarize whole societies—it is easy to see how the mainstream might be affected by accusations, innuendo, and conspiracism that challenges the very notion of observed reality.

Second, conspiracy theories help the far right identify key enemies (such as liberals, the media, Jews, academic experts, or multiculturalists) in ways that help polarize and create a sense of threat. These purported enemies are deemed to be undermining white geographies by promoting multiculturalism, liberal immigration policies, and refugee assistance. Part of what makes a theory a conspiracy theory is the notion of orchestration—such as the idea that there is an organized, coordinated effort on the part of national and global elites to manipulate populations in ways that will strengthen and maintain their own control. This reinforces ideas that disenfranchised or economically insecure working-class white communities may already have about elite bureaucrats and technocrats ignoring or undermining them. "They" are working against "us," so the logic goes, in order to solidify their own power, ensure a stream of new voters for the Democratic party, or manipulate financial markets.

Third, conspiracy theories tap into fantastical ideas about imagined territories, sacred spaces, and heroic action and layer those ideas into deep and abiding far-right ideological beliefs, such as anti-Semitism. The Soros-migrant-caravan conspiracy shows how conspiracy theories that situate an external threat to the nation or to white communities through immigration rely on the centrality of racialized territory as key to national security. Such framings rely on ideas, fantasies, and myths about sacred national space and white geographies to help mainstream extremist ideologies and violence. They require a receptivity rooted in assumptions both about who can call particular places home and who should be excluded from any claims to belonging there. They simultaneously act as a call to action for those who would defend that space, preventing imminent threats to the nation and working to restore a fantasy way of life.

Fourth and finally, conspiracy theories clearly inspire violence by fringe actors who believe the conspiracy is Truth and move from fantasy to direct action and real-life violence. This happens in at least two ways— by mobilizing individuals who believe it is their moral imperative to act and by reducing their empathy for others. "If you have found a genuine foe," Anna Merlan explains, "you are free to loathe him or her as expansively as necessary."[65] For far too many individuals, that loathing has already—or will in the future—take the form of deadly violence.

Extreme ideas, in sum, have been mainstreamed through political and campaign rhetoric and through the spread of disinformation and conspiracy theories. But they have also been mainstreamed through strategic efforts to change the presentation and packaging of far-right-extremist ideas. This is most obvious in the change in the external appearance of far-right individuals and groups, whose shift to mainstream clothing and style has been widely noted. But it is also illustrated in a transformation in how far-right ideologies are communicated, especially through the use of humor, wit, and satire online. Both phenomena reflect a new weaponization of youth culture.

Weaponizing Youth Culture: Mainstreamed Aesthetics

For a generation of adults who grew up with images of far-right extremists as racist Nazi skinheads, far-right aesthetics had clear signals: a uniform style of shaved heads, high black combat boots, and leather bomber jackets. You would be hard-pressed to find a bomber jacket in far-right youth scenes today. The past few years have seen a dramatic shift in the aesthetics of far-right extremism, as the far right has all but abandoned the shaved heads and combat boots of the racist skinhead in favor of a hip, youth-oriented style that blends in with the mainstream.[66] This shift started in Germany in the early 2000s and rapidly spread across Europe, and eventually to US youth scenes as well. The new aesthetic is wide-ranging and diverse, including both the kinds of high-quality T-shirts and sporty hoodies laced with coded far-right symbols sold by for-profit brands who market directly to far-right consumers, and the polished suits, skinny jeans, and fashy haircuts pop-ularized by the American "alt right."[67] This shifting aesthetic has been a key factor in the mainstreaming of far-right ideas. Indeed, the normal-ization of extremist ideas through the kinds of political rhetoric and conspiracy theories discussed above is significantly aided by the simul-taneous mainstreaming of the aesthetics of hate. It is simply much harder to recognize ideas as hateful when they come in an aesthetic package that doesn't fit the image people hold in their heads about what white supremacists look like or how they communicate their ideas.

There are dedicated commercial spaces facilitating this aesthetic shift in ways that are discussed in greater depth in chapter 3. But it isn't just shirts with intentional far-right messaging that have helped mainstream extreme ideas. The broader shifting aesthetic of the global far right is mainstreamed today in ways broader than dedicated brands. Main-streamed aesthetics are part of the broader set of trends supporting the normalization of extreme ideas.

Cleaning Up Extreme Ideas

Smartness has long been a smokescreen for the far right: Hugo Boss, after all, manufactured the Nazi party's brown shirts and uniforms, bringing a tailored, pristine style to military dress that marked a stark departure from the combat fatigues and drab colors typically favored by national militaries.[68] For the Nazis, black leather jackets and long trench coats, along with high black military boots, showed how fashion could be used to communicate military strength and aggression.[69] The shaved heads, bomber jackets, and high black combat boots that post-war neo-Nazis co-opted from British working-class youth in the 1980s aimed for the same impression of aggressive strength, creating a uni-form aesthetic that would come to dominate the far-right youth scene.[70] The racist skinhead look became virtually synonymous with white su-premacism and neo-Nazis for the next three decades.

You can't blame observers, then, for being surprised by the pressed khakis and white polo shirts worn by dozens of young men bearing flaming tiki torches and chanting "Jews will not replace us" as they marched across the University of Virginia campus in 2017. But the clean-cut look wasn't coincidental. Far-right leaders knew all too well that the public would struggle to connect hate with a style of dress that looked more like the kid next door than the neo-Nazi of their imagination. So, in the days leading up to the Unite the Right rally in Charlottesville, a prominent neo-Nazi blogger instructed marchers to dress respectably, noting that their appearance was more important than their ideas in getting people to listen.[71]

There are plenty of ways that the transformation in far-right aesthetics and style is organically driven from within youth scenes. But Charlottesville illustrated clearly that it is also part of a top–down tactic on the part of the far right to appear more mainstream in order to make the public more receptive to its ideas. Charlottesville, in other words, was a self-conscious and deliberate aesthetic performance—an attempt to normalize and disrupt Americans' (and the world's) ideas about what far-right extremists look like. This aimed to make it harder to interpret and recognize the ideas as extreme, since they do not fit the aesthetic package that people were used to associating with neo-Nazis, Ku Klux Klan (KKK) members, or white supremacists. Fashion and style become part of strategies to miscommunicate and hide racist intentions.[72]

The strategy wouldn't have worked if it weren't so appealing to a generation of youth drawn to the far right but eager to shed the stigma of the skinhead look and blend into the mainstream. Having come of age in the social-media and image-board era, today's youth are hyperconscious of their own appearance and personal brand. Mainstreaming the aesthetic not only helps soften the far right's message to outsiders, but also changes the conception of outsider and insider, enabling youth to move in and out of the far right in ways that would have been impossible in the past. Today's far-right youth can be mainstream in their appearance, but extreme in their ideas. This is a radical change from the racist skinhead era, when the far right's "uniform" aesthetic made extreme ideological views transparent to teachers, employers, parents, and peers. This change makes being a part of far-right scenes more palatable for a broader range of youth.

It isn't just the clean-cut look of mainstream clothing styles that nor-malizes far-right extremist ideas. Dedicated brands selling clothing with coded messaging helps socialize and desensitize consumers to far-right narratives, with ideological messaging and calls to resist, rebel, fight back, or re-migrate immigrants. But the clothing also acts as a carrier of extremist ideas into mainstream society by exposing others to the same messaging. In my previous research in Germany, for example, I found that youth learned about brands marketing to the far right from friends, classmates, older relatives, neighbors, and work colleagues. In some cases, expensive brands become status symbols, popularized by older siblings, neighbors, and friends who help establish what is "cool" and thus broaden the far-right's ideological reach. These kinds of dynamics mean that consumer preferences and youth desires can act as a kind of Trojan horse, introducing extremist ideas in unexpected ways. More-over, the growing use of social media and digital platforms for extremist communication and recruitment has meant that the kinds of emotional appeals that underpin far-right-extremist communication are carefully stylized and curated for their visual and cultural appeal to vulnerable youth. Aesthetics and style communicate emotional traits and qualities that appeal to recruits' expressions of desire, longing, anger, resistance, and rebellion and become a "gateway" into extremist scenes and subcultures.

Weaponizing Youth Culture: Humor and New Communication Styles

Part of the mainstreaming of extreme style includes a shift from aes-thetic signals that communicate emotions like anger to ones that use humor, wit, and clever codes that convey exclusionary and dehuman-izing messages.[73] For example, where the extreme far right might have previously embraced bold tattoos or posters of swastikas or racist phrases, today's far-right youth are more likely to display ambiguous messages, embedding racist or anti-immigrant sentiment in brightly colored iconography that often uses smart, historical codes. Part of this shift in communication styles is due to the wider use of humor, jokes, and irony in internet culture more broadly, especially through the creation and circulation of memes.

Memes are typically visual cultural elements that use jokes to apply witty text, labels, symbols, or alterations to images, words, photographs, cartoons, short videos, facial expressions, or other cultural bits in ways that are then shared and altered repeatedly by other users online, usually in anonymous ways.[74] The widespread creation and circulation of racist, misogynistic, anti-Semitic, or Islamophobic memes on social media—in which far-right ideological sentiments are conveyed through jokes, irony, satire, double entendres, and suggestion—have effectively weaponized humor to help carry extremist ideas into the mainstream. The use of irony and satire has helped the "alt right" open the Overton window of acceptable political ideas, as funny memes and other styles of communication in online spaces carry racist humor and white-supremacist ideas from underground, fringe places into the main-stream.[75] Jokes and funny memes create collective laughter and a sense of community among those who feel like insiders for getting the joke.[76] They create plausible deniability and depict anyone who is offended as a triggered, liberal snowflake who doesn't get the joke. In this way, humor and satire shift the far right from a defensive to an offensive cultural position and help far-right youth come across as countercultural and edgy, while simultaneously shifting public conversation to include more extreme ideologies.[77]

In some cases, memes or T-shirt messages deliberately troll the left or other groups and individuals designated as opponents. In one German T-shirt, for example, a stick figure hangs from gallows alongside the words "Dancing in the Air"—which was co-opted from an antiracist music concert by the same name. You want to dance in the air? the T-shirt seems to mock. We'll show you what "dancing in the air" looks like—the twitching of a dying man being lynched. Of all the clothing images I showed to youth in interviews for my previous book, disturbingly it was this T-shirt that produced the most laughter.

Humor can carry extremist ideas into the mainstream, helping educate and radicalize viewers to far-right ideas in a softer way. This is especially true for youth culture, where the online sharing of visual jokes and memes is already widespread. Coded references, symbols, and memes that use humor and playfully represent historical references to atrocities against Jews, Muslims, and others deemed not to belong can help socialize consumers and their peers, denigrate victims, and inform youth about far-right ideological positions. They can help youth build or strengthen racist and nationalist identification. Memes and humorous iconography desensitize youth to violence, dehumanize ethnic and religious minorities, and make light of past atrocities and contemporary expressions of hatred. Memes that compare pizza baking to putting "another Jew in the oven," T-shirts that poke fun at murders of *döner* shop owners by neo-Nazi terrorists, codes that valorize Nazi history, and iconography that celebrates the violence enacted through the Crusades are just a few recent examples. Even when jokingly embedded in witty memes and T-shirts, such iconography vilifies migrants and trivializes historical pogroms in ways that can normalize anti-immigrant, anti-Semitic, Islamophobic, and racist attitudes and beliefs. Combined with symbols that overtly and covertly express resistance and rebellion, such messages position far-right beliefs and attitudes as antiauthority and antimainstream and simultaneously help carry them into broader consumer groups. These messages don't exist in a vacuum, of course. These aesthetic shifts thrive within a broader sociopolitical context saturated with populist nationalist rhetoric, a declining trust in governments, and a loss of faith in democracy more generally. But by using humor and modern, clever, witty iconography, the new aesthetic offers broader appeal and has helped normalize and mainstream extremist ideas.

Integrated Mainstreaming

Together, these three domains where the mainstreaming of extremism is most prevalent—in political rhetoric, conspiracy theories, and aesthetics and communication styles—help establish the kinds of content that people engage with in the spaces and places where mainstreaming and radicalization are happening today. In each area, extreme ideas are being introduced to mainstream populations in new ways. But they do not act in fully isolated ways. Far-right ideologies are reinforced when similar kinds of messaging appear in other domains. A conspiracy theory may seem more plausible if it is echoed in a mainstream political campaign speech. Anti-immigration rhetoric may be more appealing to a younger generation if it is packaged in a witty meme or an expensive, well-made T-shirt. The normalization of extremist ideas is significantly aided by their simultaneous mainstreaming in multiple spheres of everyday life. In the chapters to come, I shift to a discussion of new spaces and places where these extremist ideas are encountered, focusing on commercial markets and cultural spaces, combat sports and physical spaces, educational spaces, and the online world that underpins them all.

Chapter 3

Selling Extremism

Food, Fashion, and Far-Right Markets

We were right-wing before it was cool.

—T-SHIRT TEXT AT EUROPEAN NEO-NAZI FESTIVAL,
APRIL 2018

The market for hate is thriving.[1] The days when individuals distributed self-produced music cassettes and CDs or homemade, screen-printed T-shirts out of the backs of cars and on folding tables at white-supremacist festivals are long gone. Today's far-right consumers can choose from a wide array of high-quality products that touch nearly every aspect of their lives, from the way they cook to the clothes they wear. There are dedicated YouTube talk shows and vlogs (video blogs), clothing brands, music streaming services, and a neo-Nazi coffee company owned by a white-supremacist podcaster.[2] Publishing houses produce novels and magazines laced with far-right cultural references and ideological messages attuned to modern audiences. One such German environmental magazine linked to the far right describes itself as the "magazine for holistic thinking. Environmental protection—animal protection—homeland protection."[3] Foodies can watch a German right-wing vegan cooking show or tune in to YouTube vlogs and see millennial far-right women share organic recipes while detailing their experiences growing vegetables, practicing white European paganism, being a housewife, and homeschooling children. These shows sing the virtues of joining the "white baby challenge," helping the white race reproduce.[4] In Ukraine and Germany, far-right groups run neo-Nazi summer camps for children. New genres of racist music—such as "fashwave" (fascism wave, a variant of electronic music) and white-power country and pop—have broadened far-right music scenes far beyond the hard rock style typically associated with white-power music.[5] Across the globe, the commercial and cultural spaces the far right uses to reach new audiences and communicate its ideologies have expanded rapidly—aided in no small part by social media and "brand fan" image-sharing sites that help promote and circulate new products.

This chapter takes a deep dive into new commercial and cultural spaces where far-right extremism and white supremacy are packaged and sold. Analyzing the role of these new spaces, I look here at how markets for white-supremacist products might be supporting far-right movements financially and culturally, and how the broader array of new extremist spaces may be affecting the growth of far-right extremism more generally. I rely on two extended examples to illustrate: food and fashion.

Edible Extremism: Prepping in the Kitchen, Prepping for the End Times

At first glance, the emergence in 2014 of a far-right vegan cooking show on YouTube may have seemed like a bizarre, fringe development. The show is hosted by German balaclava-wearing extremists who infuse discussions of ingredients and the virtues of a meatless diet with far-right ideology. The show was at the forefront of a transformation in the kinds of physical and virtual places and spaces where the far right engages the mainstream, as well as in the aesthetics of far-right scenes more broadly. But food turns out to be a particularly rich domain to embed messages about identity, tradition, culture, and obligations to families, households, and the homeland, as well as narratives of rebellion against an unjust state or liberal elites. Food and food-related rituals have long been understood as essential to collective belonging, emotion, memory, and national identity. This is especially obvious in a country with as many varied immigrant communities as the United States. In my Pennsylvania hometown, for example, thousands of people have shown up in a

downtown church parking lot each summer for over forty years to celebrate Lebanese Heritage Day, with overloaded plates of hummus, tab-
bouleh, and shish kabob. Indeed, on nearly any weekend day across the
United States, from church parking lots to city stadiums, the wafting
smells of Greek whole-roasted lamb on a spit, Jamaican jerk grills, and
Mexican street taco trucks accompany the thousands of ethnic heritage
food festivals that are part and parcel of every American community
today. Scores of research studies have documented the meaning-making
role played by food and its preparation, presentation, and associated
traditions, festivals, and ceremonies. From Japanese tea ceremonies to
the politics of foie gras in the United States and France, food consumption is key to the conceptualization of home, nation, and homeland.[6]

Less is known about whether and how food plays a role in extremist
identities. Food is neglected more generally in studies of youth subcultures in favor of a focus on dress, music, language and slang, and style.
And it is almost never invoked in discussions of extremism, despite its
clear connection to nationalism, nativism, and belonging. In my interviews for two separate book projects with German young people in and
around far-right scenes, food often came up as a marker of belonging,
through discussions of what young people deemed strange or foreign
smells in ethnic neighborhoods, traditional German foods, and the
issue of Muslim immigrants not eating pork. As Markus, a twenty-one-
year-old construction apprentice, explained in 2013, "a Nazi would think
a Döner (kebab) is shit, it's from the Turks. . . . I think they really
only . . . want to eat German things." More than a decade earlier, I had
spoken with Jan, an eighteen-year-old construction apprentice, who
told me that dual citizenship was an absurd notion because "if you put
a Hungarian salami in a refrigerator and then look at it after six years, it's
still a Hungarian salami and not a little German sausage." It is impossible
for a Turk to become a German, he explained, because "one is born into
a community of fate [Schicksalgemeinschaft] and one has to accept that,
you can't just write 'sheep' on a pig and have it then be a pig."[7] Food, for
Jan, is the perfect metaphor for national(ist) belonging. In fieldwork
with far-right German youth in Berlin, the anthropologist Nitzan
Shoshan had similar experiences, finding that food—and the

strangeness of foreign foods' smells, as young people walk through the city—is key to understandings of Germanness and otherness. An occasional kebab stand might be all right, but too many ethnic food options in a city or a neighborhood posed a sense of threat, harboring "unforeseen risks to the German body" and to German landscapes.[8]

The hosts of the neo-Nazi cooking show clearly recognize the powerful connection between food and identity. But they also realize that food can be a channel to connect with broader publics. Cooking shows are widely popular in the mainstream. They are, of course, places to pick up cooking tips and try out new recipes. But such shows are also lifestyle brands that convey messages about wellness, identity, and social image. Members of the group Balaclava Küche, which hosts the vegan far-right cooking show, talk about food and eating as something that enables "a healthy body" and as a "moral choice" that helps them stay "true to the National Socialist ideology."[9] In addition to sharing ideas about food and vegan lifestyles, the hosts interweave far-right references and ideological messages throughout the show, including racist and anti-Semitic comments along with antiglobalization, anti-American, and anticapitalist sentiments. They also use humor, wit, sarcasm, inside jokes, and coded messages to share and reinforce far-right-extreme ideologies in a playful, amusing way that reflects a youth-oriented style. By taking a fun activity like cooking and integrating far-right ideas in an entertaining way, the hosts both regale their audience with banter and stories that show they are having fun while simultaneously educating and guiding debate on far-right topics.[10] In this way, the Balaclava Küche hosts blend youth-oriented, hip cultural trends with far-right ideological messaging. "They fit nicely in their new IKEA kitchen," the journalist Gerda Matthies notes wryly, describing their stylish hoodies and jogging pants and noting the show is "only one of many attempts of the [far-right] scene to give itself a new image." The group has an off-line presence as well, having provided vegan catering for a large far-right music concert in 2015 and cross-promoting an extreme-right singer-songwriter by raffling off an audio CD on one of their shows. Their episodes have been viewed tens of thousands of times.[11]

Despite the show's popularity, it's hard to imagine that veganism will catch on within the broader far right anytime soon. In fact, meat consumption has recently been championed by the right as a celebration of manliness and a way of rejecting liberal calls for vegetarianism as a strategy to reduce greenhouse gases. In summer 2018, the Canadian psychology professor Jordan Peterson—whose attacks on "political correctness," snowflakes, and gendered pronouns have won him favor among the far right—publicly extoled the benefits of "carnivorism" for health reasons.[12] The trend quickly gained favor among youth who saw the diet as an easy way to thumb their noses at liberals, along with celebrating the use of plastic straws and boycotting tofu, which the far right presents as dangerous because of the potential for soy-based estrogen to emasculate young men. The all-meat diet signaled a kind of hypermasculinity and manly ideals related to primitive strength and prowess, drawing comparisons to hunters, cavemen, predators, and wolves.[13] Meat eating is used to evoke pro-American and antigovernment sentiments all at once, as Infowars founder Alex Jones did in August 2016 when he tweeted a photo of himself with a platter of raw sausages, steaks, and meat patties with the phrase "Celebrating Americana with some Red Meat, f-you Obama!" Jones's message is that Obama and other elites want "to take away America's meat, just like they were coming for guns and Confederate flags" and any of a variety of other cherished symbols.[14]

Congresswoman Alexandria Ocasio-Cortez added fuel to the fire in February 2019 when she cosponsored the Green New Deal, a plan to address climate change that raised questions about whether beef production needed to be regulated. In an interview on *Showtime*, Ocasio-Cortez tried to reassure viewers that the plan was not to "force everybody to go vegan or anything crazy like that." But, she suggested, "Maybe we shouldn't be eating a hamburger for breakfast, lunch and dinner."[15] The backlash was swift. "They want to take away your hamburgers," the far-right-linked former Trump administration advisor Sebastian Gorka warned in a speech at the Conservative Political Action Conference, "This is what Stalin dreamt about but never achieved."[16] Veggie burgers are also a perceived threat. In October 2019, the neo-Nazi podcasters Joseph Jordan and Mike Peinovich took on the "impossible burger"—a soy-based, vegetarian product from the Impossible Foods company, which now supplies products to fast-food outlets like Burger King and Red Robin. In their October 1, 2019, episode, Jordan and Peinovich argued that the soy burgers are part of a Jewish capitalist plot against white people and industrialized society, with the aim of reducing the United States "to the level of the Third World," where there will be a "mass of undifferentiated laborers that are eating soy burgers and riding around in little putt-putt cars."[17]

Hamburgers' time in the far-right spotlight isn't limited to the issue of climate change or threats from soy-based alternatives. Two years before the Ocasio-Cortez beef-production controversy, after the fast food chain Wendy's tweeted a meme of Pepe the Frog as their red-haired, pigtailed mascot—ostensibly without realizing Pepe had been co-opted by the "alt right"—the neo-Nazi blogger Andrew Anglin declared Wendy's the "official burger of the Neo-Nazi Alt-Right movement." In short order, Anglin also laid claim to Papa John's pizza as the official pizza of the "alt right," sharing a photo of a pizza pie with a sliced-pepperoni swastika. Besides Anglin's efforts, foods and food brands have been increasingly politicized in the United States over the past few years, as both the left and the right have launched boycotts of restaurant chains and food brands deemed supportive of the other side.[18]

Food is central to the far right in many other ways, including within crossover communities like extreme preppers and survivalists who are preparing for apocalyptic end times. Online guides to homesteading, techniques for growing and catching food, and ways to "transition from living in society to real off-the-grid living" are readily available.[19] Off-grid living appeals to a wide range of people across the ideological spectrum, including religious homeschoolers, doomsday preppers, environmentalists, anarchists, and anticapitalists. It represents the extreme fringe of the burgeoning popularity of organic food preparation, vegetarianism, and backyard gardening—trends that are often attributed to the liberal left even though there is ample evidence that pesticide-free food, organic farming, and healthy cooking appeal to growing numbers of individuals across the political spectrum who reject the conventional food system and large-scale corporate agriculture.[20]

The extreme end of this trend, off-grid living, is specifically appealing to a range of right-wing survivalists and groups like the Oath Keepers, a group that is "fixated on apocalyptic scenarios,"[21] whose desire to be prepared for the end times leads them down a rabbit hole of food storage, seed vaults, and solar generators.[22] Another off-grid scene is the Anastasia, or "Ringing Cedars," movement, a reactionary eco-nationalist movement that started in Russia but has grown to several overseas affiliates, including locations in Romania, Canada, Ireland, and the United States.[23] Anastasia communities are self-sustaining ecovillages that emphasize kinship networks and a retreat to nature, good nutrition, sustainable living, and paganism. Their extreme, separatist form of off-grid homesteading blends love of the land, disenchantment with the state, and protectionist nationalism that relies on a conception of humans' natural ties to homelands.[24]

Eco-nationalists aren't the only group integrating food and far-right ideologies. Extreme preppers are another key example. At this very intersection, in fact, Infowars founder Alex Jones seems to have found a market niche. "At the dark confluence of hippie and Hitler," the *New York Times* journalist Timothy Egan recently wrote, "you can buy a year's supply of earth-friendly quinoa."[25] Indeed, in addition to products with patriotic messaging sold in the Infowars store, consumers can pick up a wide array of items to squirrel away for the coming end times. Consumers who peruse the marketing text for a $17.95 bag of "Wake Up America: Patriot Blend" organic coffee are told that "The spirit of the 1776 revolution is truly alive with this exceptional *Wake Up America: Patriot Blend*. Our founders forged this nation with guts and determination, and it is with that same spirit that Infowars battles for the liberty, honor and freedoms of patriots like you everywhere."[26] Shoppers can then move quickly into other categories of products, marketed to extreme preppers awaiting the apocalypse, with categories like "emergency survival foods" and "outdoor survival gear." Consumers can buy water filtration devices, freeze dryers, emergency radios and lanterns, gun holsters, tech security devices, air filtration masks, and potassium iodine tablets, which the website describes as "an essential part of any nuclear preparedness plan." Texts for sale include guides to nuclear survival, first aid, disaster preparedness, and living off the grid. An entire "seed center" sells an organic survival seed vault, a homestead pack of forty types of organic seeds, and a wide variety of other vegetable, medicinal, and culinary herb seeds, while several books offer guidance on edible wild plants, "backyard medicine," emergency pantries, and building a "resilient farm and homestead." Customers can also purchase supplements like "Super Male Vitality," "Survival Shield X," and "Carnivore 90."[27]

Supplements may promise male vitality, but it is traditionally women who bear the brunt of far-right narratives about food, which are often linked to traditional ideals about families and women's roles as wives and mothers. Research on women's roles in far-right movements has illustrated how ideals about food, cooking, and nurturing white families have long intersected with gendered understandings of proper roles as wives and mothers within the far right. Often this is communicated through cues about women's role in producing life. Lana Lokteff, the so-called "most prominent woman" of the "alt right," refers to women as "life givers" for the future of the white race.[28] Other times the connection is more explicit, such as guidance to far-right women on their household chores, which involve cooking and maintaining their family's health. Far-right women have organized bake sales to fund white-supremacist groups and offer guidance to one another about food, cooking, and natural living. In an analysis of one white-separatist group's discourses on gender and motherhood, healthy food and a holistic lifestyle were found to be key to a "racially pure home." This guidance is shared through newsletters or websites with names like "Women's Frontier." Organic, raw fruits and vegetables are particularly encouraged, contrasted with the "billion dollar jew food industry" that threatens the "health and vitality" of white people.[29] Hate is honed, in these cases, through nutritious food and white women's role in preparing it for their families.

In the new mediascape, these messages are packaged in channels like the one run by YouTube's the Blonde Butter Maker, whose vlogs blend messaging about white European paganism with video instruction on how to make nut milk, dehydrate herbs, or preserve berries. "Complacency is poison, traditionalism is the antidote," a recent video asserts, while the channel's logo includes the tagline "Tradition-Heritage-Nutrition." The three-dozen videos have over 45,000 views.[30] Such "alt-right pioneers" package traditional notions of motherhood and femininity as a form of resistance to the mainstream.[31] "You are your own authority, and you choose which direction your life goes," the Blonde Butter Maker tells her viewers in a September 2019 video.[32]

The far right's fixation on food is not entirely new. It is part of a broader discourse linking food, national heritage, and conceptions of tradition, culture, and homeland. Food has been part of far-right mobilization in other settings globally, such as Greece's neo-Nazi Golden Dawn, whose "Greeks only" food handout program was labeled a "soup kitchen of hatred" by the mayor of Athens.[33] The German right-wing extremist party The Third Way (Der Dritte Weg) holds regular food and clothing distribution events for Germans. In its website description of a January 2018 event, the party noted that from late morning until late afternoon, German compatriots (*deutsche Landsleute*) were able to eat homemade lentil soup and pick up plenty of informational materials from their loyal-to-the-people (*Volkstreue*) party.[34] Far-right soup kitchens in France and Greece have also deliberately used pork as a way of excluding Muslims. Muslims and Jews do not eat pork, and bacon is also a frequent choice for vandals who target mosques with strips of bacon inside buildings or wrapped around door handles.[35] Soup kitchen and food outreach programs thus aim to draw in new members and build loyalty among (ethnic) national citizens by showing they can provide resources that the state cannot. But they also use food to exclude Muslims, Jews, or immigrants who do not eat pork, creating real and symbolic boundaries around who belongs in the country and who does not.[36] Pork has also been a focal point for other debates about belonging and inclusion, as illustrated by periodic controversies about whether local schools should remove pork from menus in order to be more responsive to Muslim students. In Leipzig, Germany, for example, two kindergartens received death and arson threats in 2018 after they announced their menus would be pork-free.[37]

But today's far-right fixation on food extends these traditional nationalist approaches to food and *Volk* in new ways, many of which overlap with a broad range of mainstream concerns about pesticides, healthy
living, climate change, and food waste. The modern far right's focus on
food is wide-ranging and aligned with a spectrum of views, from promoting organic food and backyard homesteading to linking red meat
with American male identity. Specific product lines and brands do exist,
such as those selling extreme-prepper products along with ideological
hints about the coming end times, but these trends are nascent, and the
targeted markets remain relatively niche. This is quite a contrast from
the sophisticated and comprehensive development of commercial markets for far-right clothing—which I turn to in the remainder of this
chapter.

Wearable Hate: Extremist Clothing

In the years since white-supremacist blogger Andrew Anglin urged his
followers to dress in "hip" and "cool" ways at the Unite the Right rally
in Charlottesville, far-right fashion has rapidly evolved.[38] The clean-cut
aesthetic of the white polo shirts and khakis that drew national attention
in 2017 has been supplanted by new brands marketing the far right, with
messages and symbols embedded in clothing to convey white-
supremacist ideology.[39] The idea that the humble cotton T-shirt—long
deployed as a walking billboard to advertise anything from the local
auto shop to children's summer camps—could be used to market extremism may seem absurd. But it turns out the T-shirt is an ideal channel for racist and nationalist messaging. Fashion has increasingly become part and parcel of the far right's outreach.

In spring 2018, an Arizona woman was indicted for burglary and other
crimes at a mosque—activities undertaken while coaching her children
to use anti-Muslim slurs and wearing a T-shirt with the phrase "you
can't coexist with people who want to kill you" written across the
chest.[40] In Northwest Washington, DC, I glanced out of my office window and saw a young man with an imperial eagle emblazoned across his
jacket—part of a British fashion brand's controversial logo, which has

been likened to the Nazi eagle symbol.[41] Later that year, I shared a campus elevator with a man wearing a "patriotic" brand T-shirt whose advertising tagline is "forcing hipsters into their safe space, one shirt at a time." Symbols and messaging on otherwise ordinary clothing help signal connections to far-right ideology and organized movements—like the torch-bearing Charlottesville marcher, for example, whose polo shirt bore a logo from the white-supremacist group Identity Evropa.[42]

The phenomenon of contemporary far-right fashion is an outgrowth of the mainstreaming of extremism discussed in chapter 2. Starting in the early to mid-2000s, expensive, high-quality commercial brands marketing clothing to far-right consumers literally transformed the face of far-right youth across Europe and North America.[43] Sometimes called "nationalist streetwear," the clothing uses coded symbols and messages to market extremist politics, turning $35 T-shirts and $80 hoodies into walking billboards to communicate with insiders and outsiders alike. The media would eventually dub the German youth who first embraced this style "Nipsters"—Nazi hipsters. The brands target broad markets of mainstream youth as well as niche subcultures like MMA aficionados. The phenomenon rapidly expanded across Europe, the former Eastern bloc countries, and Russia. Distributors and websites in the United Kingdom and the United States expanded sales into English-speaking markets,[44] and before too long, dedicated platforms like the Rise Above Movement–affiliated "Right Brand Clothing" started pushing the European products to American consumers, promoting and selling clothing through social-media sites like Instagram.[45] New brands like "Certified White Boy Clothing" showed up in the United States to sell their own T-shirts and products.

Across Europe and North America, well over a dozen brands now sell high-quality, well-made, expensive clothing with embedded far-right symbols and messages—most of which appear across the chests and backs of T-shirts and sweatshirts. Websites are often complete with translation and currency converters to help broaden markets beyond national consumers. Through symbols, coded messaging, and clever iconography, some may perceive the clothing to promote white-supremacist ideology; espouse violence against immigrants, Muslims, and Jews; and encourage consumers to rise up in revolution against liberal ideals.[46] One T-shirt tells consumers to "celebrate the real diversity" and displays nine different kinds of headgear—including a World War II gas mask and a Christian Crusader helmet. Others send straightforward messages like "zero white guilt" or simply pair a Confederate flag with a semiautomatic handgun.

Hate clothing celebrates violence in the name of a cause—often using patriotic images and phrases and calls to act like an American, along with Islamophobic, anti-Semitic, and white-supremacist messages. In this way, far-right clothing links patriotism with violence and xenophobia. On one T-shirt, a saluting, grimacing emoji wielding a semiautomatic gun replaces the stars in the American flag, overlaid with the words "locked-n-loaded;" on the back of the T-shirt, the text reads "White American/Hated by Many/Zero F#cks Given." In the "about" section of the website, the company explains it was "not founded on prejudice, seperatism (sic) or racism, but simply out of pride."[47]

The dedicated brands may have created the market for far-right-extremist products, but others quickly joined the fray. Merchandise sections of websites like Alex Jones's Infowars and Breitbart news sell political T-shirts and other products. On the Infowars Store website, consumers can buy T-shirts with political messaging like "I Stand With Trump," anti-antifa messages like "Not Today Antifa," pro–Second Amendment messages, and anti-immigrant messages like "Build the Wall, Protect Texas" alongside stickers with conspiracy messaging like "9/11 was an inside job." A baseball cap with the "OK" symbol appears alongside marketing text that refers to the "thought police at ADL and the Southern Poverty Law Center" designating the OK symbol as a hate symbol. "The new 'It's OK to be OK' Politically Incorrect Designer Snapback Hat is now available!" the website declares, "We can win the Information War by not allowing globalist drones to warp an age-old symbol of good vibes."[48]

The Breitbart store sells T-shirts with similar political messages, including "fight for freedom," "border wall construction," and "deplorable university." Like other commercial websites selling clothing, the marketing text is often even more targeted than the T-shirt iconography or words themselves. A Breitbart T-shirt with flame iconography and the words "walk toward the fire" is sold with marketing text that explains: "When the left tries to bully you . . . Walk Toward the Fire. . . . When they harass and intimidate and turn up the heat in an attempt to distract from the truth and get you to be quiet . . . Walk Toward the Fire."[49] For an Infowars T-shirt featuring the words of the Second Amendment in the shape of a gun alongside the phrase "Come and Take It," the marketing text tells customers to "Wear this t-shirt and connect with fellow gun enthusiasts. By standing together we can defeat this globalist gun grab."[50]

Other brands focus on mainstream niche markets—like veterans and the pro-gun community—infusing those communities' products with references that may be perceived as valorizing or linking patriotism with violence. The US brand Grunt Style, for example, appears to have the aim of promoting a particular kind of patriotism, based on the language and stylistic designs on its retail products. On one T-shirt, the stripes in the American flag are turned into iconography of various gun barrels, while its website explains it sells more than apparel—it "instill[s] pride," noting that "you don't have to be a veteran to wear Grunt Style, but you do have to love Freedom, Bacon and Whiskey."[51] Meanwhile, on other websites, T-shirts with messages like "Feminists don't suck enough," or that celebrate being an "infidel," appear alongside pro-veteran T-shirts, communicating Islamophobic and misogynistic positions alongside pro-military messaging. Messaging on the websites themselves often reinforces or valorizes ideological messages or violence itself, such as a website instruction on a US clothing distributor telling potential consumers to let T-shirts and hoodies express ideology in a "non-verbal" way, or a T-shirt referencing a "summer boogaloo." The term "boogaloo" is a coded reference that signals civil war.[52] Shirts and bumper stickers with Arabic text noting people must "stay back 100 feet or you will be shot" (a phrase used by military convoys in Iraq and Afghanistan) are also available. Such clothing products may directly or indirectly market hatred, sometimes couched within iconography that appeals to broader markets for its pro-veteran, pro-military, or pro-gun rights messaging.

The nationalist messaging also clearly connects local claims and concerns within a global far-right discourse. A Polish nationalist streetwear brand sells a T-shirt depicting the US Confederate flag. Other Eastern European and Russian brands widely adopt runic and Viking symbols, which appeal to German far-right groups who believe Germanic tribes descended from Nordic tribes whose origins were supposedly Aryan. References to Nazi history are common internationally, along with text celebrating or evoking violence, in phrases like "White Power," "Hate Crew," "Pure Blood," "Zero Tolerance," and "Hunting Season." All of these kinds of messages can strengthen far-right ideologies and help the far right see itself as part of a broader, global movement.

Across the board, these brands share a reliance on mainstream-style, expensive clothing and the use of coded symbols that evoke, connote, or directly reference far-right ideological viewpoints or mythic ideals. While young men are the primary target, some of the brands have developed women's lines in which the iconography and messaging are less ideological, less violent, and more sexualized. A few even sell children's clothing. Some brands use profits to support far-right movements and groups, through sponsorship of far-right musicians or concerts, offsetting legal fees for "patriots" who get themselves in trouble with the law, or funding combat-sports gym memberships. Other companies, meanwhile, are merely making money from what they have discovered is a niche, but profitable, market.

Packaging Extremist Messaging

Decades of research on far-right youth culture has shown how particular facets of subcultures and youth scenes—like hate music—can spread intolerance and prejudice against minorities, not only in expected genres like right-wing hard rock and black metal, but also in more mainstream genres like country and pop music.[53] In the same way, hate clothing can expose consumers to extremist opinions, nudging ideological views on immigration, religion, violence, and gun control toward the extremist fringe while opening the door to further engagement and more dangerous actions. Brands marketing hate offer legitimacy, signal membership, and promote ideology to far-right insiders. Far-right clothing also acts as an icebreaker for youth to strike up conversations in school, at stadiums, in bars, and at parties, when they recognize someone across the room wearing an "insider" brand. It can even act as an entry ticket to concerts and underground events where dressing normally would raise a red flag.

Clothing messages also call consumers to action in ways that have been shown to be effective in recruiting followers, whether in populist campaign promises to make a nation great "again" or in extremist calls to restore a caliphate. Across the brands, calls to action in clothing iconography include messages that express antigovernment sentiments, valorize violence, describe a "new revolution," refer to "victory or death," and call on consumers to defend the US Second Amendment. T-shirts on the same websites, meanwhile, convey messages like "White Lives Matter" or reference key white-supremacist symbols, codes, and legends like Odin, a Nordic god who evokes the fantasy of Aryan origins in the Nordic tribes. This means that as consumers scroll through the websites, messages about the need for revolutionary defense and violence are interspersed with products and marketing text clarifying just why violence is necessary or suggesting what the "new revolution" is fighting for: the defense of white civilization.

There are several ways that commercial markets for hate help build support for and engagement with the far right. I discuss three here: recruitment, radicalization, and mobilization to violent action. While I focus here primarily on the example of clothing, I draw some parallels to other examples of commercial markets, including well-developed ones like the music scene and more niche ones like prepper food products and survival gear.

Broadening the Base: Recruitment to the Far Right

Mainstreaming the aesthetic not only makes the far right's message more palatable to outsiders, it also blurs the line between outsiders and insiders in ways that help far-right recruitment. The new aesthetics and their associated commercial products enable young people to be more than one thing at the same time—mainstream in their appearance, for example, but extreme in their ideas and positions. A mainstream aesthetic allows groups and spaces to be more porous, creating easier access and reducing barriers or stigmas that might stop youth from entering. This makes for a softer, less committed, and more experimental entry—a literal trying-on of extremism that also enables plausible deniability with jokes that often carry dual meanings.

Distributors and brands selling far-right products aim for wide, profitable markets. Broadening the appeal to mainstream audiences through shared views about organic food or similar tastes in styles of dress may help win new customers and enhance profits at the same time as it embeds far-right ideology in new thematic packages. And because some far-right T-shirts are sold in general online T-shirt shops in "political" sections that also sell T-shirts promoting other ideological views, far-right views can come across to consumers as just as valid as other kinds of political views. This helps normalize and mainstream far-right ideologies, which end up seemingly "just one opinion" among many.

These trends have been under way for at least two decades in the multimillion-dollar far-right music scene, which the Southern Poverty Law Center (SPLC) describes as a "primary conduit of money and young recruits" to the far right.[54] The far-right music scene dates to the 1980s and was originally limited to hard rock, but today is present across the music spectrum, including country, pop, rap, and folk ballads. This strategy was both top–down and bottom–up, as hate-music executives worked to broaden their markets and promote bands with crossover appeal at the same time as younger generations of youth in and around far-right scenes expressed a desire for a broader range of music genres.[55] Thus the far-right music scene grew to include groups like Prussian Blue—comprising two blond, teenage sisters whose singer-songwriter folk style in the mid-2000s captivated the far right (they later renounced far-right ideology). The scene also saw new kinds of hybrid partnerships, such as a German neo-Nazi band that launched a national rap project when it saw the music appealed to a younger generation.[56] There were also music scene initiatives like Project Schoolyard, which distributed a hundred thousand copies of a pro-white sampler CD to white youth across the United States, using a network of volunteers.[57] In clear and deliberate ways, the far right adopted music early and often as a way to reach youth and inculcate far-right ideology in an youth-oriented, appealing way.

Hate clothing does much the same thing for a new generation of young people. But unlike far-right-extremist music—which was typically full of angry, violent lyrics—hate clothing also integrates humorous iconography, jokes, and insider codes that lend a sense of secrecy and amusement to the consumption process. It created a hipper, more modern way of communicating hate that ended up being a precursor to the much more widespread use of memes in online spaces. The game-playing nature of the coded messages is also fun, as youth effectively troll adults who either can't decode the messages embedded in codes and iconography, or can't enforce bans because of clever manipulation of illegal or banned symbols. Sometimes, alphanumeric sequences of numbers and letters stand in for racist or nationalist phrases, so that "2YT4U," for example, means "too white for you." Other coding deliberately plays on what youth call the "gray zone," offering plausible deniability in the face of scrutiny from law enforcement, teachers, parents, and other authorities. Thus, a purple T-shirt that says, in big, white block letters, "MY FAVORITE COLOR IS WHITE," could be read as a white-supremacist message or as a humorous play on the color of the shirt. Clever coding amuses insiders, but also helps consumers avoid the legal ramifications of displaying banned symbols.

Embodying Extremism: How Commercial Markets and Products Can Radicalize

Hate clothing radicalizes by channeling emotions and grievances toward extremist solutions. Through written messages, symbols, and iconography, consumer products marketed to the far right direct consumers to extreme political positions and help them identify perceived enemies. They suggest border closures and promote violent expulsions of Muslims. Some lash out against the left, "snowflakes," the state, or mainstream society, occasionally in violent ways. Product iconography, messaging, and website marketing language call for revolution, resistance, and defense, alongside images of skulls and weapons like brass knuckles, axes, knives, and guns. In this way, the clothing literally embodies violence and combat in the name of a cause that will be embarked upon together with other like-minded revolutionaries.

Violent references are paired with positive messaging about brotherhood, patriotism, belonging, and noble quests, making far-right positions seem heroic. They help communicate a narrative that situates far-right political positions as part of a larger cause in an epic battle against the left, the mainstream, immigrants, religious minorities, or "globalists." Hate clothing helps cement far-right activists' "us-versus-them" thinking, contrasting those whose bodies belong in the polity with those whose purportedly do not. The messaging carried through clothing iconography, symbols, and text taps into consumers' needs for belonging and (male) comradeship as well as a desire to provoke mainstream society and rebel against authority. This combination of coming together and lashing out, expressed in both coded and overt symbols and messaging across the clothing brands, is a key part of hate clothing's appeal, but also is a powerful way of making hate something that not only divides groups but also bonds people within them.[58]

Relatedly, the clothing and other products communicate normative expectations for masculinity and hypermasculinity. Catalog models sport hypermuscular bodies, with bulging biceps and shoulders stretching T-shirts to their limits. Sexualized images of women and references to brotherhood and belonging convey clear messages about manhood and its idealized qualities, signaled with language about heroism, loyalty, honor, defense, resistance, and being a warrior. While women are also attracted to the far right, it is still overwhelmingly a movement of men, particularly on the violent fringes, and the clothing is heavily produced for and marketed to men. And yet, hypermasculinity and masculinity are also constructs that appeal not only to men, but to some women in movements that express a desire for "traditional" gender roles.[59]

Hate clothing is also important for its potential to act as a gateway to more extreme content. Consumers can be exposed to far-right content when they visit websites that sell both far-right and non-far-right products. Brands targeting veterans and military communities, or focused on Second Amendment rights, for example, may primarily sell military-themed T-shirts, but also some products that are Islamophobic, misogynistic, or make fun of "fragile" snowflakes.[60] Through algorithms that recommend content based on other consumers' viewing or purchase histories, customers may encounter ever-more extreme content once they have begun to browse extremist-themed products.

Hate clothing is not the sole driver of radicalization, of course. But along with far-right music lyrics, internet forums, YouTube videos, and political rhetoric from far-right leaders, clothing can intensify exposure to ideological claims. These brands encourage consumers to accept an ideology that positions "us against them" in a war to the end, valorizing violence as the moral solution and calling on individuals to join the righteous fight to restore the nation or white heritage. They use iconography and messaging that dehumanizes migrants and minorities, legitimizes and celebrates violent revolution, identifies the "evil other," and calls on the righteous to take action. And because the act of purchasing clothing with such messages—and then wearing it—is itself a type of commitment to a cause, consumption itself may help radicalize or deepen extreme views. By wearing the clothing out and about in their everyday lives, consumers help to further market the message. Bodies become places to display clothing like a walking billboard, promoting and valorizing violence against "others" and in the name of a cause.

Mobilization: Access and Action

Clothing and merchandise sold for far-right markets is far from just a reflection of youth identity. It also helps mobilize the far right. Sometimes this happens through messaging that directly or indirectly calls consumers to action—through symbols and messaging about valiant quests, heroic engagement, restoration of the nation, sacred land and heritage, and legends about Aryan origins. Historical references abound, along with strong valorization of violence in the name of a cause. References to specific kinds of nationalist myths and violent historical events, like the Crusades or Reconquista (a Spanish pogrom against Muslims in the Middle Ages), are sometimes paired with mentions of contemporary regional tensions that hint at or call for violent expulsion of Muslims today. One Russian brand's "crusader card" T-shirt depicts a Christian Crusader stabbing a Muslim victim, with the accompanying text: "Just like back in 1099 a Teutonic Crusaders kicking in mercilessly and straight in the throats of our enemies" (*sic*).

Calls to action in clothing iconography and messages are just one way of mobilizing youth. Clothing, tattoos, and other aesthetic signals can also help open access to far-right scenes. One interviewee from my previous research in Germany explained that clothing can act as a ticket to underground concerts and events where youth aren't already known. The coded messages of their dress send signals to insiders. Far from being mere "subcultural style," clothing can be a gateway to radicalization and violence. Far-right clothing helps build connections with youth who hold similar ideological views, signaling political affiliation and attitudes toward others, allowing like-minded youth to find one another and strike up conversations in school, at stadiums, in bars, and at parties. "Maybe I'm not so alone after all," one of my interviewees explained about what it's like to see someone else wearing a T-shirt from a brand known to market to the far right, "or I'm not the only one who can't exactly identify with mainstream society."

Whether they are sold online or in physical storefronts, commercial products also facilitate extremist engagement through the creation of "brand fan" communities. People who purchase products from brands marketing to the far right may share photos of themselves wearing or displaying the products on dedicated sites set up for this purpose. This draws consumers into broader communities of "brand fans," where they can strengthen their identity and learn about brand-sponsored events like music concerts or combat-sports tournaments, where they can meet other brand fans in real life.[61] In this way, brand-fan websites can build community off-line. On one such fan group, a fellow consumer advertised a camping trip to the region said to be home to the mythical Hyperborea and Aryans.

In this sense, hate clothing and nationalist streetwear act as gateways to extremism. They socialize youth toward extremist values and ideals

while offering a noble quest and sense of purpose and identity, all the
while softening racist and xenophobic expression through humor and
clever, coded references. T-shirts are more than just T-shirts. As part of
a broader youth subculture, they can strengthen racist and nationalist
identification and mobilize extremist action and violence.

Funding and Supporting Extremism

Fashion, consumption, and style deserve renewed attention for how
they might not only reflect but also potentially constitute and mainstream extremism. The broad ecosystem of hate products online suggests that at least some individuals are partly earning a living by selling
hate and far-right ideologies. YouTube channels and product sales help
individuals in and across far-right scenes make a living, for example. But
these products also create revenue streams that help support far-right
activities beyond individual entrepreneurship. The music scene's well-
established multimillion-dollar revenue is perhaps the clearest example.
But there are more recent clues that commercial products sold to the
far right are also helping support far-right movements with income
flows and financial resources, even though in general, there is a significant gap in knowledge of the financial operations of far-right groups,
including those on the terrorist fringe, especially in comparison to what
is known about Islamist extremist milieus.[62] In addition to private donations, merchandising and event fees are the primary source for far-right-
extremist groups' financial resources, according to a recent report from
the UK-based think tank the Royal United Services Institute.[63] In some
cases, far-right individuals' personal wealth is used to augment or finance group activities that then bring in event fees and merchandise
sales profits.[64]

Other global brands and cultural festivals are also contributing to
far-right financial webs. An Eastern European antifascist watchdog
group reported in 2015, for example, that the brand White Rex offers
financial support to imprisoned neo-Nazis—referred to by the brand as
"prisoners of conscience."[65] In a section of its now-defunct website
called "Where the Money Goes," the US company Right Brand Clothing explains that the brand not only sponsors athletes and helps fund

political activism, but also offers legal support to "patriots" who "get singled out for noble actions by fake news or legal persecution," promising to "make sure those patriots are not alone and undefended."[66] Far-right products sold online, from T-shirts to bumper stickers and other items, often use far-right codes for pricing or product numbers, so that music CDs are priced at $14.88, for example, in reference to the pan-Aryan code of "fourteen words" and the Nazi code "88," for the eighth letter of the alphabet twice—HH—as a stand in for the phrase "Heil Hitler." Similar codes show up in the financial transactions of far-right groups as well.[67]

Product sales may support far-right ideologies in other ways, too. By selling a wide range of extreme-prepper products on a website where conspiracies about 9/11 and other topics are also referenced, for example, commercial markets help link ideas with action, with not-so-subtle hints about the need to prepare for an apocalypse by purchasing a seed vault and protective gear to ward off nuclear fallout and learning about preventing data and security incursions. Merchandise shops and associated products help build the brand of conspiracy theorists and far-right ideologues alike, turning consumers into advertisements that communicate ideological messages to the public in everyday ways as they are walking their dogs, going to the gym, or shopping for groceries. Consumer products that amplify conspiracy theories in multiple places may also add some degree of legitimacy by lending apparent support to false claims made elsewhere. For example, Glenn Beck, a former *Fox News* commentator who now runs the network TheBlaze, regularly promotes conspiracy theories while warning of "God's impending judgment and global chaos."[68] His store, which sells "Apparel for people who love America," includes a $30 T-shirt, available in ten colors, with Pepe-the-Frog-like iconography and the text "Stop Turning the Friggin Frogs Gay."[69] This phrase references a conspiracy theory promoted by Alex Jones that the government is using a "gay bomb" designed by the Pentagon to turn people gay with chemicals. The conspiracy became a meme—and made it onto T-shirts—when Jones later said that the government was "putting chemicals in the water that turn the friggin' frogs gay."[70] There are other, more subtle ways that commercial products can promote far-right ideologies, too. Products sold on websites marketing clothing to the German far right often carry the names of Nordic gods and goddesses, while catalog photos evoke Nordic scenes and geographies, thereby evoking the ideal of the Nordic region as sacred space for far-right consumers who see themselves as descended from Nordic tribes whose origins were Aryan.

To Ban or Not to Ban

The new aesthetics of far-right groups and the transnational growth of high-quality, expensive commercial brands marketing clothing to and for far-right youth—along with the coded nature of messaging communicated through the clothing and style—poses challenges for educators, policy makers, law enforcement, and the public, who may have difficulty recognizing ideas as extreme when the messaging comes in a mainstream aesthetic package. Mainstream-style brands, along with skinny pants and suits, are one of the ways that far-right groups use aesthetics to shape the public's receptivity to extreme ideas.

What can be done to interrupt this dynamic? In some countries, like Germany, local governments, schools, stadiums, and clubs have pursued legal bans, formal dress-code requirements that exclude particular brands, or censorship of particular brands and their logos. These strategies are less desirable or even possible in the United States because of First Amendment protections. They are also risky for the ways in which they can backfire. In the German case, banning policies have led to more game playing and coded symbols. Symbols and messaging have become ever-more coded in order to subvert bans in ways that are playful, humorous, and fun for designers and consumers. Meanwhile, the fact that the bans exist at all feeds far-right antigovernment narratives about suppression and surveillance, and the ways "they" are repressing "us."

But in the face of ever-more retail that traffics in far-right ideology, there are steps that can be taken. For decades, journalists, civil society, and watchdog groups have monitored white-power and hate music in the United States and Europe, documenting the music's production, sale, and distribution and its impact on recruitment to white-supremacist scenes.[71] The same groups can put pressure on clothing manufacturers and distributors not to produce or sell these items. This strategy worked after Charlottesville, when Spotify removed white-power music from its platform, and other tech companies—including YouTube, GoDaddy, and Twitter—pledged to monitor and remove accounts linked to white supremacists.[72]

More media literacy about how online algorithms work and how to recognize extreme content is also critical. Schools and parents have made progress in educating young people about their internet footprint, helping them understand issues of online safety, privacy, and cyberbullying. The younger generation is much better equipped than previous generations to recognize sexual predators and phishing scams, and to take steps to protect their personal information. Much less is being done to help young people recognize extremist content when they see it or understand how media manipulation and disinformation work, or how advertising algorithms may be shaping their consumer preferences or behavior. Adults need this kind of media literacy training just as much as younger people. Even casual browsing on websites selling far-right products or visits to social-media "brand fan" sites may lead consumers into a rabbit hole of additional far-right content.[73] We need broad public-education efforts that focus on educating communities about how extremist ideology is carried into the mainstream—including through high-quality, mainstream-style clothing brands and products laced with encrypted far-right messages.

No one can blame far-right violence on a cooking show or a T-shirt's message. And there are plenty of other cultural and commercial domains worthy of extensive study, of course. Entire books and special issues of journals have been dedicated to the study of hate music alone, for example, including its recent expansion into new genres, like country hate music and far-right German hip hop.[74] But like other gateways to far-right extremism—secret Facebook groups, racist music lyrics, "alt-right" conferences, and campus speaker confrontations—commercial products and markets should be taken seriously as an entry point. If we are going to find ways to disrupt radicalization toward hate, we need to identify—and intervene in—as many of these gateways as we can.

Chapter 4

Defending the Homeland

Fight Clubs and the Mixed Martial Arts

> Boxing and jujitsu always seemed to me to be more important than
> some mediocre training in shooting. You'd give the German nation
> six million impeccably trained bodies, all of whom are aglow with
> fanatical love of the fatherland and imbued with the most aggressive
> spirit . . . and in less than two years you'd have an army.
>
> —ADOLF HITLER, *MEIN KAMPF*

In mid-2017, a mixed martial arts sports bar called Reconquista Club
opened in Kiev, Ukraine. Owned and operated by the Azov Battalion—a
Ukrainian volunteer militia known for its ties to the far right—the
club's name refers to the fifteenth-century pogrom that expelled Muslims
from Spain.[1] Shortly before Reconquista Club opened, Generation
Identity launched a nationalist MMA and boxing gym in Lyon, France,
named L'Agogé—a term for training Spartan warriors in the art of war.[2]
Within the year, news broke that the Canadian far-right group Atalante
Quebec had opened a secret boxing gym in Montreal called La
Phalange—the "phalanx"—a term with dual connotations: Phalanx is
the name of a historical fascist Spanish political party as well as an ancient Greek type of military battalion.[3] Three private gyms, in three
countries: all named for historical legends and terms that symbolize
brutal combat and nativist defense, and all focused on training far-right
nationalists and extremists in hand-to-hand combat and street-fighting
techniques.

MMA is regularly described as the fastest-growing sport in the world,
its popularity evident in the rapid expansion of suburban after-school

classes as well as regional, national, and international tournaments complete with VIP lounges, celebrity fans, and lucrative commercial endorsements.[4] The sport has its origins in ancient Greece, when a hybrid sport that combined wrestling, boxing, and freestyle fighting—called "pankration"—was a part of the thirty-third Olympiad.[5] In modern times, MMA was introduced to great controversy in the early 1990s, with policy makers and the medical community describing it as inherently violent, unethical, barbaric, and dangerous to broader society. Arizona senator John McCain tried to ban the sport, calling it "human cockfighting" that was "so brutal it nauseates people."[6]

The sport operated underground for several years, unlicensed by state athletic commissions and eschewed by mainstream arenas, until the Ultimate Fighting Championship (UFC) gradually began to develop rules for the sport that reduced some of the violence, including outlawing "butting, eye-gouging and striking the throat, groin, spine or back of the head."[7] Donald Trump is credited with having rescued the UFC from likely bankruptcy by hosting two MMA tournaments at his Atlantic City hotel in 2000.[8] The next year, the Nevada State Athletic Commission sanctioned MMA.[9] Since then, the sport has grown and professionalized rapidly, with national and international federations, transnational tournaments, merchandise brands, and broad mainstream acceptance. Today, the UFC broadcasts in over 150 countries to more than a billion households.[10] Smaller tournaments pepper local regions, with names like Bare Knuckle and Cage Fury Fighting Championships.[11] An entire video game line of MMA and boxing games has developed into an industry and subculture of its own, and there are several clothing brands dedicated to MMA consumers. Importantly, although MMA remains an inherently violent sport—with fighters-in-training "introduced to giving and taking uncommon amounts of physical pain and exertion," the public face of MMA has shifted away from its early raw barbarity.[12] Instead, MMA's violent culture has been repackaged for broader audiences today by weaving in the language of solidarity, heroism, and brotherhood, albeit in the context of bloody mats, fighting bodies, and calls to be warriors.[13]

In retrospect, it isn't surprising that the far right homed in on MMA and other combat sports like jujitsu and boxing as a perfect way to channel ideologies and narratives about national defense, military-style discipline, masculinity, and physical fitness to mainstream markets. Hitler himself had advocated for the importance of combat sports for training Nazi soldiers. The National Socialist Sturmabteilung (storm division, or storm troopers) incorporated not only calisthenics but also boxing and jujitsu as a core part of training for street fights.[14] In more recent Germany history, extreme-right-wing martial arts gyms in Germany have long sought to integrate physical fitness, militancy, and extreme nationalist ideologies. The Hak Pao (Black panther) gym in Solingen, founded in the late 1980s, combined martial-arts training with plans to build a militant, nationalist, antigovernment commando unit, the Nationale Einsatzkommandos. Three of four youths charged with the murders of five women and girls in the 1993 firebombing of a Turkish family's home in Solingen were members of Hak Pao.[15]

There are plenty of other historical examples from a variety of global contexts that demonstrate the importance to far-right groups of a national citizenry that literally embodies and displays the national self as the far right imagines it. The desire for perfectly sculpted male bodies situates physical fitness and muscular manhood as expressions of both individual moral virtues like willpower, decisiveness, and courage, and desired collective traits like national strength, virility, and manliness.[16] The Ku Klux Klan adopted the practice of wearing stilts under their robes to make them appear taller. In interwar France, public attention to male toned physique and muscular power was part of "public anxieties about French national strength," while similar anxieties link nationalism, masculinity, physical and sexual prowess, and violence among Hindu nationalists.[17] In sum, extreme attention to the body has long been part and parcel of the historical legacy of nationalist, white-supremacist, and far-right movements.[18] It is equally important today as a foundational principle in far-right-extremist self-conception and subcultures.

As MMA began to grow in popularity globally, the far-right MMA world grew along with it. It became significantly more professionalized and commercially oriented, launching lifestyle brands, merchandise, social-media presence, and youth-oriented tournaments. A decade before the opening of the dedicated far-right gyms described at the beginning of this chapter, the Russian MMA aficionado and white supremacist Denis Kapustin, who goes by the name Denis Nikitin, founded White Rex, a lifestyle and streetwear brand that sponsors MMA tournaments and far-right training camps across Europe.[19] The brand's messaging and iconography promote violence and a "warrior spirit" as part of a broader defense of white European civilizations from what Nikitin views as "inferior immigrant cultures and the degenerate values of the Left."[20] A patch advertising the brand depicts a Christian Crusader against a backdrop evocative of the "black sun" symbol used by the Nazis, surrounded by the words "White Rex" and "violent athletics."[21]

After he founded White Rex in Russia, Nikitin turned to broader combat-sports markets. He personally groomed a kickboxing and MMA organization in Germany called Battle of the Nibelung (Kampf der Nibelungen), which started organizing combat-sports tournaments in 2013, coupled with an online merchandise store selling clothing with iconography and messages about healthy bodies, straight-edge (drug-free) lifestyles, and the importance of discipline. The tournaments' popularity grew rapidly, and they now regularly draw hundreds of people—the fall 2018 Battle of the Nibelungen tournament in Ostritz, in the German state of Saxony, for example, had 850 national and international attendees.[22] Like the dedicated far-right MMA gyms in Canada, France, and Ukraine, the organization's name simultaneously evokes historical legends and the contemporary far right, by referencing the Nibelungen saga from Norse mythology that became, in the form of Richard Wagner's Ring cycle, a beloved Nazi performance.[23] The organization's website describes MMA as a fundamental part of developing and spreading an alternative to mainstream society and the "decaying political system." It encourages fighters to recruit others to the cause so that more youth will "turn their backs on the system of losers, hypocrites, and weaklings."[24] Previously, the website described MMA fighters as key to the defense of "their clan, their tribe, their homeland."[25]

Nikitin also fought in the German tournaments himself, helping strengthen MMA networks between Germany and Russia.[26]

By the mid-2000s, MMA gyms across the European continent had developed a reputation as places where far-right youth were recruited and radicalized. This was a significant shift for violent far-right youth scenes, which had previously been oriented around soccer hooliganism and stadium brawls, but were now gravitating toward the MMA world.[27] Journalists, nongovernmental organizations (NGOs), think tanks, and watchdog groups have documented connections between the MMA world and white supremacists across Europe and North America. The journalist Karim Zidan has written a wide range of stories documenting connections between the MMA and the far right in Germany, France, Russia, Ukraine, Canada, and the United States. Cross-national annual tournaments with names like "Day of Glory" and "Force & Honour," for example, draw sponsorship from across the music and commercial-brand scenes in multiple countries.[28] Other far-right MMA or fitness-oriented groups periodically come to light as well, such as Wargus Christi, a Christian body-building group known for promoting far-right ideologies, which made the news in December 2019 when one of its members—a soldier—was taken into military custody in New Zealand for reasons not yet disclosed to the public.[29] In mid-2017 in East Nashville, Tennessee, a local group called "Showing up for Racial Justice" protested the opening of the Vengeance Strength Kvlt gym, telling a journalist that the gym's messaging "in their hashtags and website is a white supremacist message."[30] Vengeance, which uses the taglines "no truce" and "no surrender," along with the phrase "subversive fitness," reportedly was founded by a supporter of Operation Werewolf, a group that describes itself as "equal parts fight club, strength regimen, motorcycle club and esoteric order."[31] The gym embeds physical fitness in a broader ideology about eradicating weakness, which the gym's website describes as "a sickness which rapidly degenerates the quality of body and mind," noting that "proper training" requires purging weak people from your life and the "burning away of everything and everyone which does not benefit you."[32]

European governments are paying close attention to the phenomenon. The 2018 annual report of the German intelligence services

(Verfassungsschutzbericht) called out the "growing interest from right-wing extremists in combat sport" as a "development that vividly under-pins the violence-orientation of the right-wing extremist scene." The report specifically referred to the Battle of the Nibelungen tournament as the "largest and most important combat sport tournament of the [right-wing extremist] scene," describing the growing professionaliza-tion and steady triple-digit attendance numbers at combat-sports events as evidence for the "increased meaning of combat sports for right-wing extremists."[33] Also in 2018, the German intelligence services specifically pointed out the interest in combat sports by the small right-wing ex-tremist party "The Third Way" (Der Dritte Weg). The report notes that The Third Way's public information describes combat sports as an "in-dispensable 'part of right-wing metapolitics,'" which will use "martial arts-identity and loyalty to the people" to help attract many other young Germans to the party. Members of the party, the intelligence services note, "show a growing interest in the practice of combat sports."[34]

A 2019 Europol strategic report on rising right-wing extremism also pointed to the "important role" of MMA and combat-sports events used by right-wing extremist scenes.[35] And in September 2019, Denis Nikitin was banned from twenty-six European Union countries "because of the threat he posed to the liberal democratic order"—a clear acknowledge-ment that Nikitin is "considered the most influential figure in an increas-ingly dangerous network that links neo-Nazi football hooligans and MMA fighters across Europe."[36] In response to this growing awareness, a series of collaborative efforts between governments, national sports associations, and local gyms in places like Germany, Poland, and the United Kingdom have introduced intervention and prevention pro-grams. These are aimed at educating trainers and young people about racism and how to recognize signs of radicalization and far-right propaganda.

Serious attention to the phenomenon has been nearly absent from the North American context, however. While there has been substantial scholarship over the past decade on the ways that MMA celebrates and reinforces a kind of toxic masculinity, academic scholars and policy makers have been slower to document and analyze the rise of fight clubs and the MMA scene as places that may foment and foster white supremacy and the far right in the United States. There has been little sustained scholarship on the phenomena and no analysis that I know of exploring how fight clubs, MMA gyms, and related fight-style gyms have become significant spaces for far-right recruitment and radicalization.[37]

In part this is due to an overall failure in the American context to attend to the dangers of the far right in general, especially compared with those of Islamist extremism. But it is also because experts have been slow to recognize the changing aesthetics, styles, and engagements of the modern far right and the ways that spaces like MMA tournaments and gyms help communicate far-right ideologies and reinforce fascination with violence and national defense. US observers were largely unprepared when, in August 2017, members of the California-based Rise Above Movement (RAM)—self-described as the "premier MMA (mixed martial arts) club of the Alt-Right"—showed up at the Unite the Right rally in Charlottesville and incited violence that would later get several of them arrested.[38] The group explicitly aims to combine fashion, fight-club culture, and physical fitness regimes. RAM's founder, Robert Rundo, has described combat sports as a means to build the extreme right's "greater movement," noting that "in a time of weak men it only takes some effort to rise above all. Combat sports is that way up."[39]

Less than a year later, in April 2018, members of that same group joined a thousand neo-Nazis and white supremacists in Ostritz, Germany, for the Shield and Sword festival—an event rich with music concerts, product sales, speeches, and an MMA tournament, followed by a trip to Kiev to meet Denis Nikitin himself.[40] This isn't the only transnational connection in the combat-sports world. US-based militants from RAM, along with members of the terrorist group Atomwaffen Division, have been cultivated by the Ukraine's Azov Battalion—the volunteer militia that owns the Reconquista Club.[41] The Azov Battalion has recruited fighters from Germany, the United Kingdom, Brazil, Sweden, the United States, and Australia, and in addition to its fight club, has established "youth camps, recreation centers, lecture halls, and indoctrination programs" that teach children as young as nine years old "military tactics and white supremacist ideology."[42] Efforts contributing to the growth of a global far-right MMA and fight-club scene are evident in other countries as well. RAM members posted videos from the French boxing club L'Agogé and a Ukrainian nationalist MMA event, along with a Swiss far-right-extremist group's video invitation to Nikitin, asking him to create an MMA training workshop so they could be better prepared to defend their country from asylum-seekers.[43]

RAM's violence in Charlottesville is part of a broader far-right trend, in which extremists are increasingly moving out of the world of fantasy and utopian thinking and into the world of direct action and violent engagement. Far-right MMA aficionados are in the thick of it. Less than a year after Charlottesville, a group of masked men from the far-right group Atalante Quebec—founders of the secret boxing club La Phalange—stormed into the Montreal offices of the VICE digital media company, tossing leaflets and clown noses on the floor and shouting at journalists in an effort to intimidate them, in reaction to what they argued had been a biased article about the group.[44] Meanwhile, groups like the Proud Boys and the Fraternal Order of Alt-Knights began engaging in street fighting and brawls with antifascists at protests and public events, and small groups of fight clubs across the United States organized into a "Confederation of Volkisch Fight Clubs."[45] This fascination with MMA and street-fighting subcultures extends to more indirect cultural cues, codes, and signals popular today within the modern far right. Constant references to two key films rife with MMA and street-fighting scenes—*The Matrix* and *Fight Club*—are peppered throughout alt-tech spaces, chatrooms, and platforms, such as through the concept of being "red-pilled," which comes directly from *The Matrix*.[46]

MMA is a perfect incubator for the far right. It helps recruit new youth to the movement from adjacent subcultures, introducing key far-right messages about discipline, resistance to the mainstream, and apocalyptic battles. The combat-sports scene helps the far right motivate youth around ideals related to physical fitness, strength, combat, and violence. This mobilization calls on youth to train physically to defend the nation and white European civilization against the dual threats posed by immigrants and the degenerate left. At the same time, MMA and combat sports reinforce dominant ideals about masculinity and being a man—related not only to violence, risk, and danger but also to solidarity, brotherhood, and bonding.[47] The MMA world also helps radicalize and mobilize youth by intensifying far-right ideals about masculinity and violence and the range of exclusionary and dehumanizing ideologies that relate to the supposed incursion of immigrants, the coming of "Eurabia," "white genocide," or the "great replacement." These ideals and beliefs position offensive combat and defense of the nation as both obligations and a kind of heroic engagement to save one's people and sacred homelands from being overrun. Finally, the MMA provide ready-made, physical spaces for young people to come together in person and enact these ideals and physical engagements. Local gyms, along with tournaments, festivals, and the wide range of merchandise that accompanies them, help incubate and forge local, national, and global alliances across the MMA–far-right scenes. Video clips and live-streamed tournaments and fights, along with sophisticated MMA and combat-sport video games, meanwhile, broaden the audience well beyond these physical spaces. All told, MMA and fight-club scenes are ideal spaces for far-right recruitment and radicalization. They combine an entertainment culture that valorizes violence and hypermasculinity with a natural set of physical spaces and places where ideological messages can be intensified and experimented with.

Mixed Martial Arts as Recruitment and Regulation

MMA and other combat sports reach well beyond traditional far-right youth subcultures, helping the far right broaden its reach to new populations of youth. This is a strategic tactic, of course. In an interview with a Ukrainian website, Denis Nikitin was clear that MMA tournaments are a strategy to draw athletes into the "world of our ideas" and introduce them to new communities: "People get involved with ideas and move on to another level of development."[48] A 2019 report from the European Commission's Radicalisation Awareness Network (RAN) notes that "Far-right groups across Europe and North America use martial arts clubs to swell their numbers and boost their ideology . . . to fight their perceived enemies," describing MMA gyms and clubs as having particular "qualities that make them interesting for extremist recruiters," including an affinity for violence and a masculine culture.[49]

Modern far-right groups, both within and outside the MMA world, promote "straight-edge" living—no drugs, no alcohol, and healthy eating. Some groups eschew tattoos and body piercings and extol the virtues of physical fitness and a polished public image. White, male bodies are subject to particular kinds of regulation by the far right, as part of a strategy to produce and represent national moral and physical strength as they define it. Some modern far-right groups, like the owners of the Rise Above Movement–affiliated clothing distributor Right Brand Clothing, directly contrast the "mental and physical capacities" of far-right youth with the "left's onslaught of degeneracy and drug culture,"[50] while others, like the white-supremacist group Identity Evropa (now rebranded as the American Identity Movement, or AIM), provide formative guidance on appearance to potential members, explaining in their website's "frequently asked questions" that members are "required to keep themselves in good physical shape and generally present themselves in a professional and positive manner when in public."[51]

Messaging about the importance of physical appearance is consistent across a variety of modern far-right groups. The neo-Nazi blogger Andrew Anglin's advice to his followers to show up for the Charlottesville rally looking presentable is a clear example. As VICE journalist Allie Conti reported, Anglin argued that physical appearance is more important than ideology, noting that self-presentation "matters more than our ideas," while urging radical right activists to "go to the gym" and stay physically fit. "Fat people," he argues, "should be allowed to join groups and be involved in rallies," but only if they commit to losing weight: "continued obesity should not be tolerated."[52]

Physical fitness was thus depicted by a leader of the "alt-right" as reflective of a commitment to the movement, and to representing it in self-consciously aesthetic ways. This is why the clothing distributor associated with the Rise Above Movement, Right Brand Clothing, offered to sponsor followers' combat-sports gym memberships on their now-defunct website. Sponsorship is a way, they explained, of ensuring the movement has youth who are equipped not only with the mental but also the physical capacity for future leadership.[53] Similar messaging is communicated elsewhere online, such as through the popular body-builder and white-nationalist YouTuber known as the Golden One (Marcus Follin), whose channel shares exercises and workout regimes against Nordic backdrops, calling on men to commit to a "regimented lifestyle" and keep their bodies healthy.[54] In a summer 2019 video, Follin challenged the idea that he is spreading a hateful message, arguing that his goal is to encourage his subscribers to love themselves and commit to self-improvement. Political violence, he argued, is ineffective. He contrasts this with the "excruciatingly effective" efforts of leftist "metapolitical crusaders," who he argues have achieved dominance over institutions through cultural and intellectual control, not violence.[55]

MMA and combat-sports culture's hypermasculine, muscular aesthetic, "straight edge" philosophy, and emphasis on an alternative lifestyle align well with far-right messaging about the need to resist mainstream society, the decadent left, and combat training for a coming civil war. Far-right obsessions with the body are critical here too, as cult-like obsessions with healthy living, with no drugs or alcohol and a regimented physical fitness regime, strengthen the military-like qualities of far-right ideals and evoke racialized notions of pure bodies. This approach fits well with the overall rebranding of the far right, in terms of aesthetics and style, which has reshaped its image away from the shaven headed, heavily tattooed, and alcohol-fueled racist skinhead and toward a more clean-cut, mainstream appearance. Physical fitness, healthy bodies, and clean living are a big part of that. By recruiting heavily from soccer's violent hooligan world, the far right can use the MMA scene to transform what had long been an alcohol-laden, street-brawl subculture into a more coherent, disciplined, and regulated scene. In so doing, the movement is "turning racist hooligans into hardened fighters inculcated in a kind of race war ideology."[56] This matters, because the kinds of conflicts that the far right anticipates in the apocalyptic end phase of the "great replacement" require discipline, strength, and the ability to fight in defense of the homeland.

MMA also has the advantage of a built-in structure to reach out to groups of young men through local gyms' efforts to increase profitability and broaden their client base. Local MMA gyms in the United States, for example, regularly host live sparring demonstrations for broader communities—at open houses, martial-arts facilities, fraternity houses, and university and community centers—to promote their gyms. Fighters at such demonstrations are instructed to put on a show at much lower levels of violence and fighting in order to recruit new members and "turn the audience into customers."[57] Meanwhile, the MMA world has also developed a rich subculture outside of actual fights, with clothing lines, commercial sponsors, and a unique style to help fighters and fans build identity with the scene. This includes dedicated larger brands as well as hundreds of smaller or local vendors. At tournaments, "sexily clad" young women known as "merch girls" staff vendors' booths and act as brand ambassadors for the clothing, engaging with attendees and posing for photographs.[58] Through this broader combat-sports scene, even commercial gyms and markets not directly related to the far right can help to broaden the base of young men who are attracted to MMA and the MMA world, thus expanding the pool of potential far-right recruits.

It is important to point out that MMA is not only a channel for ideals related to discipline, violence, and fighting. Much like the new kinds of humor and game playing evident in online and commercial spaces, MMA also has the advantage of being fun. "Coupled with extremist rock music and alcohol-laden events," the journalist Karim Zidan explains, "the MMA subculture has become one of the primary forms of entertainment used to entice a younger crowd."[59] And importantly— along with its emphasis on physical strength and violence—the MMA world cultivates a set of positive emotions that appeals to youth searching for a sense of meaning and belonging, such as brotherhood, solidarity, loyalty, and community. For far-right leaders in the MMA world, this is an intentional tactic designed to draw youth in and convey far-right ideologies. Denis Nikitin, for example, described his efforts to make White Rex into a far-right MMA lifestyle brand as including a philosophy of "camaraderie, respect, strength, solidarity, honor, heroism" in order to help "bring people closer to our ideas."[60]

MMA–far-right intersections are important on their own merits. But the development of these kinds of combat-sports lifestyle brands is also key to understanding how the modern far right has evolved, and what kinds of new tactics may be helping recruitment and radicalization. These kinds of MMA lifestyle brands combine emotional cues about brotherhood and community with strategic ideological messaging about defense of homelands, physical preparation for the coming race war, and the need for disciplined warriors to engage in it. The brands help connect and normalize far-right scenes for broader publics, often by selling nonextremist merchandise in a "health-conscious lifestyle brand" package.[61]

Fight Like a Man: Violent Masculinities and Radicalization

Virtually all mass shooters and violent extremists have one thing in common: they are overwhelmingly men. Many of the messages youth encounter within far-right scenes emphasize specific ideas about what it means to be a man. Specifically, the far right's vision of manhood is typically positioned against the perceived softness, femininity, or degeneracy of the liberal left. "Be a man, not a [snowflake symbol]," commands one US T-shirt marketed to far-right consumers. "Snowflake" has a long history as an insult, and was notably used in the movie *Fight Club*, a film popular with far-right youth that glorified combat street fighting.[62] For today's "alt right," the term "snowflake" is used pejoratively, lobbed against liberals who are deemed overly soft, sensitive, fragile, or easily triggered. This kind of coaching, direct instruction, and peer pressure about manhood and physical or moral ideals is reflected in far-right movements' obsession with appearance and discipline, especially through a focus on toned physique and muscular power.

Scholars have thoroughly interrogated these questions as they relate to nationalism and the body, especially through work on modern masculinity and its intersections with nationalism and the far right.[63] We also know that physical bodies not only are reflections of nationalist ideals, but also help to shape what idealized national qualities look like.

One of the best examples is in Kristin Surak's extended ethnography of Japanese tea ceremonies, where she finds that the physical embodiments of Japanese nationhood are not only performative but also have a cultivating quality—aimed at transforming people into "better or idealized members of the nation."[64]

This is, of course, MMA's sweet spot. Scores of scholarly analyses have outlined the links between masculinity and sports, both in general and in the MMA world more specifically. Competitive sports' hierarchical culture and emphasis on strength, toughness, and winning reinforce ideals about masculinity.[65] These same kinds of themes are present in the combat-sports world. MMA fighters consistently work to perform "convincing manhood"—showcasing traits like domination and confidence; suppressing pain, empathy, fear, and shame; and aiming to be physically intimidating and instill fear in other fighters.[66] Successful fighters gain the respect of others through displays of control, skill, and competence, while showcasing idealized masculine traits related to danger and risk taking.[67] The emphasis on domination, muscularity, and physical intimidation means the MMA provides ideal sites for the construction of what scholars call "hegemonic masculinity," a concept that explains how particular views about manhood and masculinity become culturally ideal, or "hegemonic," during any given historical moment.[68] Importantly, different kinds of masculinities can coexist and interact—meaning that young men grapple with competing ideas about what it means to be a man in any given context, as they engage in communities in their schools, workplaces, homes, or other settings.[69] The culturally ideal construction of manhood that young men encounter in MMA gyms is one that suggests "real manhood" is achieved through violent, physical fights whose losers are emasculated.[70] Warriors, in contrast, exude strength, toughness, risk taking, competitiveness, and domination—a kind of a "masculine archetype" embraced in MMA culture more broadly.[71]

MMA becomes a powerful incubator for the far right when these ideas about masculinity—the notion that being a man is achieved through violent confrontation, domination, and physical intimidation of opponents—are layered onto far-right ideology about immigrant invasions and defense of the nation. Manhood itself is then linked to the idea of engaging heroically to save one's people. For example, White Rex's official "doctrine" asserts the importance of a fighting and warrior "spirit" to European values, which they suggest have been degraded by the "propaganda of alien values." In contrast, White Rex expresses a need for "WARRIORS—people who are strong morally and physically."[72] Across the board, the intersection of the far right and the MMA world helps promote intense physical fitness regimens and the resulting display of toned, muscular, masculine physiques in ways linked to white-supremacist goals. Physical health and fitness, in this sense, now represent discipline, training, and commitment to the broader far-right cause.

Meanwhile, the use of historical legends and fantastical myths from the past as gym and tournament names evokes a kind of nostalgia for a violent past. This helps romanticize the far right and encourages youth to imagine a utopian future based on the same ideals as that romantic past, positioning the far right as heroic warriors and champions for a cause, protecting and defending sacred space and restoring national homelands. In the Kiev MMA Reconquista Club, for example, the journalist Michael Colborne sat down to a table placemat with an explanation of the club's name: "Reconquista is a call for the reconquest of the World—the world to come. Reconquista will make Europe great again.... The future belongs to us!"[73] By referencing a Spanish pogrom that violently expelled religious minorities from Europe, the name Reconquista links the use of violence with aspirational racial, religious, and national purity, along with defense of the nation or of Europe more broadly.

Off the Laptop, into the Boxing Ring: MMA's Physical Spaces

Like the cultural spaces explored in chapter 3, the MMA and fight-club worlds have organizational and financial implications for the growth of far-right extremism. The sponsorship of tournaments, merchandise stores, dedicated brands and clothing lines, and training camps create significant networks of monetary and human resources. The fight-club world not only reflects and strengthens far-right ideology and messaging—it also supports them materially. The brand White Rex, for example, is sold in some thirty locations across Russia, including several stores in Moscow alone, and through international distributors like the French website 2yt4u.com. White Rex also promotes white-power music bands and concerts and organizes MMA tournaments in Russia and Europe as well as MMA training sessions for neo-Nazis cross-nationally.[74] The brand's now-defunct Tumblr page was rife with images of the brand's fans gathering in gyms, in competitive fights, or showing off their bodies, accompanied by phrases telling visitors to "train hard—look good" or that they could achieve to have "strength through beauty."[75]

These regular tournaments and training camps lend themselves well to building capacity for street fights, the apocalyptic end times, and race war. A far-right group in Britain ran a training camp in Wales, for example, that included training in self-defense, martial arts, and survival techniques.[76] Across the United States, there are plenty of backwoods militias, armed patriot groups, paramilitaries, and mercenary groups.[77] In the post-Vietnam era, the white supremacist Louis Beam created several paramilitary training facilities and boot camps that were intended to create a white-separatist army to assume control of national and regional space and expel nonwhites, creating a white homeland.[78] Beam's camps offered training in methods of decapitation, strangulation, airplane hijacking techniques, and the use of military-style firearms.[79] In the United States, however, these kinds of spaces have historically been limited to geographically separate camps in remote areas that would attract only individuals already interested in the far-right and white-power movements.[80]

These kinds of militias and paramilitaries still exist within the far right. The militant US neo-Nazi group "The Base" reportedly trains members in paramilitary insurgency techniques, including weapons and explosives training and skills for guerrilla warfare, such as ambushes.[81] But the far right has also discovered that training for combat does not require a dedicated destination or training camp: it can be done through the mainstream MMA and fight-club world. MMA's combat-style training appeals to far-right youth for the same reasons that backwoods

militias and paramilitaries appealed to a generation of returning Vietnam veterans—but with a modern twist. The combat-sports and MMA
worlds are connected to broader lifestyle brands, savvy social-media
"brand fan" sites, and "in-real-life" festivals that integrate music concerts, product and clothing sales, and MMA tournaments. And unlike
the paramilitary camps of the post-Vietnam era, MMA has the broad
advantage of being in the public sphere. This allows for more explor-
atory or experimental engagement, allowing youth to try out new political and lifestyle identities with less commitment. The rapid growth
of the MMA world both in the United States and abroad creates a steady
stream of potential recruits and a built-in system to network nationally
and globally through large tournaments and festivals.

Breaking Up the Fight

For those of us working to find better pathways to reach at-risk youth,
understanding the ways that far-right groups recruit and socialize
youth—in ways that go well beyond rhetoric and ideas—is crucial.
Having strict guidelines for physical appearance, for example, might
offer youth a sense of predictability and structure, clarity, concrete steps
for betterment, and a pathway to belonging. This may have particular
appeal for individuals who feel unmoored or disenfranchised, or lack a
sense of clear purpose. Further research into whether and how a fixation
on physical fitness and the body might intersect with other issues that
can make youth vulnerable to the far right is essential for developing
interventions that meet youth where they are.

Attempts to intervene in the combat-sports world to prevent radicalization are nascent. In Germany, the German Institute for Radicalization and Deradicalization Studies (GIRDS) has formed a network of
martial arts schools in German-speaking countries that are committed
to combatting violent radicalization across the ideological spectrum,
called the German Association of Martial Arts Schools against Violent
Extremism (DVKE). The website explains that "martial arts experts and
coaches are uniquely positioned to recognize a violent radicalization

process and intervene as mentors and respected attachment figures for teenagers and adolescents." But in order to do that effectively, coaches need training to recognize warning signs of violent radicalization and understand the psychology behind it. DVKE offers specialized workshops and training courses along with a quality seal for member gyms that can certify they have at least one trained mentor available at all times.[82]

Such efforts are few and far between, however. Robert Claus, a leading German scholarly expert on the relationship between sport and violence, has studied the relationship between MMA and violent radicalization extensively, and recently expressed concern about the lack of preparedness to address it. In a 2019 study, he found that there are not even initial approaches, much less standards, available for the prevention of violent extremism in the combat-sports world and the "trend of neo-Nazis' instrumentalization of combat sports."[83] Other countries are not much further ahead at combatting the trend, but there are some recent attempts. In the United Kingdom, the competitive Google-funded "innovation fund" grants administered through the Institute for Strategic Dialogue in 2019 included one grant to a boxing project housed at the Limehouse Boxing Academy in partnership with England Boxing KO Racism, in which young people are brought together for boxing workshops that include "open discussion about racism and prejudice."[84] Other small-scale efforts are reported to be under way in Poland and through a German activist group called "Down from the Mat," which formed "in response to the growing influence of neo-Nazis in the sport."[85] But, overall, the far-right trend of engaging, recruiting, and mobilizing through combat sports and MMA is far ahead of intervention efforts to address it.

Chapter 5

Grooming and Recruiting

Cultivating Intellectual Leadership

In April 2019, a group of white supremacists burst into a Washington, DC, bookstore, disrupting Professor Jonathan Metzl's talk on his new book, *Dying of Whiteness*, by shouting propaganda into a megaphone and chanting "This land is *our* land!"[1] The video was circulated widely on social media and the incident is listed on AIM's website under its "Activism Highlights" tab. The interruption of Metzl's talk came on the heels of an arson attack that destroyed a building at the iconic Highlander Education and Research Center in Tennessee—which houses decades of archives on the civil rights movement and hosts educational training and workshops that once drew leaders like the Reverend Martin Luther King Jr., Eleanor Roosevelt, and Rosa Parks.[2] A white-supremacist symbol—the same one that had been displayed by the Christchurch shooter two weeks earlier—was found spray painted in the parking lot next to the burned-out remains.[3] Similar attacks, such as repeated assaults on leftist bookstores in Berkeley and San Diego, have included vandalism like tipped-over bookshelves and shattered storefronts, attempted arson, and intimidation of bookstore employees.[4]

These kinds of far-right assaults on knowledge, which are comparatively rare in the United States, have long been common in Europe not only in the book burnings of the Nazi era, but also in more recent direct action against knowledge deemed threatening to far-right ideological and political goals. As the journalist Elizabeth King explains, "Attacking bookstores where authors of color or Jewish, queer, or leftist authors discuss their work, or because of the kinds of books they sell, has been a common fascist tactic since fascism rose to prominence in the 1920s, and clearly, it is still with us today."[5] After Heinz Ostermann, a bookstore owner in Berlin, joined an initiative of local bookstores against right-wing populism and racism in 2016, stones were thrown into his bookstore windows and his car was set on fire. Since his home address is unlisted, he believes he was followed home as part of a pre-planned arson attack.[6]

Bookstores and historical archives may be easy targets, but they are not the only places where knowledge is under attack. In May 2018, I found myself in the audience of an Oslo "culture café," marveling at the size of the standing-room-only crowd listening to three prominent social-science experts talking about the far right. But when the question-and-answer period ensued, it quickly became clear that the burgeoning audience was heavily populated by far-right activists from a variety of groups, whose apparently coordinated appearance at the event enabled them to hijack the discussion with hostile queries about academic bias.

Cultivating future far-right nationalists goes beyond equipping youth to fight in boxing rings or turning their chests into walking billboards for far-right messaging. It also requires developing the far right's future intellectual leadership. While the previous chapters have traced the places and spaces where the far right is mobilizing physical, cultural, and financial capacity, this chapter turns to efforts to disrupt and discredit mainstream intellectual spaces deemed threatening to the far right's worldview and create new ones dedicated to far-right ideologies. This combination—attacking educational spaces deemed to belong to the left and building educational spaces explicitly for the far right—has proven extraordinarily effective not only at building and disseminating far-right ideology, but also at working those ideological views into the mainstream. The following sections trace two major categories: efforts directed at physical places and individuals—including campuses, students, and scholars—and efforts directed at challenging, appropriating, and creating knowledge itself.

Hate Comes to Campus

In November 2019, Syracuse University found itself in the throes of a wave of hate incidents, ultimately totaling sixteen events over a two-week period, including racist graffiti and epithets against African

Americans, Asians, and Native Americans; a swastika stamped in the snow; and threatening emails.[7] Amid cancelled classes, student protests, and sit-ins to demand more serious responses from the university administration, a seventy-four-page white-supremacist manifesto linked to the Christchurch shooter was posted on a Greek discussion board and another university online forum.[8] Campus police, local law enforcement, and the FBI investigated the range of incidents, resulting in one student arrest and several suspensions, while New York governor Andrew Cuomo weighed in with sharp criticism of the university's chancellor, calling for an independent monitor to investigate.[9] In the midst of the Syracuse hate incidents, a first-year student at Georgia Southern University made a class presentation about "replacement theory" and encouraged followers to join the white-supremacist group AIM. The university defended the presentation as protected free speech.[10] The presentation was noteworthy not only because it used a mainstream college classroom to promote a white-supremacist conspiracy theory, but also for its reach outside of the campus gates. The day after the class presentation, the student uploaded a recording to YouTube, where it was viewed over 100,000 times before mid-December, garnering 8,500 "likes" and over 3,500 comments.

The Syracuse and Georgia Southern University examples illustrate how colleges and universities are struggling with rising extremism, polarization, and hate from members of their own campus communities. But campuses have also been the intentional target of organized far-right groups, as the choice of the torch-bearing white supremacists in Charlottesville to march across a university campus makes abundantly clear. College campuses are key places for the far right for both strategic and symbolic reasons. Symbolically, attacks on campuses are a part of a broader assault on knowledge, truth claims, and arguments about the liberal bias of higher education. Strategically, they are sites to challenge the limits of free speech, spread propaganda, recruit youth, and polarize campus communities in ways that contribute to overall far-right goals and create societal discord. Hateful incidents and propaganda contribute to increasingly contentious campus climates. Targeting campuses makes the public pay attention to far-right and white-supremacist ideas.

And campuses are ideal sites for the far right to recruit and cultivate young people with potential for future power and influence, who may help the far right integrate its ideas into the public domain and political spheres at some future date.

Physical attacks on campus communities by the extreme far right fall into three categories. First, far-right groups have targeted campuses with outside speakers who aim to challenge the limits of free speech or spur violence and counterprotests. Second, the extreme far right uses campuses as a site to distribute white-supremacist propaganda, primarily through paper fliers that attempt to spread hateful ideas, intimidate vulnerable communities, and recruit students directly to far-right groups and movements. And third, members of the far right or individuals motivated by far-right ideologies have initiated increasing numbers of hate crimes, hate incidents, and direct attacks on scholars and students that aim to threaten, injure, create fear, and reduce feelings of safety.

Free Speech and Far-Right Provocateurs

Over the past four years, college campuses in the United States have become central to the modern far right's efforts to foment polarization, spread disinformation, and challenge knowledge. This strategy dates at least to 2016, when Milo Yiannopoulos, a prominent provocateur and former Breitbart editor known for openly racist, anti-Muslim, and misogynist statements, launched his "Dangerous Faggot Tour" of college campuses, including planned speeches with titles like "Ten Things I Hate about Mexico."[11]

In some ways, this strategy is nothing new. After all, universities have long hosted controversial speakers, including from the far right; a 1966 talk by the founder of the American Nazi party, George Lincoln Rockwell, generated tremendous protest.[12] Far-right groups and individuals often deliberately push the boundaries of US free-speech laws, which have been central to far-right-extremist scenes for decades—relying on the fact that the US Constitution protects hateful speech and symbols in ways that go well beyond other democracies' more restrictive policies and practices on racist speech and symbols.[13] But when Yiannopoulos, who was later banned from entering Australia after he referred to Islam as a "barbaric" and "alien" religion in the wake of the Christchurch shootings, showed up for these speeches, some campuses erupted in violence. At Berkeley, violent protesters threw Molotov cocktails and commercial-grade fireworks, breaking windows and starting fires, while a Yiannopoulos supporter shot a protester outside a speaking event at the University of Washington.[14] White supremacist and "alt-right" founder Richard Spencer, who heads the far-right National Policy Institute (NPI) think tank and advocates for a separate white ethno-state and re-migration for ethnic minorities, began his "Danger Zone Tour" of major US universities during the same period as Yiannopoulos's tour. Spencer, who has been banned for five years from the United Kingdom and twenty-six European countries for his white-supremacist views, intended for the speaking events to help recruit followers, challenge university free-speech practices, and provoke campus communities through arguments about white oppression and the need to protect white people, among other topics.[15] These efforts are consistent with Spencer's overall focus on college-student recruitment at his annual events and NPI conference—an effort that has been successful, according to the ADL.[16]

The issue of provocative speakers has put university campuses in the center of increasing national political polarization and contentious debate about the tension between free speech and hate speech.[17] Controversial speakers are often invited by mainstream-conservative or right-wing student groups, while violent protests have been driven at least in part by groups coming from off-campus. Berkeley, for example, described the violent protesters at Yiannopoulos's February 2017 talk as masked outside agitators who arrived on campus and disrupted peaceful protests—likely members of antifa, an anti-fascist movement.[18] The cancellations of some of these events—often over security concerns[19]—have helped fuel arguments made by far-right individuals and groups about suppression of free speech, with President Trump weighing in by tweet to suggest that if Berkeley can't protect free speech, it should lose federal funding.[20]

In November 2019, the far right's engagement with campus speakers took a new turn when a group calling itself the "groyper army" began to show up at campus speaking events featuring mainstream-conservative speakers. The groypers, a part of the far right self-named in reference to the Pepe the Frog meme, are led by YouTuber Nick Fuentes, who has urged his followers to show up to conservative speakers and events on college campuses and commandeer the question-and-answer period to push far-right ideological views. Groypers have made up as much as a third of the audience at some events.[21] The focus has primarily been on events organized by Turning Point USA (TPUSA)—a conservative group active on over 1,500 college campuses across the United States that aims to promote ideas about free markets, individual liberty, and limited government.[22] Targets have included TPUSA founder Charlie Kirk as well as congressional representatives, pundits, and writers. Donald Trump Jr. was heckled at a California speaking event.

Their goal is to show that these conservative speakers—and the Trump administration more generally—have become too moderate and are out of line with "true" conservative thought.[23] By tripping up Republican speakers with leading questions about immigration, Israel, and LGBTQ+ issues, groypers try to show that mainstream Republicans, or what they call "Conservative, Inc.," are "insufficiently homophobic, anti-Semitic, or racist."[24] This turn of events shows clearly the kinds of tensions between conservative and mainstream politics and the far right, and makes clear that protests and tensions on campuses around provocative speakers are not only emerging from traditional leftist–far-right conflicts, but also from fragmentation, dissent, and tension within the broader conservative and right-wing spectrum itself, including between conservatives and the far right.

The higher education sector has scrambled to come up with effective responses to provocative and extreme speakers, often struggling to balance issues of free speech and academic freedom with condemnation of hate speech and support for vulnerable campus community members.[25] Hate incidents, attacks, and white-supremacist propaganda have an immediate and negative effect on campus climate issues in ways that challenge universities' ongoing efforts to improve racial equity.[26] In addition, the financial burden of providing adequate security for controversial outside speakers is substantial. The University of Florida spent half a million dollars and brought security personnel in from forty-five agencies to patrol an event where Richard Spencer was scheduled to speak—but was eventually heckled off the stage. After the event, a man in a car fired gunshots at a group of protesters and was later arrested.[27] Some universities have tried to use financial costs and security concerns to prevent controversial speakers from coming to campus, but these attempts have not always been successful, particularly if university policies allow the renting of campus space to outside groups. After Auburn University tried to ban Spencer from speaking at a campus event that was organized and paid for by a nonstudent, it was sued by Spencer's representatives and forced to allow the talk. Afterward, it changed its space rental policy to require current student organizations or faculty to sponsor any outside group, with the aim of reducing the likelihood of outside provocateurs using the campus for their own purposes.[28]

There is no question that American college campuses have become a focal point for the far right. Soliciting invitations that bring far-right provocateurs and speakers to campuses builds on a long history of controversial and far-right speakers in higher education. But in-person visits to colleges and universities are not the only strategy to physically bring far-right ideas to college campuses. Another prominent tactic is the targeting of campuses for white-supremacist and far-right propaganda, through paper fliers, stickers, and posters with white-supremacist messaging, along with efforts to recruit students to join far-right movements and organizations.

Far-Right Paper Fliers and Campus Recruiting

"You have [college] classes wanting white people to apologize for being white," Lance told me on the phone, arguing that the political left has undertaken a "strategy of marginalization" against "the white male." It was shortly after the 2017 Charlottesville Unite the Right rally, and I was taking listener calls on a Wisconsin public radio show. Lance sounded irritated and a little bewildered as he described political and campus climates that leave white men feeling as though they have done something wrong. Far-right groups capitalized on this sentiment, plastering fliers with the phrase "It's OK to be White" on college campuses across the country. As Richard Baker, assistant vice chancellor and vice president for equal opportunity services at the University of Houston told *Inside Higher Ed* in late 2018, the fliers' intent is to imply that "whites are a marginalized group and are being made to feel 'not OK' in their whiteness," noting that the aim is to recruit people who may be "sympathetic to that position but may not respond to a swastika or other traditional symbols of white nationalism or direct recruitment."[29]

With all that is known about the importance of online radicalization, one curious development has been the surge in old-school paper fliers posted by white-supremacist groups across the country, with college campuses a particular target.[30] The "It's OK to be White" fliers are just one of many examples. The fall 2019 semester saw more than double the number of extremist propaganda incidents (410) on US college campuses compared with any prior semester, as documented by the ADL. Overall, 2019 saw a record-high number of white-supremacist propaganda incidents nationally, a quarter of which took place on college campuses: there were approximately 630 incidents of fliers, stickers, and posters on 433 different campuses in forty-three states and the District of Columbia.[31] This is part of an unprecedented rise in far-right propaganda on college campuses—with nearly 300 incidents in the 2017–18 academic year alone, representing a 77 percent increase from the previous year. Increases continued in the 2018–19 academic year, although at a slower pace, reflecting a 7 percent jump from the previous year.[32] A variety of groups use the strategy, including neo-Nazi groups like American Vanguard, white-supremacist groups like Patriot Front, and Identitarian groups like Identity Evropa (now AIM). Fliers typically include a URL to drive potential recruits to places where they can get more information about membership, activities, and the group's ideology.

Distributing paper fliers is just one part of a broader higher-education marketing and recruitment plan for far-right groups. In summer 2018, *NBC News* reported that the white-supremacist and Identitarian group Identity Evropa's efforts to spread recruiting fliers on college campuses was part of a broader strategy to "seed college Republican groups with Identity Evropa members as a stepping stone to careers in politics." This is a long-term plan, explained the group's executive director, Patrick Casey, who (in journalist Anna Schechter's words), views "politics rather than protests as the prime vehicle to carry his brand of white identity politics into the mainstream." The plan involves group members running for office as Republicans "without broadcasting their polarizing views on immigrants and nonwhites." Casey described the plan as intending to "take over the GOP as much as possible." The strategy is known as "entryism"—the use of mainstream political parties and systems by radical individuals outside the system for their own purposes—originating in communists' attempts to infiltrate socialist parties to bring them further toward communism.[33] The far right's efforts to mainstream extreme ideas by carrying them in on elected Republican platforms is the latest example of entryism.[34] For example, restrictions on immigration is an area where the far right finds agreement with Republicans and conservatives, so the far right pushes proposals more moderate than its own ideology calls for as a "stepping stone to reframing the national discussion around race and immigration and gaining access to a larger base of White conservatives."[35] College campuses are a key part of this strategy. The "alt right" in particular has seen conservative campus groups as a "vehicle to influence broader politics and cultures."[36] As Richard Spencer explained to *Mother Jones*, college students are especially "open to alternative perspectives, for better and for worse. I do think you need to get them while they are young."[37] In the NBC *Today Show* segment referenced earlier, Identity Evropa leader Patrick Casey explained that the group's ideas are controversial "at this point, but that doesn't negate their validity. Quite often, controversial ideas start off as being very taboo and people have to be very careful with them, but they can skillfully insert them into the mainstream."[38]

One such effort stumbled, however, when Identity Evropa member James Allsup—who had been the leader of the College Republicans at Washington State University—was too open about his white-supremacist views. Although Allsup won a local election on the Republican ticket, he was subsequently condemned by local Republican leaders; the county's Republican Party chairwoman resigned after she was criticized for defending him. Recalling the experience, Casey noted, "Allsup is a capable and intelligent man, but ideally our members interested in getting involved in politics will do so covertly—that is, without openly identifying as identitarians, at least not upfront."[39] Notably, Allsup had been quite open about his strategy of entryism, using student Republican clubs to help gain legitimacy and recruit more students. On a 2017 episode of a white-nationalist radio program, Allsup explained that by taking over a college Republicans group and moving it "essentially to being an alt-right club," you gain access to resources and "political credibility. It gives you all of these things that come along with the name of being a Republican."[40]

Propaganda, white-supremacist fliers, racist graffiti, and provocative speaking tours have brought hate to campuses across the country in new ways, exposing hundreds of thousands of students to far-right ideologies. This kind of hate intimidates and threatens members of vulnerable groups, unsettles campus climates, and creates significant anxiety around student safety and well-being. Students at Syracuse University who staged a sit-in in November 2019 following more than a dozen hate incidents at the university told journalists that they didn't feel safe on campus. "I absolutely do not feel safe here, and I think a large number of students also don't feel safe here," one student told Anderson Cooper on CNN, noting, "I personally, and I know I speak for a lot of people when I say I don't even feel safe walking back to my own residence hall."[41] The safety of students of color and members of other vulnerable groups is a major concern across the country on college campuses, where in some cases hate has moved beyond graffiti, propaganda, and paper fliering to direct attacks on individual students and scholars, sometimes in violent and even deadly ways.

Hate Incidents Directed at Students and Scholars

Classes had just ended in spring 2017 and Taylor Dumpson was in the first day of her new role as the first Black female student-government president, when nooses holding bananas were hung in three different places at American University's campus in Northwest Washington. The bananas had messages written on them: "Harambe bait" (a reference to the Cleveland zoo gorilla who had been shot and later became the subject of racist memes), and the letters AKA—for Alpha Kappa Alpha, an African American sorority. The FBI investigated the incident as a hate crime—unsuccessfully—but the damage quickly spread beyond the original event: prominent far-right blogger Andrew Anglin directed his followers on social media to unleash a troll storm of harassment that caused Dumpson and her family to be placed under police protection.[42]

The fall semester was no sooner under way when a second major hate crime took place on American's campus. While Professor Ibram X. Kendi was speaking to share the vision for his new Anti-Racist Research and Policy Center, someone hung Confederate flag fliers affixed with stalks of cotton on bulletin boards in four campus buildings. This time, clear video evidence caught the suspected perpetrator, who was a middle-age white man not identifiable as a member of faculty or staff. He was never found. Other hateful incidents on campus in the two years prior—including swastikas on classroom whiteboards, bananas thrown at Black students, and anti-immigrant and misogynistic fliers posted on campus—made it clear that the incidents targeting Dumpson and Kendi were part of a broader rise in hate on campus.[43] And American University is not atypical. The same month that Taylor Dumpson was targeted, just a few miles away from AU's campus, an African American Bowie State University student, Richard Collins III, was fatally stabbed by a white college student near the University of Maryland's campus, only a few days before Collins was scheduled to graduate. The alleged murderer was a member of a Facebook group called "Alt-Reich Nation" and had racist memes on his phone.[44]

College campuses have endured hundreds of hate crimes and hate incidents across the country over the past three years, from swastikas stamped in the snow and spray painted on buildings to racial slurs and physical assaults on students, staff, and visitors. "It's unsettling at best, it's terrorizing at worst," said Lecia Brooks of the SPLC in response to two hate incidents at Duke University in fall 2018.[45] National data on campus hate are inexact, in part because they are officially tracked in at least three places: through reports compiled by nonprofit watchdog groups like the SPLC and the ADL, through mandated disclosure to the US Department of Education (DOE) under the Clery Act, and through campus-police-department reports to the FBI. There is variation in the numbers across these data sets, but all show increases over the past three years. In addition to the rise in white-supremacist propaganda documented earlier, DOE data track a 25 percent increase from 2016 to 2017 in campus hate crimes. FBI data—which constitute the most conservative account—show a steady rise in hate crimes on campuses, up 9 percent from 2016 to 2017 and 44 percent since 2015, with nearly 280 hate-crime reports from campus police departments in 2017, including 31 assaults, as well as over 75 incidents of intimidation. Over half of the incidents involved vandalism or destruction of property.[46]

Online attacks are particularly common. Over the past few years, academics have increasingly faced violent threats for their scholarship and public engagement. The typical trajectory starts, according to a report by *Inside Higher Ed* journalist Colleen Flaherty, with a professor's comments on a politicized topic appearing "on a right-wing website such as *Campus Reform*," which is followed by further appearances on "other, similar websites and news outlets and, finally, Fox News." After that, she reports, scholars receive "death threats, the threats of sexual violence, calls for them to be fired and lose their jobs."[47] There have also been attacks on individual faculty members' teaching and research, and an expansion of faculty surveillance websites like Campus Watch and Professor Watchlist.[48] City University of New York professor Jessie Daniels described a "tsunami of sustained chaos" when she was attacked online by the far right. She received hundreds of daily messages including rape and death threats. In her essay reflecting on the deluge of hate, she warns college faculty members that if a far-right attack against some member of their campus hasn't happened yet, "chances are it will."[49]

Higher education is not only a physical place that is valuable to far-right groups and individuals for its potential role in recruitment, polarization, and attacks on individual scholars and students. Universities are also key to the far right because they play a critical role in creating knowledge and claims to truth. The far right's attacks on expertise and knowledge, while more refined and intellectual than vulgar paper fliers and violent hate crimes, are nefarious in different ways.

"Cultural Marxism" and Attacks on Knowledge

Far-right attacks on higher education expertise are rooted in both ideology and conspiracy. Ideologically, the far right depicts universities as bastions of liberal brainwashing, where professors with leftist agendas churn out generations of students hostile to capitalism and critical of the government (despite evidence showing that liberal professors do not produce more liberal students).[50] But ideology alone doesn't explain the far right's virulent hostility to mainstream expertise and higher-educational institutions. Far-right attacks on expertise are embedded in global conspiracy theories suggesting that communists and progressives are engaged in secret efforts to undermine capitalism and control mass opinion through thought control. Higher education, in this frame, is said to regulate and restrict how people think in order to reproduce an intellectual elite that will perpetuate progressive control and promote multicultural societies to the detriment of whites.[51]

It is not only that universities are undermining Western values, according to far-right groups and individuals—they are doing so as part of an orchestrated effort by global communists to overthrow capitalist and Western societies from the inside. This is cultural Marxism—a coded catchword that has already made it from the far-right fringes into the mainstream. In a traditional Marxist revolution, communists would overthrow capitalism by a revolt of the laboring classes—the factory workers whose labor the system depends on. But since those revolutions were unsuccessful, the idea of cultural Marxism suggests that a new plan is afoot to disrupt and dismantle Western and capitalist values from within. The far right invokes the phrase "cultural Marxism" in spaces like Breitbart or Infowars as a way of arguing that the left is trying to destroy Western society. Feminism, a disrupted gender binary, multiculturalism, Muslim immigration, and gay rights are all invoked as part of a "plot to finish the job" that communist labor organizers couldn't pull off, ultimately undermining the West, the nation, capitalism, and traditional Christian values.[52]

Universities, of course, are seen as ground zero for this plot. In fact, if there's one thing that the American far right can agree on, it's this: higher education is the predominant site of the culture wars that are undermining far-right ideological values and Western, Christian civilization more broadly. And they are doing so at the direct expense of white men. The Proud Boys' founder Gavin McInnes calls college "totally and utterly useless," while far-right favorite Jordan Peterson tells people to "abandon universities (which have been hopelessly corrupted by their adoption of 'women's studies') in favor of trade schools."[53] Far-right provocateur Milo Yiannopoulos created a post-secondary-education "Privilege Grant," for which white men were exclusively eligible, so that they could be "on equal footing with their female, queer and ethnic minority classmates."[54]

Higher education is not the only target, of course. It is merely at the center of a broad assault on specialized knowledge more generally. Tom Nichols's The Death of Expertise traces a decline in respect for expertise through what he calls a "campaign against established knowledge."[55] Some of this decline happens through conspiracism, because the new conspiracists target the institutions that produce knowledge—including the media, higher education, research institutions, and government experts—in order to undermine the credibility of people, facts, and arguments. Specialized experts are regarded as suspect, accused of partisan bias, or disregarded entirely, including expertise from scientists, social scientists, public health and education professionals, and the free press.[56] The overall effect is to weaken "the legitimacy of sources of knowledge" and undermine shared ways of understanding and explanation.[57]

These far-right attacks on higher education do not exist in a vacuum, of course—rather, they have grown in the context of broader conservative critiques of the academy, as painstakingly documented by historians of higher education.[58] From Joseph McCarthy's hunt for communist academics in the 1950s through critiques on social science under the 1980s Ronald Reagan administration, the mainstream political right in the United States has long raised concerns about liberal political bias in US universities.[59] But unlike conservative criticisms of higher education, the extreme right wing links its attacks on mainstream expertise to far-right conspiracy theories framing higher education as part of a nefarious global plot by Marxists or communists to exert thought control over the public and thereby secure future power. This is consistent with fascist attacks on knowledge and expertise, which are a critical step in undermining the public's source of factual information and creating broader receptivity to propaganda and extreme ideologies.[60]

The broader phenomenon of declining public trust and confidence in American higher education provides important context for these ongoing far-right assaults on expertise. Republicans have particularly poor views of higher education, with 59 percent (compared to 18 percent of Democrats) reporting in 2019 that colleges have a negative impact on the way things are going in the country.[61] A climate of declining public trust, anti-intellectualism, and attacks on expertise has created fertile ground for more-extreme attacks on higher education to thrive among far-right groups and individuals. But in the midst of so many attacks on knowledge, facts, and claims to truth itself, the far right figured out something very important. Even as it works to discredit scientific knowledge, it could also appropriate that knowledge for its own ends.

Appropriation of Knowledge

"Discover what your professors never taught you in school," the website of the American white-supremacist group Identity Evropa once declared. Many of the "education" links on that site, predictably, led to white supremacist or far-right publications. But tucked in between descriptions of books with titles like *White Identity* and *The Perils of Diversity* was a link to Robert Putnam's mainstream scholarly treatise *Bowling Alone*—a book that traces the steady decline in Americans' civic and community engagement over the last half of the twentieth century.[62] Social science, it turns out, can be used to support far-right-extremist ideas—in ways that most scholars have probably never considered.

The far right is not only attacking academia—it is also deploying its scholarship for its own ends, using scholarly analyses of demographics, race, immigration, crime, and identity to make arguments in support of white-supremacist ideologies and platforms.[63] Herein lies the appeal of *Bowling Alone*: when interpreted through a far-right, anti-immigrant lens, Putnam's arguments about Americans' increasing disconnection from civil society and local communities may be viewed as helping the far right make claims about the supposed consequences of increasing diversity and immigration on community cohesion and identity.

The social sciences aren't the only scholarly domain that appeals to the far right. The past few years have also seen significant appropriation of art, antiquities, and history for far-right ideological ends. In a May 2019 advertising campaign, the German far-right political party AfD used the nineteenth-century French painter Jean-Léon Gérôme's *The Slave Market* painting, which depicts a naked white women having her teeth and mouth probed by a turban-clad man. In billboard-size posters, *The Slave Market* image was accompanied by text urging voters to learn from history and vote for the AfD to prevent Europe from turning into Eurabia—a reference to a conspiracy theory about the orchestration of future Islamic rule in Europe.[64] Elsewhere, far-right groups have embraced an ancient Spartan symbol, the lambda, as an emblem representing heritage, ancestry, roots, land, blood, and identity.[65] Symbols referencing the Spanish *Reconquista* are so frequent that the pogrom itself has become largely divorced from its historical context. Instead, *Reconquista* has become a tool for political mobilization by comparing modern Europe to resistance against Muslim conquerors in the Iberian Peninsula.[66]

Greek and Roman statues, temples, and ruins are also popular. The neo-Nazi website Stormfront uses images of the Parthenon.[67] The posters that Identity Evropa put up on college campuses included images of classical white marble statues.[68] Richard Spencer called for a North American white ethno-state that would be a "reconstitution of the Roman Empire."[69] In an essay that unleashed significant harassment against her from the far right, the classicist Sarah Bond argued that the public has falsely associated Greek and Roman peoples with whiteness, helped along by museums and scholars who have failed to communicate the ways that white marble was used during ancient times, not as the final sculptural product, but rather as a canvas that was then painted with a variety of colors.[70] Today's antiquities have lost their original paint, she explained, so their creamy white appearance became associated with classical beauty and left generations of modern observers with the false impression that ancient Greek and Rome were racially homogeneous, perpetuating "ideas of whiteness that never existed in the ancient world."[71] As a result, white-supremacist groups adopted classical statuary as symbols of white male superiority.[72]

This appropriation hasn't gone unnoticed by mainstream scholars. Classicists and historians have decried the use of Greek and Roman antiquities and medieval history by white-supremacist groups,[73] with one group of scholars even setting up an entire website, called "Pharos: Doing Justice to the Classics," devoted to documenting and challenging hate groups' appropriations of Greco-Roman culture. The Pharos website aims to challenge distortions and errors in hate groups' interpretations of historical time periods and ancient material.[74] But the use of classical antiquities, along with Greek and Roman history and symbols, continues to be popular among the far right.

Mainstream academic scholarship and historical narratives are useful to the far right because they can help legitimize and justify white-supremacist and antidemocratic goals. Almost anything can be interpreted through this lens with the right kinds of massaging. Data on declining civic engagement or rising crime are used to frame those issues as products of immigration. Research on the environment has been used to justify violent acts of terror with the argument that, in the face of climate change, national space must be preserved for citizens. "For those with a political ideology to sell," Angela Saini writes, "the science (such as it is) becomes a prop. The data itself doesn't matter so much as how it can be spun."[75] Many readers will be skeptical of authors whose extremist leanings are easily detectable through publishers or titles with obviously racist goals. But arguments that draw on reputable scholars or sources are harder to dismiss outright. The use of mainstream scholarship also helps far-right groups have better "optics," which is part of broader strategies to blend into the mainstream.

Far-right groups and individuals may well detest higher education and show themselves to be anti-intellectual, but they have also shown that they can use social scientific and historical research to present themselves as more mainstream. But political change won't come about only by delegitimizing existing expertise and using mainstream scholarship to support far-right policies. To effectively lay the groundwork for the political changes that will stop immigration, re-migrate ethnic minorities, and create a white ethno-state, the far right needs its own independent intellectual base and the means to shape public opinion. The creation of dedicated institutions to cultivate expertise and knowledge by and for the far right has been a decades-long project that has recently started to bear fruit.

Knowledge for and by the Far Right

Although far-right intellectuals have existed for centuries—dating at least to the French Revolution—following World War II, writers and scholars on the far right were largely discredited and disappeared from the mainstream.[76] But around the turn of the twenty-first century, far-right intellectual movements began to gain renewed strength, helping shape the ideas and policies of far-right political parties and election campaigns across the globe. These ideas have been honed and disseminated through an ever-expanding intellectual ecosystem of dedicated think tanks, publishing houses, research grants, magazines, conferences, and more.

The roots of modern far-right intellectualism date at least to the late 1960s and the Nouvelle Droite (new right), a group of far-right intellectual thinkers in France who promoted the idea that political change could come about only as a result of cultural change.[77] They were sometimes called the "Gramscians of the right" because of how they adopted the Marxist Italian scholar Antonio Gramsci's notion of hegemony, which suggested that revolutions would not come as a result of violence or physical overthrow but only through gaining control over ideas and education in order to transform how people think.[78] These ideas remain popular today, with one far-right group in the United Kingdom even referencing Gramsci's *Prison Notebooks* on its website to signal the importance of cultural change as a precursor to political revolution.[79] The modern far right has acknowledged, as Andrew Breitbart put it, that politics is downstream from culture.[80]

Enter metapolitics—the term far-right groups and individuals use to refer to a prepolitical cultural and intellectual project to shape mainstream ideas in ways that will lead to social transformation and political change.[81] Metapolitics is a long game, focused not on immediate political power but on the slower incubation of ideas that will, as the far-right group Generation Identity UK describes, "shape public debate, promoting ethno-nationalist ideas, and their goal the ethnic cleansing of Europe."[82] Metapolitics aims to seed the cultural changes and ideological foundation required for the public to accept the establishment of a white ethno-state.[83]

Metapolitics is more than just ideology. Big cultural ideas, as far-right leaders well know, can disseminate only if they have intellectuals to develop them and spaces where they can be disseminated.[84] Public education is essential to the project of political change. Greg Johnson, founder of the widely read far-right Counter-Currents website that views "metapolitics as pivotal to dislodging the Left's control of culture,"[85] once wrote that "today's White Nationalist movement might work best on the model of a Montessori school, not a Hitler Youth rally."[86] For Johnson, knowledge is key to the kinds of value shifts that will help accelerate the passage of the current Dark Age into the "Golden Age to come," in which separate homelands will exist for every race and ethnicity.[87]

Far-right intellectuals have been chipping away at the problem for decades, but their ideas are being received differently now. Jared Taylor, who runs the white-supremacist publication the *American Renaissance* (*AmRen*) and describes himself as a "white advocate" who "understands that the races are not identical and equivalent," recently told National Public Radio (NPR) reporter Joel Rose that after decades of work, he felt his ideas were finally starting to gain traction. "I've been injecting my ideas into the general conversation patiently and diligently for the last 30 years," he explained, "and I can assure you that more and more people agree with me." Indeed, the context of Taylor's media appearance was the recent revelation that White House advisor Stephen Miller had recommended articles from *AmRen*, along with other white-supremacist sources.[88]

The dissemination of far-right ideas was undoubtedly helped by the creation of new kinds of spaces online to communicate with broader publics. Blogs like *Unqualified Reservations*, launched in 2007 by Mencius Moldbug (pen name for Curtis Yarvin), who appropriated the phrase "taking the red pill" from the film *The Matrix* as a metaphor for an awakening to far-right ideas, quickly showed that online spaces were an ideal platform to reach new audiences and popularize far-right ideas among a broader public.[89] Before long, blogs were supplanted by a wide range of social-media platforms, which even parts of the far right not typically viewed as intellectual or academically focused quickly embraced as a means to recruit and persuade. In a 2018 interview with the *Guardian,* the white nationalist and founder of MMA brand White Rex Denis Nikitin laid out his virulent anti-immigrant views, explaining that killing "one immigrant every day" would never be enough because "tens of thousands more will come anyway. I realized we were fighting the consequence, but not the underlying reason. So now we fight for minds, not on the street, but on social media."[90] Younger generations are paying attention. In 2019, PragerU—an online video portal that shares short, five-minute videos promoting a mix of conservative and right-wing content—counted over one billion views.[91]

Online spaces were only part of the strategy. In short order, far-right intellectuals have worked to establish dedicated think tanks, research institutes, publishing houses, and training academies. Think tanks like the NPI—established in 2005 and led today by Richard Spencer—engaged in public speaking events and political lobbying to promote pan-Aryan and white-nationalist ideas.[92] The Swedish scholar Daniel Friberg established the far-right publishing house Arktos Media, now widely considered to be the "foremost producer of English-language Traditionalist and New Right literature."[93] In 2017, Friberg and Spencer combined their efforts, forming the "Alt Right Corporation" under the website AltRight.com, merging content from European and American writers.[94] Steve Bannon was thwarted by a local Italian town when he tried to turn an old monastery into a right-wing training academy, mod-eled as a counterpoint to George Soros's Open Society Foundation. "Soros has done an amazing job," Bannon told the *New Yorker* in a spring 2019 interview about the initiative, describing Soros as a "role model" for how he has seeded liberal political thought in NGOs, government, and the media in ways that have created "immense political power."[95] Bannon's vision was to finance young professionals to spend time in residence in his academy in Italy as a similar strategy for bringing more right-wing views into media and government.

These mostly American far-right intellectuals have an outsized influ-ence on global far-right knowledge and expertise, in large part because English-language text can be readily consumed across many different countries. But similar developments are afoot across Europe. Although Bannon's academy failed to get off the ground, there are other models already in existence. A political training school in Lyon, France, called the Institute for Social Sciences, Economics and Politics (ISSEP), is run by far-right political activist Marion Maréchal. The school offers master's degree courses in subjects like "the art of disinformation" and "Islam and Islamic civilizations: analysis of a new global trend."[96] Several far-right European political parties have organized summer schools, which include physical activities as well as lectures from far-right speakers.[97] A new Ukrainian "Education Assembly," founded by two members of a group identified as neo-Nazi, runs lectures and seminars focused on youth development and partnered with a mainstream think tank in Es-tonia, which was apparently unaware of the group's far-right connec-tions.[98] In Germany, a network of think tanks, publishing houses, writ-ers, and scholars is working to create the intellectual base for the new German right and an "alternative civil society network" to legitimize and normalize far-right-extremist ideas.[99]

A decades-long far-right intellectual project to seed extreme ideas in mainstream culture has been under way, with the eventual goal of shift-ing the "Overton window" of acceptable public policy solutions. This is where the fragmentation across the broader far right becomes especially clear, of course. Unlike the violent far right, for whom political change will come about through apocalyptic race war, the intellectual far right sees cultural revolution as imperative to political change. It is this kind of internal division and ambiguity that can make discussions of the "far right" particularly challenging. On the violent and accelerationist fringe, working within the mainstream political system is anathema to extremist goals to collapse current governments and societies and rise anew as a restored white civilization. But for much of the far-right spectrum, metapolitical change and the shifting of mainstream culture are the primary goals. Generation Identity's Europe/UK website sums up the far right's view of the importance of developing a far-right intellectual base when it says that this is a fight of "words, ideas and politics."[100] There is perhaps no better example of how this works in practice than in the gradual return of eugenics and race science into the mainstream.

The Return of Race Science

Most people are probably aware that national socialism and its policies, including the eventual murder of millions of Jews and others deemed biologically inferior to ethnic Germans, were underpinned by racist scientists—biologists and geneticists who manipulated interpretations of data to create eugenicist claims about the physical and intellectual superiority of whites. In the United States, too, scientific racism was produced and reproduced through miscegenation laws, for example, which criminalized interracial marriage.[101] Less well known, however, is that racist scientists did not completely disappear after World War II— on the contrary, a small group of white-supremacist scientists worked under the radar in the postwar era to create an international network to fund, review, publish, and comment on one another's work. Dedicated journals like *Mankind Quarterly*, an international association, and even a private foundation all supported the cause. Taken together, the science journalist Angela Saini recently explained, these activities worked to keep "scientific racism alive" in the postwar era.[102]

For the first few decades after the war, race science was largely relegated to the fringe of mainstream scholarship and social science. There were periodic surges of scientific publications arguing for a genetic basis to intelligence, but they were typically met with a swift backlash and protest. Arthur Jensen's 1969 *Harvard Educational Review* article on race, IQ, and scholastic achievement, for example, led to international protest, death threats, and even students burning him in effigy.[103] Such research still had an impact, though. Despite the protests, Jensen's article opened the door to a renewal of race science, allowing "other racist psychologists to crawl out of the woodwork."[104] In the years that followed, Jensen continued to produce research with "increasingly overt racist content," receiving over a million dollars for his work from the Pioneer Fund, an endowed fund that supports studies of race, intelligence, eugenics, and race science more broadly.[105] In the 1990s, the *Los Angeles Times* reported that the Pioneer Fund was by then distributing approximately a million dollars of scientific grants per year, primarily to academics "looking for genetic differences between races."[106] Indeed, the Pioneer Fund's financing over the past eighty years shows "an enduring thread from the eugenics movement of the previous century to the alt-right today."[107]

Saini's account of these postwar developments tells the story of an insular, closed circle of committed race scientists who were largely shunned by mainstream academia. But over the course of the 1980s and 1990s, she documents, these scientists gradually began making inroads into the world of public policy. An Iowa professor, Ralph Scott, who was a Pioneer Fund recipient and organizer of an anti-busing campaign, was appointed by the Reagan administration to chair the Iowa Advisory Commission on Civil Rights, even as he continued to write articles arguing that "integrated schools were holding back white students." Following an exposé in the *Nation*, Scott resigned.[108] But his was not an isolated case.

Over time, science that has sometimes been relied upon by white supremacists began having an influence on public policy, occasionally through other social scientists' work. The case of Richard Herrnstein and Charles Murray's 1994 book *The Bell Curve* is perhaps the best-known example. *The Bell Curve* argued that IQ is primarily genetic and is unevenly distributed across racial groups because of genetic differences that result in lower cognitive ability, or intelligence, on average, among Blacks. The book became a bestseller, widely discussed in the mainstream media and in scholarly and public-policy circles, even though it was critiqued and largely discredited for "spinning" data, exaggerating findings, drawing faulty conclusions, and relying heavily on a small group of race scientists as sources.[109] Indeed, as Saini and Evans both point out, *The Bell Curve* cited seventeen researchers who had contributed to the white-supremacist journal *Mankind Quarterly*, including ten who had served as the journal's advisory board members, along with five articles from the journal itself.[110] One of the scholars cited liberally in *The Bell Curve* was J. Phillipe Rushton, who had also written for the white-supremacist newsletter *American Renaissance* and had spoken publicly of the "genetic problem" of Islam and the "innately aggressive Muslim personality."[111] Rushton died in 2012, having published to the end of his life with well over a million dollars in financial support from the Pioneer Fund, which he also headed as president from 2002 to 2012.[112]

Herrnstein died before *The Bell Curve* was published, leaving his co-author Murray to field widespread critiques that the book's argument was "intellectually shoddy, racist, and dangerous,"[113] even as it continued to influence far-right policy makers.[114] In the wake of the critiques, Murray was more or less out of the public spotlight for nearly a quarter of a century (although he wrote another bestselling book in the interim). But in 2017 he was back in the news when a conservative student group at Middlebury College invited him to speak on campus on his new book, alongside a left-leaning Middlebury professor, Allison Stanger. The talk was immediately interrupted by chanting protesters and forced to move to—and then broadcast from—an undisclosed location, after which Murray and Stanger were physically attacked. Stanger ended up with whiplash and a concussion as a result of the altercation.[115] The protests made international news and were roundly critiqued across the political spectrum. But the attention launched Murray into the "alt-right" world as a "hero and martyr to the cause of free speech."[116] In short order, a 2015 interview between Murray and YouTuber Stefan Molyneux was recirculated, ultimately receiving over three hundred thousand views.[117] The popular podcaster and author Sam Harris invited Murray to join him on an episode he called "Forbidden Knowledge," whose four hundred thousand listeners heard Murray portrayed as a "valiant truth-seeker and his critics as cowardly, dishonest, hypocritical witch-burners."[118] In the episode, Harris frames critiques of Murray as attributable not to weak science or faulty data conclusions, but to "dishonesty and hypocrisy and moral cowardice," even suggesting that "there is virtually no scientific controversy" about Murray's claims.[119] This, in turn, launched a flurry of back-and-forth publications and responses with academic scientists, who argued that "Murray was peddling pseudoscience and Harris had been irresponsible in representing it as the scientific consensus."[120]

The "alt-right" celebration of Murray and his work as valiant truth telling is just one example of the revival of race science. Despite strong scientific evidence that race has little biological basis at all—such as the finding that 99.9 percent of the human genome is identical across races[121]—race science has continued to surge in popularity among the far right. Claims about genetic predispositions to crime or lower intelligence among nonwhites pepper far-right discussion boards and comment threads, underpinning a "proliferation of race science on social media" that has paralleled the rise of the far right across the United States, Europe, and elsewhere.[122] Such race science is often presented in ways that cherry pick data or draw on "pseudo-social-scientific theory" to support racist claims.[123] These efforts are helped along by far-right narratives that position racist opinions as legitimate facts that are being censored by the liberal media, politically correct culture, university "snowflakes," and Democratic elites—sometimes with conspirational frames that link the suppression of race science to supposed orchestrated efforts by global elites to eradicate white societies and replace them with multicultural ones.[124]

Long before the 2017 events at Middlebury College, though, race science had been steadily marching toward the mainstream, underwritten in part by the Pioneer Fund's financing of basic research linked to extreme far-right ideologies and platforms, including funding to two anti-immigration groups designated by the SPLC as hate groups.[125] Additional funding went to the Foundation for Human Understanding (FHU) and the Testing Research Fund (TRF), which, according to some scholars, helped publicize research on race, heredity, and intelligence, along with a range of other "efforts to prove the superiority of the original white 'stock.'"[126] More recently, the Pioneer Fund has supported the white supremacist Jared Taylor's newsletter, *American*

Renaissance, as well as the Ulster Institute for Social Research, whose publications include a book on racial difference in sporting ability.[127] In 2018, a student newspaper exposed a secret conference on eugenics and racially inherited IQ , which had been held on the campus of University College London (UCL) without permission, called the "London Conference on Intelligence." Topics included discussions of racial mixing and population quality. The program included speeches by the editor-in-chief of *Mankind Quarterly.*[128] In the wake of the ensuing scandal, UCL issued a statement pledging an investigation and condemning eugenics.[129]

In the first two decades of the twenty-first century, in sum, scientific racism continued its steady march into the mainstream, so brazen today that it can only be described as a "revival."[130] This development surprises even those who had tracked it. As the anthropologist Jonathan Marks told Saini: "I was working on the assumption that these guys were a lunatic fringe. If you had told me twenty years later that they would be part of a political mainstream wave, I would have said you are absolutely crazy . . . they are clearly ideologues for whom empirical evidence isn't important. But I think they were a lot cleverer than us professors."[131]

Scientific racism appeals to the far right for many reasons. At the most basic level, of course, scientific racism reinforces and validates white supremacy. By extension, though, scientific racism supports calls for white protection, separation, and segregation. Preserving the uniqueness of racial and cultural diversity thus becomes a justification for the white ethno-state. If each racial group is unique, it must be protected from endangerment through race mixing.[132] Keeping racial groups separate, of course, requires that each has a homeland of its own.

Responses to Rising Hate in Higher Education

Clearly, there are a variety of factors being deployed by far-right individuals and groups as part of a broad effort to confront higher education and academic expertise. These tactics range from physical and symbolic hate attacks to propaganda directed toward students and scholars, as well as efforts to delegitimize knowledge-producing institutions and develop an alternative ecosystem to train a new generation of far-right intellectuals. The response of university communities to these developments has been mixed and is worthy of much greater discussion than space allows here. Mainstream scholars have been actively focused on how to respond to far-right attacks on individual scholars, providing guidance on how individuals, universities, and disciplinary associations can take steps to protect themselves and respond to threats in the event of harassment or abuse.[133] But universities are also working across a range of other domains to address the rise of far-right and white-supremacist engagement on their campuses. Some have also worked to acknowledge their own historical roles in eugenics research, ownership of slaves, and naming of buildings after racists and white supremacists.

Within individual campuses, universities have run training workshops for faculty to better prepare for contentious classroom conversations that might include far-right statements or political views that fall outside of the mainstream, and have ramped up orientation programs designed to help students engage in civil dialogue across differences. Disciplinary groups have run special sessions at conferences on responding to attacks, and launched scholarly campaigns to counter misinformation and misuse of scholarship. National higher-education associations have also tackled campus polarization and attacks on higher education as key parts of their work. Senior leaders have worked to develop new guidelines for responding appropriately to controversial speakers' events and campus hate. Overall, however, these efforts have been largely reactive, as campuses scramble to respond to rapidly changing campus political climates and to all-too-frequent attacks, hate speech, and propaganda.

These efforts to dismantle knowledge deemed to come from the left and build intellectual capacity for the far right are critical aspects of the overall transformations in far-right extremism. They have taken place alongside the development of new markets and financial capacity and efforts to train youth physically for future battles. But all of these domains rely on new media ecosystems to communicate. The transformations in online spaces, in other words, underpin all of these other changes in important ways that I analyze in the next chapter.

Chapter 6

Weaponizing Online Spaces

For all the lack of attention I've suggested that spaces and places have gotten in the quest to better understand youth radicalization, there is one exception. Online spaces are constantly invoked in discussions about pathways to extremism, in policy discussions, and in media headlines that warn parents and educators of the dangers of online exposure to extremist propaganda and persuasive recruiters. Indeed, the public could not be faulted for thinking that radicalization happens primarily to isolated, lone teenagers who stumble into nefarious parts of the dark web from a gloomy corner of their bedroom lit only by the glow from their screen. And like many stereotypes, there is some kernel of truth to this. More than ever, exposure to extremism requires no physical destination at all—its virtual spaces beam right into our homes and schools in social-media memes, imageboards, chatrooms, and online games. But stereotypes are also debunked for good reasons. And if ever there was a fantasy in need of demystifying, it is the idea that radicalization happens only or primarily in fully isolated, online domains. The story of how the far right has created, cultivated, and weaponized the internet is much more complex, relying on a strategic combination of online and off-line activities that enables the far right to maximize the circulation, communication, and effectiveness of far-right ideologies.[1]

As the previous chapters have shown, the modern far right is working to build muscular warriors equipped with the physical capacity to fight, along with "alt-right" thinkers with the intellectual capacity to lead and the commercial ecosystems that help market, brand, and financially support these actions. Underpinning all of these activities, though, is the modern far right's rapid adoption—and creation—of a broad new tech and media ecosystem for communication, dissemination, and mobilization. Groups and individuals across the far right were early users of the internet and have quickly capitalized on new media's ability to broaden recruitment and exposure to political ideologies beyond the physical spaces of MMA tournaments, music concerts, and rallies.

This chapter aims to unpack the complex set of factors that have made online spaces so central to the growth of the far right. It's important to note that any discussion of online phenomena—especially in a print publication—is made more difficult by the rapid evolution of far-right landscapes both online and off-line, particularly the constant changes in how far-right leaders and influencers communicate and the degree to which they are regularly "outmaneuvering" traditional channels and platforms for communication.[2] There will always be new spaces, channels, and platforms enabling online communication and mobilization. Moreover, much of the ecology of hate online is self-organized rather than engineered from the top down. Clusters of individuals constantly migrate across different platforms in response to banning and "de-platforming"—a term that refers to individuals or groups being denied access to a particular site, or to a forum like 8chan losing technical support from the website company that had been supporting it.[3] This chapter focuses on the strategies and modes of communication enabled by online spaces, using examples of channels and platforms to illustrate. The reader should bear in mind, however, that even by the time these words are in print, the specific ecosystem enabling these modes and strategies will have evolved. New and emerging platforms, however, are likely to only extend and deepen the new modes of communication that online spaces have made possible.

Going Online: How the Internet Fuels Far-Right Extremism

By the time the media revealed that the Pittsburgh synagogue shooter had been partially radicalized on a fringe social-media website (Gab) with a reputation for extreme-far-right content, it was already clear that the growth of far-right extremism was directly linked to online spaces, including social media and digital platforms for extremist engagement.

Indeed, online spaces are foundational to the growth of the far-right movement; the spaces and places talked about in the rest of this book all rely on digital communication and online technology to thrive. Brands sell commercial merchandise laced with far-right codes on dedicated websites and online distributers; MMA and combat tournaments are advertised, ticketed, and live-streamed online; attacks on scholars and the creation of new knowledge rely heavily on internet platforms for communication and distribution. The ecosystem of tech platforms where the far right is engaged is vast and ever-evolving.

Like any other ordinary citizen, far-right individuals connect and communicate through mainstream social media and imageboard sites like Facebook, Twitter, Instagram, and Pinterest. There are Tumblr blogs dedicated to far-right merchandise and brand communities, and far-right influencers building collaborations on YouTube.[4] Such sites and channels have proven strategically useful not only for recruitment and radicalization of young people, but also for their mobilization. After a German man died in a street-fight stabbing and a Syrian and an Iraqi asylum seeker were arrested for the crime in September 2018, a spontaneous crowd protesting "criminal migrants" grew overnight—largely through social-media recruiting—to six thousand protesters.[5] But as hate speech, vile rhetoric, dehumanizing language, and threats against individuals and their families began to escalate on mainstream platforms, tech companies started to revise their terms of service and ban users who violated them. Spotify and Apple removed white-supremacist hate music from their platforms, while website-hosting platforms like GoDaddy kicked white-supremacist sites like The Daily Stormer off their sites.[6] Other tech companies—including YouTube and Twitter—pledged to monitor and remove accounts linked to white supremacists.[7]

Enforcing terms of service made these mainstream platforms safer and more pleasant for the mainstream and helped companies draw a line that clearly conveys what they stand for, sending an unequivocal message that hate groups' beliefs, statements, and actions are so incompatible with mainstream values that their members and organizations are unwelcome as consumers, guests, speakers, or visitors. But the bans also turned out to have an unintended consequence: they backfired, further fueling extremism by driving it underground and reinforcing the far right's narrative of suppression, censorship, unfairness, and injustice. As mainstream platforms cracked down on users who violate their terms of use, those users migrated to unregulated, alternative platforms that more deeply incubate a hate-filled, dehumanizing culture; celebrate violence; circulate conspiracy theories; and help translate resentment, shame, or frustration into anger and calls to action. The concentration of extreme views on unregulated sites (combined with a lack of moderate ones), along with the kind of heightened polarization brought on by the relative anonymity of social media and the lack of oversight, makes fringe platforms especially ideal places to incubate and radicalize individuals.[8] Even in off-line spaces, when individuals spend time in groups of only other like-minded individuals, their opinions and views become more extreme and they are less open to opposing views.[9] The effect is similar online. Alternative platforms thus become what scholars refer to as "echo chambers" of extreme content and hate—places that intensify extremist ideology and further radicalize new members. Research evidence supports this. In an analysis of over a hundred million comments and ten million images posted to Gab and the "politically incorrect" (/pol/) 8chan message board between July 2016 and January 2019, the Network Contagion Research Institute found that anti-Semitic slurs and content doubled after the 2016 election, along with a surge in racist expressions and the n-word slur.[10]

De-platforming and banning are processes more complex than many observers realize. Migration between platforms, for example, is more complicated than a simple one-way move. In some cases, bans on mainstream platforms drive users to more extreme options, as data on the relationship between Twitter de-platforming and increased engagement on Gab has shown.[11] Banned individuals and groups not only move between platforms, but sometimes also circle back to the places from which they were originally banned, after they discover ways to circumvent the bans. For example, the KKK, which had been banned from Facebook, was able to thrive in nearly sixty separate clusters on the Russian social-networking site VKontakte.[12] But when the Ukrainian government banned VKontakte, some KKK groups migrated from that platform back to Facebook, but with "KuKluxKlan" written in Cyrillic in order to circumvent English-language detection algorithms.[13]

Banning policies also fuel an entrepreneurial spirit within the far right. When fundraising and crowdsourcing platforms like Paypal, Patreon, GoFundMe, and Kickstarter proved too restrictive (by banning racist or sexist campaigns, for example), the far right moved to Hatreon, GoyFundMe, MakerSupport, and Wesearchr—which either had fewer restrictions on who could raise money or were designed as dedicated platforms for the far right.[14] Wesearchr, for example, recently hosted a fundraising campaign for Andrew Anglin's legal expenses against the SPLC, raising over $155,000 in less than two months. As Wesearchr's cofounder, Charles Johnson, described, de-platforming policies created an opportunity for the company, which takes a 15 percent cut of funds raised, explaining that they are "basically the monopoly for people on the right," since there is "literally nowhere else for them to go."[15] At its peak in 2017, Hatreon was reportedly collecting approximately $25,000 per month.[16] However, subsequent efforts by mainstream companies that support online payment processes—including Paypal, Stripe, Apple Pay, Google Pay, and Visa—have increasingly restricted, suspended, or banned card payments in ways that have reduced the ability of the far right to fundraise on websites.[17] One consequence of this development is the far right's increasing use of peer-to-peer transactions, both through personal checks and bank transfers as well as through cryptocurrency donations, which allow for more anonymity or discretion in donations.[18]

As sites are de-platformed, others quickly spring up in their place. Endchan welcomed "8chan refugees" after 8chan was shut down in the wake of the 2019 El Paso shooting (after the El Paso and Christchurch shooters posted their manifestos there). Almost immediately, a Norwegian extremist posted a manifesto on endchan and attacked a mosque outside of Oslo, where mass tragedy was prevented by security measures that had been put in place after Christchurch.[19] Meanwhile, the far right broadened the online spaces where recruiters and sympathizers could communicate, using gaming platforms like Steam or Discord, which feature text, audio, and video communication options between players, and encrypted free-speech platforms like Telegram, which had been created for prodemocracy activists but was then adopted by far-right influencers who had been suspended from other platforms. Proud Boys founder Gavin McInnes, who was banned from mainstream platforms like Twitter, Instagram, and Facebook, has a Telegram channel with nearly seven thousand subscribers, while Milo Yiannopoulos's channel boasts over eighteen thousand followers.[20] Growth in these platforms is rapid and recent. Vice journalist Tess Owens recently analyzed a sample of 150 "alt-right" and neo-Nazi Telegram channels and found that 94 of them had been created in the first eight months of 2019, with a clear spike in the month after the Christchurch shooting. The newer channels, Owens found, are heavily accelerationist and terror focused, including 19 that talk openly of a coming "boogaloo," a term used to refer to "an impending civil war or government overthrow." Owens also found that images and memes from Ukraine, where the far-right Azov Battalion is active, were especially popular.[21]

The widespread sharing of memes, video clips, propaganda, planning tips, and more across borders is part of the global nature of the modern far right. The global interconnectedness of hate is used to help build "intertwined narratives that cross languages and causes," resulting in groups and clusters with membership from multiple countries and ideological rationales that are not always consistent. This means that the global online ecology of hate "acts like a global fly-trap that can quickly capture new recruits from any platform, country, and language, particularly if they do not yet have a clear focus for their hate."[22] Meanwhile, new software, platforms, and channels emerge constantly, so that virtually every mainstream platform has an alternative counterpart catering to users who want less regulation, more security, or more privacy. Thus, banned Twitter users, for example, migrate to Gab or the new "free-speech" alternative Parler.[23] Alternative search engines, encrypted email platforms, streaming services, and imageboard sites help round out a broad alternative ecosystem with particular appeal to the far right. Alternative online modes of financing, such as cryptocurrencies, often align well with far-right ideological views, such as a "historical mistrust of global financial systems" and conspirational thinking about Jewish "globalist" architects of financial institutions and global markets.[24]

Even on mainstream platforms, the ever-expanding numbers of social-media, gaming-platform, and imageboard sites struggle with trolls, racists, and far-right users in ways that shed light on how young people might encounter hate content and white-supremacist messaging as they engage in ordinary activities online. The popular Russian-owned meme-sharing site iFunny, for example, includes accounts called "Race-War" and "Traditional_Nationalist," which share neo-Nazi and white-supremacist propaganda—the latter has nearly twenty thousand subscribers.[25] The online game Roblox, which has over a hundred million global users, is a popular children's game but also includes users who valorize the Holocaust and spread white-supremacist propaganda.[26] The gaming problem is particularly substantial: in one recent national survey by the ADL, 23 percent of online gamers reported encountering white-supremacist propaganda while gaming.[27] Even children's games are a target for extremists, who take advantage of user-generated-content features to insert racial slur words, swastikas, and extremist symbols and expressions into geometry games and online games like Roblox, where an August 2019 investigation found over a hundred accounts with racist and extremist content.[28]

Taken together, the broad range of mainstream gaming and social-media platforms, alongside alternative imageboard sites and communication channels, makes up a broad tech ecosystem that underpins far-right growth. So-called alt-tech spaces garner a lot of attention from the media and the general public for how they have enabled reactionary online discourse and harassment,[29] including in prior forms of online trolling that played a key role in the modern far right's online engagement, like the Gamergate saga. Gamergate's 2014 torrent of misogynistic hate, online threats, and abuse against women in the gaming industry was readily incorporated into the "alt right" and broader attacks on PC (politically correct) culture, feminism, social justice warriors, and the liberal left's supposed efforts to indoctrinate youth.[30]

Despite the key role such alt-tech spaces have played, it is important to remember that these platforms and channels themselves are just the most visible feature of what is essentially an entirely new mode of engagement, communication, and mobilization enabled by the internet and social media. These new modes of communication have fueled far-right growth in at least two ways. First, online spaces broaden exposure to and amplify extreme content and far-right ideas. Second, they help those on the far right communicate with one another, broadening networks; building resources that support activism, violence, and movement growth; and bridging online connections with off-line engagements and networks.

Exposure and Amplification

There were many horrific aspects to the murder of fifty-one Muslim worshippers in Christchurch, New Zealand, in March 2019, but among the most shocking was the fact that the seventeen-minute attack was live-streamed on Facebook Live and then rapidly circulated globally, downloaded, and reposted on other sites, including YouTube, Twitter, Reddit, and Instagram.[31] This turned an already-terrible terrorist attack into a global performance, exponentially increasing the ways in which terrorism is a "type of bloody political theatre."[32] In the twenty-four hours following the attack, Facebook alone removed 1.5 million instances of the videos.[33] Similar patterns hold true for less violent local activism as well, which far-right groups deliberately design as, or rapidly convert to, marketing stunts. After a group of AIM activists disrupted author Jonathan Metzl's book talk in spring 2019 at a Washington, DC, bookshop, chanting "This land is *our* land!" and shouting far-right propaganda, the group circulated the video and posted about it on the AIM website under examples of activism, where it remains as of this writing.

For decades, white-supremacist and far-right movement leaders have created reams of propaganda and marketing materials—in pamphlets, newsletters, videotapes, radio programs, and even cable-access shows, but, as extremism expert J. M. Berger describes, "virtually no one saw it."[34] Such materials were produced for and circulated to small audiences and shared with known lists and groups of individuals, making for a limited reach. The internet opened new modes of communication, and white supremacists jumped on the bandwagon early, running dial-up forums in the 1980s and creating more sophisticated white-supremacist message boards like Stormfront as early as 1995. But while these new online modes of communication facilitated conversation among white supremacists, they were not "engines of growth."[35] This all changed with the advent of social-media platforms and the sudden ease with which propaganda and marketing materials could be distributed, circulated, retweeted, shared, and connected with the mainstream.[36]

The vegan far-right cooking show discussed in chapter 3 is a good example. In the past, "such amateur videos would have never been available to a global audience (including the ability to network within their movement)."[37] Traditional media outlets such as radio and television were limited to mainstream content by design. The limited number of channels and the lack of openness to user-generated content meant that all entertainment and news media were necessarily centralized and mediated through professional journalists aiming for broad, mainstream viewership. But today, the barriers to entry are low: all it takes is a decent smartphone camera and a strong internet connection to broadcast almost any content a given individual desires. This creates "previously unimaginable opportunities for the promotion of extreme right messages" along with more direct ways of engaging audiences. The vegan cooking show, for example, enables viewer engagement through a chat function, creating direct contact to hosts that would have been impossible in traditional media formats of the past.[38]

The internet in general and the broad ecosystem of new media platforms it has enabled—social-media sites, gaming platforms, encrypted communication channels, crowdfunding and money transfer sites, and content-sharing and streaming sites—have rapidly and radically transformed the spread of extremist propaganda and opportunities to communicate online. The broad range of online spaces is used to expose new audiences to extremist content, through live-streaming or sharing videos, posting manifestos, circulating memes, and sharing other content. YouTube has proven an especially useful platform, both because of its broad popularity—it rivals traditional television in viewership—and because the medium allows far-right "e-celebrities" to engage with popular influencers by appearing as guests on other pundits' channels. This, in turn, lends legitimacy and validation to sexist and racist rhetoric, which they frame as merely attempts to "'trigger' liberals and fight for 'free speech.'"[39] It is not only dedicated far-right videos, vlogs, podcasts, and talk shows with names like "White Genocide Explained" that have radicalized audiences, but also guest appearances on shows in adjacent and overlapping communities, such as the shows of YouTube stars in the gaming, men's rights, conspiracist, and trad wife (traditional wife) worlds. These audiences are diverse, including not only dedicated far-right activists but also groups who are on the margins of the far right. Online spaces thus bring together antifeminist misogynists, trolls, hackers, online gamers, the anime-sharing users of 2chan, and the meme makers of 4chan.[40]

The broad variety of online platforms has helped the far right weaponize the internet for the intentional purpose of recruiting, radicalizing, communicating with, and mobilizing followers, as well as raising or crowdsourcing the funds to support its efforts. Critically, surges in online hate are associated with more violence off-line, meaning that hateful communication and spikes in hate in online spaces correlate with spikes in violence in the real world—"more violence occurs where a large amount of hatred is disseminated on social media."[41] But online spaces have also helped the far right in ways that are much less intentional, related to the nature of social media itself and how individuals engage with it. One of the more unexpected developments in the internet age is how the structure of social-media and online communication platforms have amplified and intensified exposure to extreme content through filter bubbles, echo chambers, recommender systems, search algorithms, and social-media personalization algorithms.

Two Clicks from Extremism: Algorithmic Radicalization

The public's first inkling that algorithms might play a role in extremist radicalization came about in the wake of Dylann Roof's 2015 murder of nine African American parishioners in a Charleston church. As the flurry of information from law enforcement and media investigations about Roof's background made its way to the public domain, the news broke that Roof's radicalization pathway started with a Google search about "black on white crime," when the results took him to a white-supremacist website. Roof had typed that phrase into the search engine after becoming curious during the trial of George Zimmerman, a Florida neighborhood-watch captain who had shot and killed seventeen-year-old Trayvon Martin while he was walking on a neighborhood street. Roof was curious about whether Zimmerman was justified in feeling a sense of threat from Martin, and wanted to know more about crime statistics and racial groups. But his Google search directed him to the Council of Conservative Citizens, which like other white-supremacist groups uses a tactic of framing an "epidemic of black-on-white crime," sometimes described in shorthand as "black crime." Such frames use language that depicts crime as including mobs of unprovoked attackers, typically arguing that the media and government are censoring crimes committed by Blacks against whites by describing them as isolated events and not classifying them as hate crimes.[42] In the manifesto Roof posted online as well as in FBI interviews, he singled out the importance of that Google search, noting that "I have never been the same since that day."[43]

Google has made efforts to change its search algorithm, such as removing the auto-fill options in the search bar after researchers like Safiya Umoja Noble pointed out the racist and misogynistic bias that led searches using the keywords "black girls," for example, to prioritize pornography sites. Noble labels these kinds of data failures "algorithmic oppression," showing how Google searches and page-ranking search protocols reinforce stereotypes that marginalize women and people of color.[44] But there are some aspects of online searches that tech companies can't control. After I gave a talk on youth radicalization recently, an audience member approached me to explain how she had searched online for tips on prepping food in Tupperware containers and was directed to a site for "extreme preppers," whose doomsday, apocalyptic fantasies have created a subculture of stockpiling survivalists, some of whom believe in accelerationist strategies to hurry the coming apocalypse. It's hard to imagine how tweaks to an algorithm could prevent that from happening.

The problem is far bigger than search engines alone. Social-media and commercial shopping platforms, for example, use recommender systems that guide users to other content, products, or people. When consumers purchase a book on a distributor's website, for example, an algorithm shows them what other people who bought that book have also looked at or bought. In theory, this can be a useful (and profitable) feature—if I'm searching for gluten-free cookbooks, shopping sites' algorithms will almost always direct me to products similar to the one I viewed or purchased, sometimes describing these as items that others also viewed. Similar algorithms recommend people to follow on Twitter, videos to watch on YouTube, and friends to connect with on Facebook. But left unregulated, the same algorithms can guide casual or coincidental viewers to extreme content that they might otherwise not have encountered.

While personalized recommender systems significantly increase the "possibility of system-driven promotion" of extreme content, the effect is uneven across platforms.[45] In an investigation of YouTube, Reddit, and Gab, researchers found that only YouTube "prioritizes extreme right-wing material after interaction with similar content," increasing the likelihood that an individual who interacts with extreme content on YouTube will subsequently encounter further extreme content as a result of being on that platform. This reinforces previous research that showed users who follow YouTube's recommendation system "can be propelled into an immersive ideological bubble within a few clicks."[46] An in-depth *New York Times* analysis of former "alt-righter" Caleb Cain's YouTube history showed how recommendations created a spiral of ever-more extremist content.[47] YouTube isn't the only problematic platform, though. Researchers have found that Twitter's "who to follow" recommendation system and Facebook's "recommended friends" feature have helped connect violent extremist accounts or terrorist sympathizers with one another.[48]

YouTube made changes to its algorithm in 2019 that were aimed at reducing viewers' exposure to "conspiracy theories and partisan content," although it is too early to know much about the impact of those changes.[49] What is important to know is that for several years during the rise of the new far right, personalization algorithms helped shape the choices that people make, influencing their actual behavior by recommending other accounts, products, videos, or people to follow, watch, and connect with. And algorithms filter content in ways that significantly reduce the likelihood that youth who engage with extreme content will also encounter views, information, or news sources that challenge those views. Personalization algorithms curate news, timelines, feeds, and information for every user, acting as gatekeepers in ways that create "filter bubbles"—"personal, unique universe[s] of information that you live in online" that an algorithm edits for you based on what it already knows about your preferences.[50] While intended to create results that better reflect what people want, the end results are unbalanced, limiting the breadth of perspectives individuals are exposed to, tailoring search results and information in ways that limit what people see and read in their feeds, reinforcing their worldviews, and restricting opposing viewpoints. Personalization algorithms box users who engage with extremist content into echo chambers that reinforce their emerging worldview—and reduce the chance that they will encounter information to challenge those views.[51] Algorithms alone are not responsible for radicalization, of course. Algorithmic recommendations interact with viewers' and users' behavior, helping shape the universe of choices people have—and the ones they actually make—as they continue to engage online. Recommendation systems and personalization algorithms interact with human preferences and behavior in ways we do not yet fully understand—shaping what information individuals search for, how they receive it, and their behavior afterward. The consequences of this development are vast—for dialogue, for civic education, and for democracy itself—but are only starting to be understood.

What I refer to as "algorithmic radicalization," then, refers to changes in human attitudes, beliefs, or behavior as individuals are directed to extremist content, networks, groups, or other individuals as a result of guided searches, filtered news feeds, recommended videos, and connections from extremist adjacent sites. But individuals can engage with extreme content even when algorithms do not drive them to do so. People encounter extreme content and an extreme culture on a site like Gab, for example, simply because there are a lot of extreme individuals there.[52] Encounters with extremist content on fringe and unregulated social-media platforms, imageboard sites, and YouTube channels are more likely because of the high volume of extremist accounts and individuals sharing that content, not (only) because of algorithmic recommendations. Crossover content also helps the situation by linking individuals motivated by a single issue—like gun control or abortion—with broader far-right-extremist content. This is true in commercial spaces too, such as on the website gunbroker.com, where customers can pick up swastika Christmas ornaments, Hitler youth belt buckles, and other Nazi paraphernalia along with their military-grade weapons.[53] Platforms that lack regulation or moderation are especially problematic, but platforms that do regulate or ban often push individuals into more underground or egregiously extreme platforms and discussions. And even regulated sites may host videos that do not violate any terms of service, but act as gateways to more extreme content by offering links or URLs that take users to encrypted channels for more information.

Finally, while exposure to and filtering of information, content, and connections to extreme individuals are key to the earliest phases of radicalization, online spaces also play a critical role in intensifying and deepening extreme views. Online spaces can connect users, visitors, and observers to one another in online and off-line spaces. Consumer goods, brands, and musicians marketing to the far right often maintain Twitter feeds, Facebook and Tumblr pages, and Instagram accounts. Those pages then become a constantly updating feed of posts from "friends" and others who share information, update followers on new products, and issue announcements about political actions, events, rallies, and festivals that take place in off-line spaces—even, in one case, advertising a "study tour" trip to a region of Scandinavia sacred to the far right for its Norse mythological ties to supposed Aryan origins.[54]

Weaponizing Humor: Memes and Emoji

One reason the new ecosystem of online spaces has been so effective in spurring growth in the far right has to do with the entertainment value of social media and the ways that humor has been weaponized, especially through the creation and circulation of memes, jokes, and emoji.

The far right has figured out that young people are motivated not only by serious, planned action but also by spontaneous and humorous engagements. Humor, memes, and jokes thus become tactics for engaging youth.[55] Rapidly evolving emoji become signals for insiders and provocations for outsiders. "Alt-right" Twitter users began adopting a red X in their handles, for example, to signal their belief that they were being "shadow banned" (oppressed by an orchestrated group of political elites); they also used a glass of milk emoji, reflecting milk's brief popularity as an "alt-right" symbol, based on the belief that white people can digest milk better than other ethnic and racial groups and to celebrate dairy milk over soy milk, which is viewed by the far right as emasculating.[56] The Syrian flag became a popular emoji in social-media handles in support of a Trump-ordered air strike in Syria, followed by the "OK" hand gesture, which was officially named a hate symbol by the ADL in 2019.[57] It is worth noting that all of these symbols can be understood only in the context of their usage; there is nothing inherently far right about the "OK" symbol or a milk icon. These kinds of ordinary symbols only become "far-right symbols" when they are deployed with specific white-supremacist intent. And the meanings of any given symbol or emoji are constantly in flux, driven by an online youth culture oriented around provocation and visual engagement.

One of the clearest illustrations of how unpredictable this use of humor can be is the story of how Pepe the Frog—a cartoon character with no relationship whatsoever to the far right—became co-opted by the far right. Originally created by cartoonist Matt Furie for the comic *Boy's Life*, Pepe's original character was an affable if crass frog whose antics revolved around life with his three roommates and the pranks that characterized their everyday interactions.[58] Sometime in 2015, the nascent "alt right" decided to "remake Pepe" as a "white nationalist icon."[59] Memes began to circulate on sites like 4chan and Reddit that adapted Pepe the Frog in varied right-wing-extremist ways—wearing a Nazi uniform and a KKK hood and robe, among other caricatures.[60] By the time the election campaign was well under way, the connection between Pepe the Frog and the US far right was so strong that Hillary Clinton denounced Pepe publicly, and the ADL added the cartoon character to its hate-symbols database.[61]

Pepe's popularity with the far right was not only due to the iconographic representation of the frog with Nazi and far-right symbols but also because of the way it symbolized a kind of superior nonchalance toward others, helping to normalize hostile attitudes toward minorities and political opponents.[62] Part of the growing use of memes as "emblematic representations of words and images" that act as "short-hand tools for political communication online," the Pepe meme communicated both far-right ideological positions and kind of anti-elite arrogance and condescension.[63] By the time a meme of Pepe as Donald Trump was retweeted by the Trump campaign during the 2016 election, Pepe the Frog had become a clear symbol of the "alt right," not only through online memes but also through the use of the cartoon character in emoji, pins, patches, and more.[64] But around the time Pepe became an official hate symbol in fall 2016, things got even stranger.[65] Someone discovered that there is an Egyptian god who is depicted as a frog-headed man—named Kek. (The letters KEK had already evolved as a popular stand-in for LOL to indicate online laughter.) Soon, the far right created an imaginary country called Kekistan, complete with flags that began to show up at off-line gatherings, including at the Charlottesville Unite the Right rally.[66] A civilian contractor working in Afghanistan with the US armed forces was fired after a video alleging he was wearing the Kekistan flag on his helmet was circulated online.[67]

Pepe is an extraordinary case, but there are other examples where elements from the off-line world are co-opted, infused with new meaning, and circulated online for and by the far right. The appropriation of the tiny Swedish industrial town of Finspång into a fantasy far-right "execution meme" is one such case. Sometime in mid-2017, as Andreas Önnerfors explains, a far-right website posted a meme of two people dressed in protective clothing and gas masks entering a doorway leading to a "white reservation" named Finspång, described as a place established to protect the "biological exceptionalism" of white Swedes.[68] Subsequent images and text depicted a polluted, collapsed "multicultural Sweden" outside the walls of Finspång, in contrast to the "clean" and "free" white reservation. In this future fantastical world, tribunals in Finspång will lead to executions of "traitors of the people" in streetlamp hangings lining the roadways. The real town of Finspång was thus appropriated into a meme of a fictional place where national traitors would be executed under a future fascist regime. This evolved into a broader Finspång meme used to convey various far-right ideological positions and threats against groups and individuals through the phrase "See you in Finspång," alongside images of hangings, echoing German far-right extremists who use the phrase "See you in Walhalla," the hall of the dead in Norse mythology. The meme moved out of niche far-right subcultures into more mainstream usage, as Önnerfors describes in greater depth, when it was deployed by the leaders of a right-wing alternative news site that reaches 8 percent of Swedish news readership.[69] In this way, a real place rooted in the off-line world became a fantastical place in online spaces and was infused with far-right meanings.

The Pepe and Finspång memes show how a particular kind of dark humor, relying on insider jokes or fantasies of mythological spaces, is part of a shift toward playful, creative modes of offensive provocation in far-right communication styles. An entire series of memes and jokes compares Jews to pizzas (with images of stone pizza ovens, and phrases like "another Jew in the oven") or uses wordplay to communicate anti-Semitic messaging, like "Jewnited States" or "Jewpreme Court."[70] But it is not just that the far right uses irony, satire, jokes, and innuendo to carry extremist, racist, and hateful ideas and images into the mainstream. Just as important is how it frames this as countercultural pushback.[71] The far right's success online is at least partly attributable to the ways it has managed to make racist, misogynist content come across as "edgy rebellion."[72] This has had particular appeal to disaffected young white men, for whom participation in racist "counterculture" offers a sense of power and supremacy that they may find lacking elsewhere.[73]

Online spaces have turned out to be a perfect incubator for far-right-extremist ideas. They have helped introduce and intensify racist and white-supremacist beliefs and created a far-right youth counterculture that weaponizes humor, valorizes provocation and trolling, and delegitimizes critiques by framing them as coming from oversensitive liberal snowflakes and "social justice warriors" who are triggered by jokes.[74] But online spaces turned out to be useful to the far right in ways that move far beyond recruitment and radicalization: they also helped build national and transnational networks, share tactics and strategies, and build financial resources that help support far-right influencers, finance activism, and cover legal expenses.

Building Resources, Training, and Global Networks

Online spaces, as this chapter has documented, can expose new audiences to far-right ideologies, deepen and intensify far-right ideas, and help channel unfocused hate toward political goals. They facilitate the spread of conspiracy theories, racist memes, and hateful attacks on scholars, journalists, and political opponents. And they intensify and amplify hateful rhetoric from the mainstream, as political hate speech and polarizing mainstream news speech lead to a flurry of social-media hate that then inspires fringe actors to engage in violence.[75]

But online spaces also provide critical domains through which far-right groups meet one another, build resources, and share lessons learned across movements and countries. They are places where far-right leaders, influencers, and organizers communicate, fundraise, and build networks transnationally.[76] Mainstream, moderated platforms like Twitter and Facebook have been especially key here, offering an initial place where the far right delivers information, coordinates activity, circulates reports of actions, attacks opponents, and disrupts public discourse.[77] Online spaces offer guidance and training in how to carry out acts of violence, share terrorist manifestos, celebrate violent acts, and spur on new ones.[78]

Early engagement on mainstream platforms proved useful to the far right, as it saw rapid growth in follower counts and an expansion of networks. But as mainstream, regulated platforms began to block content and remove extremists from their sites, the new ecosystem of smaller, unregulated platforms that sprung up in their place brought together previously disparate groups from across the far-right spectrum. In this way, on the "alt-right Twitter equivalent" Gab, for example, "populist political candidates, Identitarians, neo-Nazis and alt-right trolls mingle, allowing for the transfer of ideas which leads to a more cohesive ideology."[79] Online spaces help share visible successes, amplifying local operations and demonstrating tangible results that help recruit new followers to what they perceive as effective activism.[80]

Groups and individuals share manuals and "how-to" guides for acquiring weapons, making bombs, and planning attacks. They coordinate efforts ideologically, aiming to shape prepolitical ideas among the general public in ways that will eventually make inroads into public policy and bring previously fringe ideas like ethnic re-migration or border closures into the mainstream.[81] Supporters of far-right parties in the Netherlands and France have "borrowed tactics employed by the alt-right in the US elections," including "the organized use of trolling armies, fake accounts and social media bots to spread memes, disinformation, and engage in a range of psychological operations." These efforts are known among extremism experts as examples of "tactical convergence," showing how far-right networks use "common tactical playbooks with which to manipulate the public and disrupt democratic processes."[82] The global networks and rapid evolution of online spaces and ecosystems of hate make them ideal places to disrupt and undermine democracy. As the technology enabling realistic "deep fake" videos becomes better and it becomes increasingly difficult to separate fact from fiction, such disinformation campaigns and fake news accounts will become all the more dangerous. Fake news is not only an online problem, of course—mainstream news outlets certainly also play a role.[83] But the online ecosystem allows for the rapid creation and circulation of fake news in ways that deserve particular attention.

Online spaces have also created significant means through which the far right can raise funds and resources. An online store selling clothing for the "alt right" in the United States notes on its website that a portion of the profits will be used to fund the legal expenses of "patriots" who find themselves in trouble with the law. The May 2017 Defend Europe mission—in which members of Génération Identitaire in France chartered a ship intended to interrupt migrant boats crossing to Europe from Libya—raised over $200,000 over Paypal, Patreon, and Wesearchr through small donations from over three thousand individuals from eight European countries and the United States. Key far-right leaders in the United States, including David Duke, Grand Wizard of the KKK, urged their social-media followers to support the mission.[84] Andrew Anglin crowdsourced a legal defense fund for a lawsuit brought by the SPLC, raising over $150,000.[85] A crowdfunding campaign raised about $100,000 Canadian dollars to fund a YouTube video series produced by The Rebel Media—which then launched a pay service of $8/month for access to the YouTube shows—now seen by more than eight hundred thousand people per day.[86] Lauren Southern, a Canadian far-right activist who was previously a contributor to The Rebel Media, is reported to have made a large share of her income through crowdfunding on Patreon, where she earned over $5,000 per month.[87] Similar revenue streams have been reported for other YouTubers as well.[88] Hosts of YouTube shows can earn significant amounts of money through advertising and other features that allow video creators to keep some of the revenue they create, while viewers can pay for their comments to appear more prominently in the "live chat" next to videos.[89] This Super Chat feature is now the top revenue stream for YouTube, which takes a cut of the earnings.[90] Allowing video creators to earn profits from their content has created a significant financial incentive to churn out material.[91] And because salacious content gets more clicks, being provocative, edgy, or offensive quite literally pays off for hosts.[92]

Finally, online spaces facilitate communication and mobilization to violence and protest. While previous social movements mobilized through tedious telephone chains, today the far right can rapidly mobilize over encrypted and unencrypted channels, as the protests in Chemnitz, Germany, in 2018 illustrated clearly.[93] By posting manifestos, livestreaming attacks, and circulating videos of protest or activist engagements, far-right groups and individuals help inspire "disciples" to launch similar attacks or actions of their own. In this way, the Christchurch shooter noted he was inspired by the Oslo attacker, while the El Paso and Poway shooters and Norway mosque attacker said they were inspired by the Christchurch shooter. Such inspiration is clearly facilitated by online spaces.

Online Spaces as a Battleground

The internet is useful at building and amplifying far-right ideologies and growing the movement, but it also offers a wide range of opportunities to attack the mainstream or the left, as well as spaces for counterengagement, intervention, and prevention work. The use of social media and online spaces has proven especially useful for quickly mobilizing troll armies who harass, dox (make private addresses and information public), and otherwise abuse individuals. In Germany, recent law-enforcement raids on far-right groups have turned up lists of tens of thousands of names of politicians, journalists, and activists deemed "enemies" to the cause, which include some of the targets' home addresses and phone numbers along with titles like "We will get you all." In June 2019, a German politician who had been named on one of the "enemy" lists was assassinated by a far-right extremist, leading a group of journalists to write an open letter to the interior minister asking for more measures to protect the safety of journalists.[94] In addition to scholars, political opponents, journalists, or antifascist activists, other targets have included those who were already victims of hate crimes who the far right decides should be even bigger targets.

Online spaces are not the domain of only the far right, of course. They have also proven key to de-radicalization and intervention initiatives and to efforts to increase media literacy, for example. And the public also uses online spaces in its reaction to the far right. The same viral nature of online spaces that led to Pepe the Frog's rapid adaptation into a far-right icon also provides the means for the rapid development of public outrage and protest. Viral tweets of offensive products and symbols generate anger as consumers and observers share photos and videos on social media, often tagging brand representatives and CEOs in ways that force a more rapid response from companies than might have been the case through traditional media reporting. Both the fast-food hamburger chain Wendy's and the Spanish clothing chain Zara have issued public apologies after customers shared social-media images linking their logos or products to Pepe the Frog, for example.[95] There also have been some viral efforts to combat the use of coded and co-opted symbols by the far right. For example, in 2016 the "alt right" began using triple-parentheses "echo" symbols around Jewish names online. Both Jews and non-Jews aiming to show solidarity quickly began to claim the echo symbol directly, placing $((( )))$ around their names on Twitter and other social-media sites, effectively removing the anti-Semitic purpose of the symbol.[96]

Impact and Interventions in Online Spaces

The nature of engagement in online spaces changes how we can understand the boundaries of far-right movements, as well as efforts to intervene in them. The nature of far-right engagement online is often described more like a "swarm" or "loose coalition of like-minded people" than as a traditional social movement.[97] Online spaces have opened up entirely new modes of communication that ease entry into far-right scenes and change the way individuals engage within them. It is hard to imagine neo-Nazis raising a flag representing the fantasy nation of Kekistan—or embedding frogs on those flags—a decade ago. The rapid creation, evolution, appropriation, and circulation of far-right memes, even when they later appear in off-line spaces, is a product of online worlds.

At the same time, "online radicalization" is a misnomer. Like communities in real life, online spaces play a key role in exposing individuals to ideas that inspire them, desensitizing them to violence, engendering a sense of urgency, and spurring them to take what they see as vengeful or heroic action. There is always an interaction between online and off-line worlds, however, just as there is between algorithms and human behavior. Recommender systems may direct users to extreme content, but individuals' preferences, beliefs, and behavior also change as they absorb that content, leading them to make choices that may well be different from the ones they would have made earlier. Significant research is needed to disentangle the complex web of interactions that characterizes the mix of online and off-line influences in radicalization toward violence.

Discussions about how to intervene effectively in online spaces are nascent. We need more policies and programs that address some of the root issues that underpin radicalization, including improved media literacy on issues like disinformation and manipulation and conspiracy theories. We need better measures of impact and effectiveness to gauge whether and how individuals change their behavior, beliefs, or choices as a result of these interventions. The rapidly evolving nature of online modes of communication and new platform creation make it especially difficult for policies and programs to keep up. If we accomplish little else over the next several years, at the very least we clearly need a more nuanced picture of radicalization in virtual and real-life contexts.

Conclusion

Whose Homeland?
Inoculating against Hate

During a recent citywide debate on a new ethics and diversity curriculum for Berlin schools, a local Green Party politician of Turkish-German background criticized the prevailing approach to teaching about diversity. An inclusive curriculum is typically presented in instrumental terms, as something that will either help native citizens better navigate diverse future career environments or help immigrant children better integrate into their new countries. What if, instead, he suggested, we simply approached diversity education with one question in mind: What would it take to ensure that everyone feels at home in the country where they live?[1]

This is such a simple question. And yet, to acknowledge how far we are from achieving that goal requires looking deeply at a number of assumptions in any given society. Who gets to claim membership in, or ownership of, imagined and real territories? Whose homeland is the homeland of this book's title? Why do national spaces and places engender such defensive and racialized protectionism from so many people? Can homelands—or the spaces and places that foster them—help us better understand the rise of the far right and its move from the fringes to the mainstream? In this book, I have tried to show that any efforts to understand the growth of far-right extremism, in the United States or elsewhere, must include a focus on real and symbolic geographies, and the local, national, virtual, and youth cultural spaces and places that create and sustain them.

What this means is that the global growth of the far right can't be explained by focusing only on the *how* and *why* of extremism. Most research and policy efforts have attempted to explain rising white-supremacist and far-right-extremist movements by developing better understandings of cognitive radicalization within those individuals (bottom–up approaches) or improved knowledge of the strategies and tactics of extreme-far-right organizations and groups (top–down approaches). In short, we tend to approach the puzzle of rising extremism by asking why young people are radicalizing and how far-right groups are organized and mobilized. Shifting our gaze to a new set of questions focused on the *where* and *when* of far-right extremism, I argue here, offers a fresh way of understanding pathways in and out of extremism for a generation of youth not bound by traditional or fixed understandings of identity and social-movement engagement. Looking at questions of *where* and *when* also trains our eyes on geographic claims and everyday engagements in ordinary spaces and places. Extremist narratives are not only a destination to be arrived at through deliberate and targeted searches and travel to particular places. They are also encountered in ordinary interactions in the mainstream spaces and places of the everyday.

There has been some previous attention to space and place as they relate to white supremacy over the years, especially in work discussing white-supremacist geographies, the proposed re-migration or deportation of immigrants and ethnic minorities, the obsession with border walls, and the imagined separation of races into regional, racial ethno-states. A range of historical and ethnographic research studies, as discussed earlier in this book, have traced the impact of specific far-right-extremist physical domains, like paramilitary training camps, white-supremacist prison gangs, and right-wing music festivals. But over the past several years, a new range of cultural spaces and places cultivating far-right and white-supremacist ideology—not only in the fringes but also within the mainstream—has gradually changed the cultural landscape of the far right. In order to truly understand the rapid growth of the modern far right, we need to look beyond the study of traditional spaces and places known to foment far-right extremism. Faster and more innovative exposure and recruitment are happening in a broader range of mainstream spaces, from clothing companies marketing to veterans to fight clubs, MMA gyms, and college campuses.

An approach that focuses on these kinds of places as a means to better understanding far-right radicalization requires de-centering our fixed understandings of far-right youth. It means paying attention to youth at the peripheries of far-right movements. This is the crux of my argument: youth on the margins of the far right are mobilized through quotidian, flexible engagements in mainstream-style physical and virtual spaces that the far right has actively targeted for this purpose. In this book, I have shown how the far right has become a market in its own right, producing and selling merchandise and products from clothing to coffee in ways that deserve closer attention. I've documented how far-right groups globally are leaning on the burgeoning popularity of combat sports and MMA as spaces to recruit and radicalize young men in particular toward violent combat and ideologies about a coming race war. I have traced how the far right is attacking higher-education spaces and knowledge at the same time as it is appropriating and creating new knowledge institutions, publishing houses, think tanks, and summer schools to train the next generation of intellectuals to lead the movement. And I've examined how online spaces help foster the growth of the modern far right by introducing an entire ecosystem of alt tech that makes use of new modes of communication to weaponize youth culture, creating and circulating memes, propaganda, and misinformation, crowdsourcing funds, and trading cryptocurrencies. In each of these cases, I've argued, new spaces and places for far-right engagement show how the far right is not only a destination for isolated individuals on the fringe, but is also a set of narratives and ideas that mainstream youth and adults increasingly encounter in their everyday lives. Extremist messages are not limited to violent manifestos but are also carried in banal and everyday ways, from the dog-walker's T-shirt in the neighborhood park to the paper fliers hanging on a campus bulletin board.

What New Spaces and Places Mean for the Growth of Far-Right Extremism

There are four key takeaways from this book about these new spaces and places of far-right extremism. First, by putting space and place at the center of our analysis, I call on scholars and policy makers to focus on hate groups and far-right extremism not only as bounded, formal social-movement groups and terrorist organizations, but also as flows of individuals who move from the margins into the core of extremist scenes and back again. People may share a far-right meme online or forward an anti-Semitic conspiracy theory while taking a break from a class assignment or work project. They could don a T-shirt with coded anti-immigrant messaging, but pull a sweater on top, obscuring the message until they decide to reveal it. Competitors may spend a weekend at a far-right MMA tournament, but return home to ordinary lives that show no signs of extremist engagement.

Understanding the hard-core, violent center of extremist movements is critical, of course. But so too is developing a better comprehension of where and when early encounters with extreme ideas take place. For many—perhaps even most—modern far-right youth, I argue, extremist engagement happens through spiraling engagement in and out of far-right scenes over time, across their adolescence and early adulthood. Such an approach requires broadening our understanding of far-right youth beyond members of terrorist cells or formal extremist groups at the hard core of violent white supremacism. Radicalization pathways begin at the peripheries, and finding the spaces where youth first encounter far-right-extremist messaging may shed light on flows in and out of extremism during initial and sometimes casual encounters with white-supremacist extremist narratives and propaganda. We need better ways of understanding how youth on the margins of far-right movements are drawn into far-right ideologies and movements, especially through encounters in mainstream physical and virtual spaces. Understanding how those mainstream spaces work, I've suggested, also requires moving beyond the prevailing tendency to separate the study of physical from virtual places. Instead, we need to look more carefully at how online and off-line spaces work in tandem and together have constitutive power for shaping far-right youth engagement and identity.

Second, a focus on space and place opens up pathways to better understand the normalization and mainstreaming of far-right-extremist narratives that help shift the Overton window of acceptable political discourse and public policy. Looking at mainstream spaces and places where far-right ideologies intersect is one way to do this. In those spaces and places, everyday encounters with extremist messaging happen in many different ways. I've traced three that have been particularly successful: the mainstreaming of extremist political discourse, the mainstreaming of conspiracy theories, and transformations in far-right aesthetics and communication styles. In each of these areas, the increasing prevalence of extremist messages—about border closures, immigrant invasions, the threat of demographic replacement, and the role of global elites in orchestrating it all—has broadened the kinds of repeated exposure to far-right ideology that youth and adults encounter in ordinary spaces and places.

Third, by looking at ordinary and everyday encounters with extremist messaging, we raise new possibilities for intervention and prevention work. Most work countering violent extremism has focused on improving law enforcement or surveillance and monitoring efforts, or on de-radicalization programs—all of which target youth at the hard core of movements rather than at their periphery. De-radicalization programs are known to be widely variable in their effectiveness, in part because they are unlikely to reach individuals before they are ready to come out of extremist milieus.[2] And law-enforcement approaches will always be a Band-Aid solution, intervening at a moment when extremist activity has already moved far along the pathway toward criminal violence. Shifting our gaze to the physical and virtual spaces where ordinary individuals engage with the far right in more flexible, everyday ways on the peripheries of extremism may help us find at-risk youth and better meet them where they are. Youth within mainstream spaces and places may be more reachable with educational interventions than youth already in the harder core of organized groups. Thinking about interventions as specifically existing in particular places and spaces from the beginning, moreover, raises a new set of questions. Who is most likely to be able to reach youth in these places? What kinds of training might they need in order to recognize signs of radicalization and know how to respond? Focusing on space and place helps open up the possibilities of preventative educational work, as a precursor to law enforcement and surveillance and monitoring initiatives.

Fourth and finally, a focus on space and place forces us to look more carefully at the importance of territory and geography and their intersections with identity, a sense of belonging, and the appeal of calls to defend, guard, or fight back against incursions and invasions. Even though national homelands and their defense are at the very heart of conspirational thinking about a "great replacement," there is little research and even less policy discussion about territory and identity and its intersections with masculine ideals around heroism, warriorhood, and defense as playing a central role in the appeal of far-right rhetoric and propaganda. We need more attention to the deeply emotional roots of ideas and ideals related to national homelands, regional heartlands, and a range of racialized geographies that evoke an organic connection to "motherland," "fatherland," "roots," and "soil." Attention to space and place can help illuminate these emotional connections and raise questions about whether it is possible to shift national narratives in ways that are not only more inclusive, but also oriented toward that question of what it would take, in the end, for everyone to feel at home.

How to Reach Youth in Particular Spaces and Places

The far right's successful weaponization of humor, irony, and youth culture more broadly over the past few years has made one thing abundantly clear: if we are going to address the problem of rising far-right violence, we need innovative, flexible, and youth-driven ideas. One place to start is by meeting youth where they already are—in their schools, college campuses, fitness clubs, social-media sites, gaming platforms, or consumer goods stores. Targeting more mainstream places logically raises a new set of questions for interventions. Who already spends time in those spaces and places—like coaches, trainers, school counselors, clothing designers, merchandisers, or online content developers—in ways that might create new preventative pathways or intervention partners? Who should be involved and what are the kinds of places where they can be reached—professional associations, competitions, fashion shows, or trade schools? How can we potentially engage youth in these new spaces and places or find youth who are on the peripheries of extremism more generally? What would interventions look like that engaged coaches, combat-sports trainers, clothing manufacturers and retailers, high-school teachers and counselors, or college faculty and advisors? What might parenting interventions look like that helped parents and guardians recognize the signs of online radicalization? The repeated and regular appearance of the far right in the new places and spaces I analyze in this book disturbs many, of course, because it is easier to think of extremist messaging as happening in fringe subcultures rather than in a middle-school classroom or an MMA gym. But these new spaces and places are also an opportunity to reach youth before and during the radicalization process, instead of afterward.

Acknowledging the mainstream nature of these places and spaces highlights the need to take a "herd immunity" approach to prevention against extremist messages and radicalization pathways. A range of new prevention and intervention approaches are doing just this. These initiatives take a public-health approach to hate, focusing on early immunization and inoculation against hate in order to reduce overall vulnerabilities to extremist radicalization and change the trajectory of rising hate and extremist violence. This approach focuses on early and ongoing education, combining awareness and knowledge of the dangers of extremist rhetoric with focused efforts to reduce vulnerabilities. It starts with a holistic understanding about youth, including ways to address rising alienation, anxiety, isolation, and the lack of belonging that can create susceptibilities to extremist promises, along with the need for mental-health resources to help young people process and heal from prior trauma or exposure to violence. Such preventative work takes seriously the need to create pathways for all young people to enact meaning and make a difference in the world. In order to build resilience to extremist narratives that try to convert individual grievances into a sense of anger and blame vis-à-vis the government, elites, or ethnic minorities and immigrants, youth need a sense of purpose and a way to imagine a future for themselves that includes economic stability and physical and mental wellness. Research and evaluation are critical here, too.

Acknowledging the importance of emotional needs and young people's deep desire for human connection and belonging, for example, raises important questions about how to engage youth on the peripheries of extremism in ways that don't just dismantle existing relationships to extreme groups, but also help build new bonds. Interventions also need to take seriously the emotional lives of young men, including desires to be a part of something bigger and better than themselves or to engage heroically. There are programs that offer positive channels for these emotions, for example, such as a German pilot project pairing at-risk youth with firefighters to enact heroic action in a different way, but little is known about their scalability or transferability to other national and local contexts.

The "herd immunity" approach to hate prevention means working to improve empathy, cross-cultural openness, understanding, and a sense of human connection with peers and others. There are some existing efforts in these areas, such as the $20 million investment of Daniel Lubetsky, founder of snack-bar company KIND, in an educational initiative to teach empathy, and broader global efforts to build socioemotional learning into educational reforms.[3] But most of this work has been disconnected from specific issues of radicalization and deradicalization and needs to better align with the experience of local experts who know youth best, including social workers, educators, mental-health counselors, and youth development specialists, and not just counterterrorism experts. Improving empathy and meaning among young people is important for preventative work, but there is also evidence that empathy is key to radicalization and disengagement of individuals already involved in extremist movements.[4]

Working with youth on the peripheries, or even in the hard core, of extremist groups has to start with our viewing them with some empathy—which is not a simple proposition in an era when social-media memes like "it's OK to punch a Nazi" are common. We need to acknowledge that some of the moral decisions made by far-right actors are driven not only by simple emotional desires like anger or resentment, but also by complex yearnings such as feelings of nostalgia or a desire for order.[5] Intervention efforts ought to therefore locate common ideals—like the desire to make a difference—and find ways to reorient those ideals away from exclusionary solutions.

Youth (and adults) also need more awareness and knowledge about extremist propaganda and disinformation campaigns that work to destabilize the public's trust in government by claiming elections were illegitimate, news is fake, or all politicians are corrupt. On the one hand, this includes serious media literacy and internet safety education for youth and adults to help people understand what they are encountering when they run across extremist content online. While adults have made great strides in educating young people about internet predators and privacy concerns, youth get virtually no information about what to do when they encounter extremist content online. Parents and educators need training to help youth recognize and respond to extremist content.

More awareness about extremist narratives and recruitment techniques won't make a difference, however, if young people do not have a basic understanding of the national histories around racism and white supremacy. In the United States, this requires an understanding of the legacy that white-supremacist policies and practices have had on structural inequality, racism, and injustice.[6] Youth learn far too little about the policies and practices of the pre-civil-rights era that disenfranchised and disadvantaged generations of Blacks and other ethnic minorities relative to whites in the United States in ways that still affect communities today. Students need better understandings of residential and school segregation, the history of discriminatory mortgage and lending policies (redlining), the impact of congressional district gerrymandering on voter disenfranchisement, and how those policies and practices affected everyday life in areas like school quality, neighborhood crime, home ownership, and inherited wealth. Young people—and their teachers—also need better global understandings of the impact of historical and contemporary geopolitics and colonialism on immigration patterns from the global South to the United States and Europe. Teaching about global white-supremacist atrocities like the Holocaust, moreover, is also crucial to helping young people understand the anti-Semitic intent behind memes like "another Jew in the oven" (with an image of a pizza being put in the oven), which so many youth retweet and share, often without fully understanding the violent and horrific content being conveyed.

Policy Solutions

The kinds of preventative work described above are critical to long-term reduction of white-supremacist and far-right violence. But there are also more immediate steps that local, state, federal, and global actors can take to stem the rise of extremist violence from the far right. Local engagement with law enforcement and advocacy groups, educators, parents, social workers, and mental-health experts can start with education to improve knowledge and understanding of white-supremacist groups and messages, including the kinds of symbols and codes used to communicate and the social-media channels and platforms used to recruit and radicalize. We also need improved channels for collaboration, and ways for experts and the federal government to work with governors, mayors, local law enforcement, local educators, parents, and religious leaders. Engagement with NGOs and watchdog groups as well as the private sector is critical. Innovative, creative approaches need investment and encouragement, along with public attention. For example, when the British clothing company Lonsdale was co-opted by German far-right youth (who discovered that a half-zipped bomber jacket over the logo would reveal the first four letters, NSDA, of the Nazi party, NSDAP), Lonsdale struck back. The company refused to deliver clothing to shops associated with the far-right scene, funded counter-far-right programs, and launched a pro-tolerance campaign, "Lonsdale loves all colors."[7] In turn, mainstream and antiracist supporters decided they should support Lonsdale and started wearing the brand. This effectively disrupted the significance of the logo, making it impossible to identify only with the far right.

We need a rethinking of the division between international and domestic terrorism, and paths for cross-national collaboration with experts overseas. Federal and local law enforcement need resources and direction. The US government's recent inclusion of white-supremacist extremism as part of the DHS's counterterrorism strategy is a starting point, but we need broad action, including considering options to work with allies overseas to monitor and sanction foreign terror organizations, if far-right extremists meet that threshold; pressure social-media companies to do more to prevent hate speech, harassment, and incitement to violence; and improve communication and interagency collaboration to share knowledge and information. We also need structured strategies to share what has been learned about Islamist radicalization that might apply to white-supremacist extremism and terrorism. There are strong similarities in what draws youth to both movements—a desire to belong, to contribute to something bigger than themselves, a need for purpose and to enact meaning, and also expressions of anger, a sense of betrayal, resentment, and the desire to resist and rebel against adults and mainstream society. Far-right and Islamist extremists share a belief in an apocalyptic end phase, idealized sacred territory, and the fantasy of a phase of rebirth, whether expressed through the restoration of white homelands or the Caliphate. Might there also be shared strategies around prevention and de-radicalization approaches that could better interrupt radicalization pathways before they turn violent?

Across all of these efforts, we need a sustained focus on improved national research capacity and expertise. In the wake of 9/11, millions of dollars were spent on building capacity in the United States on Islamist extremism—funding research centers, university departments, think-tank divisions, and staff teams in government agencies. The Norwegian government committed millions to create the Center for Research on Extremism (C-REX) in the wake of the 2011 terror attacks that killed seventy-seven people in Oslo, which has resulted in what is now widely recognized as the most comprehensive center for scholarly and public-policy expertise on far-right extremism globally. Hundreds of NGOs, research centers, private and political foundation initiatives, and intervention projects exist in Germany, while the United Kingdom has implemented broad, national preventative surveillance and intervention programs like Prevent and Channel. The United States is comparatively far behind virtually all of its peers in addressing and building capacity for understanding white-supremacist and far-right extremism and terrorism.

Across the board, we need a sustained commitment to long-term capacity building for expertise about global issues that affect national security. We need expertise not only on the strategies and tactics of financing, planning, and enacting mass terror attacks and violence, but also in-depth knowledge of local places and dynamics overseas. The recent rise of white-supremacist terror attacks has made these global connections all too clear, as violent far-right actors around the world are inspired by one another, cite one another's manifestos, and draw on similar conspiracy theories around the great replacement, the idea of an organized group of global (Jewish) elites orchestrating multicultural societies, and the need to accelerate violence toward the end times. There can be no question that white-supremacist extremism and far-right movements are decidedly global in nature. Addressing the evolving nature of hate and terror requires a steady pipeline of future experts who are well versed in global issues, not only local ones.

This requires investments in undergraduate and graduate training, but also partnerships with funding agencies overseas to incentivize comparative and global research on terrorism and white-supremacist extremism. We need research in a wide variety of other areas, too. We need evidence demonstrating what kinds of early interventions are effective at building resilience to extremist narratives, building empathy, and improving cross-cultural understanding. We need to know more about the modern places and spaces where young people encounter extremist messaging, and ways to intervene in those places. We need more systematic, national-level data on the far right, so that scholars are not left piecing together a picture of the threat from a variety of sources, including federal agencies, watchdog groups, and research centers. We need collaborations with the private sector to help combat "algorithmic radicalization," by tweaking or gaming the algorithms in ways that might prevent youth from entering the rabbit hole of far-right radicalization. And we need more research to help disentangle how algorithms and human choices interact and mutually influence behavior and beliefs.

Focusing on the new kinds of spaces and places I analyze in this book is not an easy task. The mainstreaming and normalization of far-right ideologies into more ordinary spaces pose a challenge for traditional interventions as well as for law enforcement and surveillance, raising important questions related to First Amendment and free-speech rights as well as issues of privacy. It is arguably more straightforward to surveil, shut down, and de-platform dedicated far-right spaces and identifiable white supremacists than it is to address the far right within the mainstream. The success that federal government authorities and the SPLC had decades ago in forcing the Aryan Nations to give up their Idaho compound following a personal injury lawsuit, for example, would be much harder to achieve for mainstream spaces.[8] The good news, however, is that we do not need to fully reinvent the wheel. There are extraordinary examples of how prevention and intervention work can be done on a broader scale. Germany is one such place.

Lessons from Elsewhere

Decades of work to rebuild democracy in Germany after the Nazi era—along with the need to respond to a wave of right-wing-extremist youth engagement in the 1980s and 1990s—has led to what is now unquestionably the broadest and most comprehensive approach to combatting right-wing extremism globally. What the German approach makes clear is that a national strategy focusing predominantly on surveillance and monitoring of extremists will never be enough. Successfully countering right-wing extremism requires deep integration of that work into the strengthening and protection of democracy itself.

Framing extremism prevention as part of broader democratic practice directly integrates it into the mandates of a broad range of federal, state, and local actors. Domestic German intelligence agencies are literally called offices for the protection of the constitution (*Verfassungsschutz*), which situates security work within a charge to protect democracy.[9] German police are trained to assess crimes for right-wing-extremist motivation. Teachers have a mandate to prevent right-wing extremism as part of their broader obligation to reinforce democratic values, which often manifests through direct engagement and counterargumentation with right-wing extremist youth in classrooms.

This approach naturally leads to a greater focus on space and place. But it also requires serious investment in professional training, especially for educators.[10] Classroom teachers and educators in Germany receive significant guidance to improve knowledge of extremist youth culture and learn new strategies to engage those at risk. A recent three-year pilot project in Dresden, for example, offered intensive coaching for vocational school teachers to improve their knowledge of right-wing extremist youth culture and to collaboratively develop pedagogical strategies for engaging right-wing youth in classrooms.[11] Similar training, seminars, and workshops are widespread and consistently frame schools' engagement with right-wing extremism as part of the broader promotion of democratic values and practices.[12]

The approach goes beyond the classroom and operates across all levels of society, embedding counterextremism education into a variety of mainstream places, from local theater and arts programs to football teams, concerts, work with religious groups, and more. Making intelligence, prevention, criminal enforcement, and de-radicalization work part of shared regional and national strategies to strengthen democracy clearly communicates that prevention of extremism is not just a niche approach to combat a fringe group, but is rather part of the entire nation's obligation to the greater good. This approach makes it easier to situate counterextremism work within comprehensive public education about the dangers right-wing extremism poses to a healthy democracy. It makes ensuring an informed citizenry a community responsibility, rather than relegating it to narrower groups, such as history and social studies teachers. In Germany, federal and state agencies for civic education, along with local organizations, provide a constant stream of public education about extremism, radicalization, and violence prevention, offering regular events, workshops, subsidized books, and materials to the public as well as specific training for teachers, social workers, parents, and others.

In this way, counterextremism work is integrated into every region and small town. There are hundreds of federally funded NGOs, state agencies, local organizations, initiatives, and projects nationwide working with schools, youth centers, and communities to provide outreach, counseling, and rehabilitation support to at-risk youth and drop-outs from far-right scenes. There are local "mobile advisors" for right-wing extremism across the country, offering training, consultations and on-the-ground advice based on local, regional, and state needs. This includes free and confidential counsel for anyone concerned about right-wing extremism in the local area and advice on addressing immediate crises, as well as long-term prevention strategies.[13] One local mobile advisor's website, for example, offers support for situations such as right-wing-extremist youth trying to take over a local youth club, trying to organize a right-wing concert, or when right-wing or hateful incidents happen in workplaces or schools.[14] Thematic diversity is present too. Public and private funding supports research, arts- and theater-based programs, and public debates to increase awareness and critical engagement among the general public. A national network of churches and religious associations pursues right-wing-extremism prevention as part of broader missions to promote respect for human rights and an inclusive society, and to be places for "everyday democratic culture" (*demokratische Alltagskultur*).[15]

Importantly, the German approach recognizes that effective interventions require meeting at-risk youth where they are. Scores of preventative programs are situated in the places where at-risk youth are most likely to encounter extremist messaging. At least a dozen of these initiatives target online radicalization alone. There are antiracist programs for soccer clubs, including initiatives to organize soccer tournaments against racism and violence and efforts to advise sport halls against renting space to right-wing extremist groups.[16] There are programs for teachers in vocational schools, and a network of MMA gyms that commit to counter-radicalization work in a variety of ways, such as promising to have an on-site, trained mentor who can recognize signs of radicalization and intervene. Federal and state agencies maintain searchable databases to enable easy access to programs and expertise.[17]

This principle—of meeting people where they are—applies even to Holocaust memorial work, which is a part of everyday practice in

Germany. Spaces to remember victims of right-wing violence are integrated into ordinary life, in the names of streets and in the simple *Stolperstein*—cobblestone—memorials placed outside residences from which Holocaust victims were deported. Through such everyday confrontations with lived history, the consequences of right-wing extremism become integrated reminders in daily German life.

Most of the rest of the world treats counterextremism as a law-enforcement problem. This work is critical, of course. And indeed, Germany is also leading the charge on investing in law-enforcement approaches to countering violent far-right extremism, announcing a major overhaul of domestic intelligence approaches in 2020, including the addition of six hundred new federal intelligence and criminal-law-enforcement positions dedicated to combatting far-right extremism.[18] But countries that rely primarily on intelligence efforts to counter violent extremism will always be playing catch-up, because even the best monitoring systems are at best a Band-Aid solution—leaving plenty of openings for violent individuals to slip through. The United States and other countries would do far better to model counterextremism efforts on the German approach—by acknowledging that preventing extremism is not just a law-enforcement mandate. We all contribute to environments in which extreme views flourish or are expunged. Situating deradicalization and prevention strategies within broader democracy- and civil-society-building efforts helps ensure extremism remains marginalized and makes clear that we all have a role to play.

The German approach isn't perfect, and it hasn't solved right-wing extremism, which is rising in Germany, just as it is across Europe.[19] It requires resources, and there is duplication and competition across local initiatives, which could be better coordinated. Moreover, the emphasis on preventing right-wing extremism has arguably overshadowed the need to promote diversity and inclusion as part and parcel of democracy, too. But as imperfect as the German approach may be, attacks like the ones in New Zealand or El Paso are made less likely by integrating counterextremism into broader democracy-building efforts.

We can start by recognizing that prevention of extremism and the protection of democracy go hand in hand. This means finding ways to integrate the values of democratic culture into everyday life such that every individual feels an obligation to promote inclusivity, protect minority rights, and fight racism wherever it exists, in the spaces and places of their ordinary lives. New Zealand's prime minister Jacinda Ardern already knows this. In a speech to a Christchurch high school just days after the shooting, she told students that preventing future extremist violence will require "every single one of us" to commit to combatting racism, which "breeds extremism."[20] Preventing another white-supremacist attack, in other words, is more than the work of a specialist few. It is part of everyone's obligation to a thriving democracy.

———

The approach to far-right extremism and radicalization I take in this book significantly broadens what we know about the far right, and how and when people engage with it. Asking why we are seeing so much rising extremism and violence and how organized far-right-extremist groups recruit and mobilize followers is important, of course. But, as I have argued here, we also need to ask questions about where and when young people encounter far-right-extremist ideologies, especially in mainstream and everyday spaces and places. We need to better understand how defensive ideas about territory and belonging shape people's sense of ownership over nation and homeland, and their ideas about who is eligible to belong there. And we need to better understand the impact of these new spaces and places on how youth communicate and engage with the far right. The spaces and places I have analyzed here have introduced or capitalized on entirely different modes of communication (such as meme sharing) or reinforced messages that are aligned with far-right narratives (such as the warrior mindset and physical-fitness regimen of the MMA and fight-club scenes). Each of these new spaces and places has figured out ways to weaponize youth culture, using humor, irony, satire, wit, innuendo, and jokes to shape the far right into a counterculture that is not only provocative and rebellious, but also fun for people who engage in it. This is a radical shift from previous kinds of spaces and places known to foment and foster white-supremacist and far-right extremism, including backwoods militias, prison gangs, and hard-rock white-power music concerts and festivals, where emotions like anger and rage were plentiful but irony and humor much less so.

There are, of course, other spaces worthy of sustained attention for their potential intersections with the contemporary far right—from evangelical churches to gun shows, nightclubs, soccer stadiums, and even the domestic sphere of private homes.[21] The same could be said for public space, which has been a particular target of the far right in the past few years, including an increase in white-supremacist propaganda in parks, city centers, and commercial spaces.[22] The examples I've given here only scratch the surface of the new spaces and places that are fomenting the far right. Over time, I hope such an agenda will challenge and change how scholars and the general public alike see the far right and the spaces and places where it is growing.

Notes

Notes to Preface

1. This work is derived in part from the article "The Global Dimensions of Populist Nationalism," published in the *International Spectator* (2019, copyright the Istituto Affari Internazionali, Via Angelo Brunetti, 9-00186 Rome, Italy, available online, https://www.tandfonline.com /doi/full/10.1080/03932729.2019.1592870, doi:10.1080/03932729.2019.1592870).
Portions of this work are excerpted from "What Makes a Symbol Far Right? Co-opted and Missed Meanings in Far-Right Iconography," by Cynthia Miller-Idriss, from *Post-Digital Cultures of the Far Right: Online Actions and Offline Consequences in Europe and the US*, edited by Maik Fielitz and Nick Thurston. Copyright © 2019 by Transcript Verlag, Bielefeld. This work is licensed under the Creative Commons Attribution-NonCommercial-No-Derivatives 4.0 (BY-NC-ND), which means that credit is given to the author. Reprinted by permission of Transcript Verlag.

Introduction

1. Parts of this chapter are adapted from Cynthia Miller-Idriss, "Gun Reform Alone Won't Address White Supremacist Extremism," *Boston Globe*, August 4, 2019, https://www .bostonglobe.com/opinion/2019/08/04/gun-reform-alone-won-address-white-supremacist -extremism/qCtK0RrDx01A2NHjbz7lLJ/story.html, and from my congressional testimony on September 18, 2019, at the hearing "Meeting the Challenge of White Nationalist Terrorism at Home and Abroad," held by the Committee on Foreign Affairs' Subcommittee on the Middle East, North Africa, and International Terrorism and the Committee on Homeland Security's Subcommittee on Intelligence and Counterterrorism. For my full written testimony see Miller-Idriss, "Statement."

2. James Fields was sentenced to life in prison for the crime. See, for example, "Charlottesville: White Supremacist Gets Life Sentence for Fatal Car Attack," *Guardian*, June 28, 2019, https://www.theguardian.com/us-news/2019/jun/28/charlottesville-james-fields-life -sentence-heather-heyer-car-attack. For a chronicle of the Charlottesville events, see "A Timeline of the Deadly Weekend in Charlottesville, Virginia," *ABC News*, August 10, 2018, https:// 6abc.com/a-timeline-of-events-in-charlottesville-virginia/2305769/. Also see McAuliffe, *Beyond Charlottesville*, and Spencer, *Summer of Hate.*

3. Beirich, "Year in Hate."

4. See reporting from the Anti-Defamation League (ADL) and the Southern Poverty Law Center (SPLC), along with widespread mainstream media coverage, such as the overview in Meghan Keneally, "Extremist-Related Killings in 2018 'Overwhelmingly Linked to Right-Wing' Movements: ADL," *ABC News*, January 23, 2019, https://abcnews.go.com/US/extremist -related-killings-2018-overwhelmingly-linked-wing-movements/story?id=60568464.

5. For coverage of the spring 2019 events, including the arrest of a member of a border patriot group who was arrested for impersonating a United States officer, see Lucas Peerman,

"Border Patriot Groups Spokesperson Charged with Federal Crimes," *Las Cruces Sun News*, June 22, 2019, https://www.lcsun-news.com/story/news/local/2019/06/22/jim-benvie-border -patriot-groups-spokesperson-charged-federal-crimes/1538156001/, or Catherine Shoichet, Deanna Hackey, Geneva Sands, and Paul Murphy, "A Militia Group Detained Migrants at the Border: The ACLU Calls It Kidnapping," CNN, April 19, 2019, https://www.cnn.com/2019/04 /19/us/border-militia-migrants/index.html. For a discussion of the challenge of private militias illegally operating at the US border, see Mary McCord's discussion, "Governors Can Stop Private Militias from Massing at the Border," CNN, November 7, 2018, https://www.cnn.com/2018 /11/07/opinions/border-state-governors-should-stop-militias-mccord/index.html, and Russell Contrera's "AP Explains: Militias Have Patrolled US Border for Decades," Associated Press, May 12, 2019, https://www.apnews.com/12dd5d7564304f35860efe3a64fc6f93.

6. See Cas Mudde's varied analyses for a cogent explanation of the difference between extreme far-right and radical far-right groups and the distinction between antidemocratic and illiberal ideals, such as in Mudde, *Far Right Today*.

7. As articulated in Plattner, "Illiberal Democracy." See especially Plattner's explanation of liberalism and democracy on pp. 6–7.

8. See, for example, Anna Schecter, "White Nationalist Leader Is Plotting to 'Take Over the GOP,'" *NBC News*, October 17, 2018, https://www.nbcnews.com/politics/immigration /white-nationalist-leader-plotting-take-over-gop-n920826.

9. D. Smith, *Less Than Human*, 5.

10. D. Smith, 264.

11. Manne, *Down Girl*, 156–57, 168.

12. Pitcavage, *Surveying the Landscape*, 3.

13. See Pitcavage for a full discussion of these groups.

14. See the October 3, 2019, press release issued by the Institute for Research on Male Supremacism, "Neo-Nazi Website Attacks Female Founder of Institute for Research on Male Supremacism," https://www.malesupremacism.org/2019/10/03/neo-nazi-website-attacks -female-founder-of-institute-for-research-on-male-supremacism/.

15. Hailey Branson-Potts and Richard Winton, "How Elliot Rodger Went from Misfit Mass Murderer to 'Saint' for Group of Misogynists—and Suspected Toronto Killer," *LA Times*, April 26, 2018, https://www.latimes.com/local/lanow/la-me-ln-elliot-rodger-incel-20180426 -story.html. I am also indebted to Erin Miller for analysis of the Elliot Rodger case, as described in endnote 48 below.

16. See Alba and Barbosa, "Room at the Top?"; William Frey, "The US Will Become 'Minority White' in 2045, Census Projects: Youthful Minorities Are the Engine of Economic Growth," *The Avenue* (blog), Brookings, March 14, 2018, https://www.brookings.edu/blog/the-avenue /2018/03/14/the-us-will-become-minority-white-in-2045-census-projects/; for statistics on European demographic changes, see "People in the EU—Statistics on Demographic Changes," Eurostat, last updated November 18, 2019, https://ec.europa.eu/eurostat/statistics-explained /index.php/People_in_the_EU_-_statistics_on_demographic_changes.

17. This section is indebted to the thorough discussion of the Great Replacement theory, along with its precursors "white genocide" and "Eurabia," in J. Davey and Ebner, *"The Great Replacement."*

18. See Michael, "David Lane."

19. See Ye'Or, *EurAbia*. Also see review discussion of Ye'Or's 2010 book, *Europe, Globalization and the Coming Universal Caliphate* (Madison, NJ: Fairleigh Dickenson), in Rubenstein, "Bat Ye'or."

20. See J. Davey and Ebner, *The Great Replacement*, 7–8.

21. Catherine Hickley, "US Museum Criticises Use of Gérôme's *Slave Market* in German Right-Wing Campaign," *Art Newspaper*, April 30, 2019, https://www.theartnewspaper.com/news/us-museum-protests-use-of-gerome-s-slave-market-in-german-right-wing-campaign.

22. Tenold, *Everything You Love*, 166–67.

23. In the following sentences and throughout, I deliberately exclude the names of terrorists and violent actors, in keeping with a growing call to journalists and academics to avoid contributing to fame or notoriety for terrorists. I also use the language "allegedly," even in cases with confessions or video evidence, if court cases are still ongoing.

24. See Fekete, " Muslim Conspiracy Theory," along with discussion in J. Davey and Ebner, *The Great Replacement*.

25. Yasmeen Abutaleb, "What's Inside the Hate-Filled Manifesto Linked to the Alleged El Paso Shooter," *Washington Post*, August 4, 2019, https://www.washingtonpost.com/politics/2019/08/04/whats-inside-hate-filled-manifesto-linked-el-paso-shooter/.

26. See J. Davey and Ebner, *The Great Replacement*.

27. I am indebted to Julia Ebner's articulation of acceleration in a US State Department lecture on July 22, 2019; also see J. Davey and Ebner, *The Great Replacement*; Ebner, *Rage*.

28. Busher and Macklin, "Interpreting 'Cumulative Extremism.'"

29. See ADL, "White Supremacists Embrace Acceleration."

30. I am thoroughly indebted to Brian Hughes for ongoing discussions about acceleration-ism and its manifestations inside and outside of the far right, including several rounds of feedback on my description of the phenomenon in this book. There is insufficient space here to fully explore the roots of far-right accelerationism and its various iterations, but these are extensively documented in Hughes, "'Pine Tree' Twitter."

31. Agence France-Presse in Berlin, "Neo-Nazi 'Terrorist Cell' on Trial over Alleged Berlin Attack Plot," *Guardian*, September 30, 2019, https://www.theguardian.com/world/2019/sep/30/neo-nazi-terrorist-cell-revolution-chemnitz-trial-germany.

32. "Chemnitz Neo-Nazi Group in Court over Germany Attack Plot," *Deutsche Welle*, September 30, 2019, https://www.dw.com/en/chemnitz-neo-nazi-group-in-court-over-germany-attack-plot/a-50636603. Also see "Revolution Chemnitz: Right-Wing Group Charged with Terrorism," *Deutsche Welle*, June 25, 2019, https://www.dw.com/en/revolution-chemnitz-right-wing-group-charged-with-terrorism/a-49352436.

33. For a brief overview of Atomwaffen in general and of the five recent murders, listen to Ari Shapiro's interview with Joanna Mendelsohn, National Public Radio, March 6, 2018, https://www.npr.org/transcripts/590292705.

34. Ware, *Siege*, citing Hatewatch, "Atomwaffen and the SIEGE Parallax: How One Neo-Nazi's Life's Work Is Fueling a Younger Generation," SPLC, February 22, 2018.

35. Derek Hawkins and Hannah Knowles, "Alleged Members of White Supremacy Group 'The Base' Charged with Plotting to Kill Antifa Couple," *Washington Post*, January 18, 2020, https://www.washingtonpost.com/national-security/2020/01/18/the-base-white-supremacist-arrests/.

36. Quotes are from J. M. Berger's March 25, 2019, interview on National Public Radio's *Fresh Air* with Terri Gross in the wake of the Christchurch attacks: "Author Says New Zealand Massacre Points to a Global Resurgence of 'Extremism,'" https://www.npr.org/templates /transcript/transcript.php?storyId=706482037. Also see J. M. Berger's discussion of extremism and radicalization in *Extremism*.

37. See Pitcavage, *Surveying the Landscape*.

38. See Byron Tau, "FBI Abandons Use of Term 'Black Identity Extremism,'" *Wall Street Journal*, July 24, 2019, https://www.wsj.com/articles/fbi-abandons-use-of-terms-black-identity -extremism-11563921355.

39. See my congressional testimony on September 18, 2019, where I made this point, at the "Meeting the Challenge of White Nationalist Terrorism at Home and Abroad" hearing: Miller-Idriss, "Statement."

40. McGarrity, "Statement."

41. Lecia Brooks's congressional testimony on June 4, 2019, for example, urges the US government to understand white supremacy as a "global terrorist threat." See Brooks, "Testimony."

42. See especially the discussion by Joan Donovan and Jessie Daniels in Denise-Marie Ordway, "10 Tips for Covering White Supremacy and Far-Right Extremists," *Journalist's Resource*, July 22, 2019, https://journalistsresource.org/tip-sheets/reporting/white-supremacy-alt -right-wing-tips/.

43. In the end, it may be best if scholars, policy makers, and the media agree to disagree about which terms best reflect these phenomena. There is an argument to be made that spending too much time mired in definitional debates can be a barrier to getting on with work that might help interrupt or intervene in the prevention of violent extremism.

44. See especially the discussion by Joan Donovan and Jessie Daniels in Ordway, "10 Tips." Despite these concerns, the term "alt-right" carries a specific connotation to a unique development in the far-right scene in the United States since 2015, which is distinct from older factions of the American far right such as the Ku Klux Klan and the Aryan Brotherhood. I have opted to deploy the term here but use quotation marks around the phrase to signal its contested nature. Similarly, the "alt lite" is a term coined by members of the "alt right" to distinguish what they perceived as authentic, hardline views from paleoconservatives, libertarians, and others deemed to be profiting off the "alt right" but trying to reform it. See Tenold, *Everything You Love*, 234. For more on the emergence of the "alt right," see Main, *Rise of the Alt-Right*.

45. The far right denotes an extreme fringe and not ordinary political conservatism or radical-right populism, although there have been occasions when mainstream political leaders have used words and arguments that legitimize far-right ideas and there are key ways in which previously extreme ideas are increasingly moving into the mainstream.

46. Miller-Idriss and Pilkington, *Gender*.

47. See Pitcavage, *Surveying the Landscape*, for example.

48. I am indebted to the scholar Erin Miller for her comments on the Elliot Rodger case and its later analysis as part of the broader far-right spectrum, in remarks at a May 2, 2019, Women in International Security moderated panel in Washington, DC, which helped my understanding of these overlaps.

49. ADL, "Extremism in the United States in 2019."

50. See ADL, "Extremism in the United States in 2018."

51. Lecia Brooks's June 2019 congressional testimony notes eighty-one murders since 2014: Brooks, "Testimony." The deaths of twenty-two people in El Paso in August 2019 put this number above one hundred, without counting other attacks still under investigation at the time of this writing, such as the three people allegedly killed at a Gilroy, California, garlic festival shooting by a young man whose last social-media post encouraged people to read a white-supremacist novel, or the deaths of three people in Canada in summer 2019 allegedly at the hands of two young men who were later found to have posted far-right comments online; one had been photographed wearing a Nazi armband. For media coverage of these two cases see, for example, David Ingram, Brandy Zadrozny, and Corky Siemaszko, "Gilroy Garlic Festival Gunman Referred to 'Might Is Right' Manifesto before Shooting," NBC News, July 29, 2019, https://www .nbcnews.com/news/us-news/gilroy-garlic-festival-gunman-referenced-might-right-manifesto -shortly-shooting-n1035781; Mack Lamoureux, "Teens Sought for Multiple Murders Have Far-Right Links: Report," Vice News, July 22, 2019, https://www.vice.com/en_us/article/8xzzeb /teens-sought-for-multiple-murders-have-far-right-links-report.

52. As cited in Brooks, "Testimony," and documented in the SPLCs Intelligence Reports magazine. See especially Beirich, "Year in Hate."

53. Christopher Mathias and Ryan J. Reilly, "Over 40 People Have Been Arrested as Potential Mass Shooters since El Paso," Huffington Post, August 31, 2019, https://www.huffpost.com /entry/mass-shooting-plot-arrests-el-paso_n_5d66d1eae4b063c341f9f2da.

54. See video clip from Wray's July 23, 2019, testimony where he made this point in response to a question from Senator Dick Durban, in Morgan Chalfant, "FBI's Wray Says Most Domestic Terrorism Arrests This Year Involve White Supremacy," The Hill, July 23, 2019, https://thehill .com/homenews/administration/454338-fbis-wray-says-majority-of-domestic-terrorism -arrests-this-year.

55. See the ADL's Oren Segal's statement in Montanaro, Domenico: "Democratic Candidates Call Trump a White Supremacist, a Label Some Say Is 'Too Simple,'" NPR, August 15, 2019; also see "ADL: White Supremacist Propaganda Distribution Hit All-Time High in 2019," ADL, February 12, 2020, https://www.adl.org/news/press-releases/adl-white-supremacist -propaganda-distribution-hit-all-time-high-in-2019.

56. As noted in George Selim's May 15, 2019, congressional testimony before the Civil Rights and Civil Liberties Subcommittee of the House Oversight and Government Reform Committee, at a hearing on "Confronting White Supremacy (Part I): The Consequences of Inaction," citing the ADL report "White Supremacists Step Up Off-Campus Propaganda Efforts in 2018," https:// www.adl.org/resources/reports/white-supremacists-step-up-off-campus-propaganda-efforts-in -2018. See George Selim's full written testimony: "Congressional Testimony."

57. Propaganda was linked in 2018 to Identity Evropa (which regrouped in 2019 as the American Identity Movement, AIM), Patriot Front, Loyal White Nights, Ku Klux Klan, Daily Stormer, Atomwaffen Division, National Alliance, National Socialist Legion, National Socialist Movement, and Vanguard America. See Selim, "Congressional Testimony."

58. Personal correspondence with Liz Yates in January 2020, based on updated data from the University of Maryland's START Center.

59. This figure comes from personal and small group discussions with Oren Segal, director of the Center for Extremism at the Anti-Defamation League.

60. The most recent annual German intelligence services report, *Verfassungsschutz 2018*, is available in German here: https://www.verfassungsschutz.de/de/oeffentlichkeitsarbeit /publikationen/verfassungsschutzberichte. See charts detailing potentially violent right-wing extremists at: https://www.verfassungsschutz.de/de/arbeitsfelder/af-rechtsextremismus /zahlen-und-fakten-rechtsextremismus/rechtsextremistisches-personenpotenzial-2018.

61. As documented in my US congressional testimony, Miller-Idriss, "Statement." I am indebted to Stephen Tankel for helpful discussions on these five categories.

62. J. Davey and Ebner, *Fringe Insurgency*; Keatinge, Keen, and Izenman, "Fundraising."

63. See the written and oral testimony of Ali Soufan at the hearing "Global Terrorism: Threats to the Homeland (Part I)" before the House of Representatives Committee on Homeland Security on September 10, 2019. Soufan, "Written Statement."

64. See Brooks, "Testimony."

65. Department of Homeland Security (DHS), *Strategic Framework*.

66. Definitions of youth vary, with some researchers focusing on the teen years through the early twenties, and others including young people up to their mid-thirties. I tend to split the difference, using the term to refer to people from early adolescence through about the late twenties. See, for example, Mudde, *Youth*, 4; Miller-Idriss, "Youth." For a discussion of youth culture in fascism, see Valencia-García, *Antiauthoritarian Youth Culture*.

67. According to the University of Maryland START Center's PIRUS data set of radicalized violent extremists in the United States, nine of the twenty-two far-right offenders who have killed someone since 2010 were age forty or older, and the median age of far-right extremists is older compared with those who adhere to other extremist ideologies. I am indebted to Elizabeth Yates for pointing me to the PIRUS data set and for helpful exchanges on the issue of youth versus older adults in US extremism.

68. For example, PIRUS data show that of the 292 successfully executed violent far-right extremist plots in the United States up to 2017, 144 of the perpetrators were under thirty at what they label "age of exposure," defined as typically the time of the incident or arrest. See the data visualization tool: https://www.start.umd.edu/profiles-individual-radicalization-united-states -pirus-keshif. For global statistics on youth violence in general, see the World Health Organization's data at https://www.who.int/news-room/fact-sheets/detail/youth-violence. For more on youth vulnerabilities to far-right-extremist rhetoric and youth engagement in hate see Kelshall and Meyers, *Normalization of Extremism*, especially 34–36; Julie Norman and Drew Mikhael, "Youth Radicalization Is on the Rise: Here's What We Know about Why," *Washington Post*, August 28, 2017, https://www.washingtonpost.com/news/monkey-cage/wp/2017/08/25 /youth-radicalization-is-on-the-rise-heres-what-we-know-about-why/.

69. Altier, Boyle, and Horgan, "Returning to the Fight."

70. See Miller-Idriss, *Extreme Gone Mainstream*; Steinberg and Chein, "Adolescent Impulsivity"; Baier, Pfeiffer, and Rabold, "Jugendgewalt in Deutschland." Also see Hall et al., *Culture, Media, Language*; Muggleton, *Inside Subculture*; Nayak, *Race, Place and Globalization*.

71. Dinas, "Opening 'Openness to Change'"; Siedler, "Parental Unemployment."

72. For a good overview of recruitment and radicalization in youth-oriented spaces, see Wiegel, "Rechte Erlebniswelten."

73. For a comprehensive discussion of Gamergate, see Salter, "Geek Masculinity to Gamergate." For discussions of Gamergate's evolution into the "alt right," see Matt Lees, "What Gamergate Should Have Taught Us about the 'Alt-Right,'" *Guardian*, December 1, 2016, https://www.theguardian.com/technology/2016/dec/01/gamergate-alt-right-hate-trump; Evan Urquist, "Gamergate Never Died," Slate.com, August 23, 2019, https://slate.com/technology/2019/08/gamergate-video-games-five-years-later.html.

74. Miller-Idriss and Pilkington, *Gender*.

75. Flint, introduction to *Spaces of Hate*, 4.

76. I rely on a variety of sources in this book, as documented in endnotes throughout. In addition to media and nongovernmental organization (NGO) reports, association newsletters, government agency reports, and public federal data, I draw in illustrative ways on prior empirical research conducted over twenty years in Germany in and around far-right youth scenes, as well as (especially in sections on aesthetic mainstreaming and youth culture) 1,400 screenshots of T-shirts gathered in 2018–19 from ten clothing brands marketing products with far-right ideological messages, and a limited review of these brands' and brand-fans' social-media feeds.

Chapter 1

1. Rössler, "Blut und Boden."

2. Anderson, *Imagined Communities*.

3. I am indebted to Daniel Koehler for helpful feedback and discussions about the bonds linking geography, race, ethnicity, and culture in far-right ideology.

4. See, for example, the review of the field in Hubbard and Kitchin, "Why Key Thinkers?" Also see Entrikin, introduction to *Betweenness of Place*, 1.

5. Gieryn, "Space for Place," 463.

6. Agnew, "Space and Place," 27; Sack, " Power of Place," 329; Lefebre, *Production of Space*, 34.

7. Flint, introduction to *Spaces of Hate*, 1.

8. I am indebted to Brian Hughes for this reflection.

9. Tuan, *Space and Place*. Also see Cresswell, *Place*.

10. Cresswell, *Place*, 1.

11. Flint, introduction to *Spaces of Hate*, 7.

12. Flint, esp. 7.

13. N. Smith, "Blood and Soil."

14. On space and mobility, see Massey, "Power-Geometry," as discussed in Cresswell, *Place*.

15. See Belew, *Bring the War Home*.

16. Stern, *Proud Boys*, 34–35.

17. Perry and Blazak, "Places for Races," 33.

18. Tuan, *Space and Place*, 154.

19. See, for example, Castells, *Informational City*, and the discussion in Duyvendak, *Politics of Home*, 8–10.

20. Duyvendak, *Politics of Home*, 11.

21. Goodhart, *Road to Somewhere*; Jonathan Freedland, "*The Road to Somewhere* by David Goodhart—a Liberal's Rightwing Turn on Immigration," *Guardian*, March 22, 2017,

https://www.theguardian.com/books/2017/mar/22/the-road-to-somewhere-david-goodhart
-populist-revolt-future-politics.

22. For more on the connection between industry and local or regional identities, see the case studies in Wicke, Berger, and Golombeck, *Industrial Heritage*; also see Materna, Hasman, and Hána, "Acquisition of Industrial Enterprises."

23. Tenold, *Everything You Love*, 164–65.

24. For a discussion of the role of resentment in mobilizing far-right extremism, see McVeigh and Estep, *Politics of Losing*.

25. Bonds, "Race and Ethnicity II."

26. Bonds, 4, 2.

27. Bonds, 5.

28. Malkki, "National Geographic," cited in Duyvendak and Verplanke, "Struggling to Belong."

29. Grandon, *End of the Myth*.

30. For a lengthier discussion, see chapter 2 of Miller-Idriss, *Extreme Gone Mainstream*.

31. See, for example, Griffin, "Fixing Solutions," on the relationship between postmodernity and fascism.

32. Stern, *Proud Boys*, 52, citing Roberto Ramón Lint Sagarena, *Aztlán and Arcadia: Religion, Ethnicity, and the Creation of Place* (New York: New York University Press, 2014); and American Renaissance, "Wakanda: The Perfect Ethnostate?" featuring Jared Taylor, YouTube, March 7, 2018, https://www.youtube.com/watch?v=JL6Zgw4FZVA.

33. Stern, *Proud Boys*, 53, citing an essay by Johnson that was originally titled "The Slow Cleanse": Greg Johnson, "Restoring White Homelands," Counter-Currents Publishing, June 24, 2014, https://www.counter-currents.com/2014/06/the-slow-cleanse/.

34. Perry and Blazak, "Places for Races," 32.

35. See Miller-Idriss, *Blood and Culture*; also see Kalen Goodluck, "Far-Right Extremists Appropriate Indigenous Struggles for Violent Ends," *High Country News*, August 27, 2019, https://www.hcn.org/issues/51.16/tribal-affairs-far-right-extremists-appropriate-indigenous
-struggles-for-violent-ends.

36. Goodluck, "Far-Right Extremists."

37. On the 2014 example see Günther Lachmann, "AfD kopiert die NPD und blamiert sich," Welt.de, June 21, 2014, https://www.welt.de/politik/deutschland/article129330115/AfD-kopiert
-die-NPD-und-blamiert-sich.html; the 2019 case is discussed in "AfD empört mit rassistischem Kommentar zum neuen Nürnberger Christkind," Focus.de, November 1, 2019, https://www
.focus.de/politik/deutschland/kreisverband-muenchen-land-afd-empoert-mit-indianer
-kommentar-zum-neuen-nuernberger-christkind_id_11299731.html.

38. "Outrage after AfD Scorn Mixed-Race Girl Playing 'Christ Child,'" *BBC News*, November 4, 2019, https://www.bbc.com/news/world-europe-50287563.

39. Goodluck, "Far-Right Extremists."

40. Goodluck, "Far-Right Extremists."

41. Goodluck attributes this idea to Frank Usbeck, curator for the Americas at the State Art Collections in Dresden.

42. See Liulevicius, *German Myth*, 2.

43. Tuan, *Space and Place*, 157–58.

44. Miller-Idriss, *Extreme Gone Mainstream*.

45. For more on national imaginaries, see Billig, *Banal Nationalism*. On collective pasts, see von der Goltz, *Hindenburg*; Williamson, *Longing for Myth*.

46. As documented by Throop, "Engaging the Crusades." See especially p. 129.

47. Miller-Idriss, *Extreme Gone Mainstream*. Also see Miller-Idriss and Johnson, "Free Advertising."

48. Bonds, "Race and Ethnicity II," 2.

49. Eller, "Matriarchy and the Volk."

50. For more on the far right's use of the environment see, for example, Beth Gardiner's recent op-ed, "White Supremacy Goes Green," *New York Times*, February 28, 2020, https://www.nytimes.com/2020/02/28/opinion/sunday/far-right-climate-change.html?referringSource=articleShare.

51. "Betsy Hartmann: An Environmental Essay on the Greening of Hate," Climate & Capitalism, August 31, 2010, https://climateandcapitalism.com/2010/08/31/the-greening-of-hate-an-environmentalists-essay/. Also see Joel Achenbach, "Two Mass Killings a World Apart Share a Common Theme: 'Ecofascism,'" *Washington Post*, August 18, 2019, https://www.washingtonpost.com/science/two-mass-murders-a-world-apart-share-a-common-theme-ecofascism/2019/08/18/0079a676-bec4-11e9-b873-63ace636afo8_story.html.

52. Stern, *Proud Boys*, 60.

53. Bonds, "Race and Ethnicity II," 7.

54. Flint, introduction to *Spaces of Hate*.

55. See, for example, discussion in Julie Turkewitz and Kevin Roose, "Who Is Robert Bowers, the Suspect in the Pittsburgh Synagogue Shooting?" *New York Times*, October 27, 2018, https://www.nytimes.com/2018/10/27/us/robert-bowers-pittsburgh-synagogue-shooter.html.

56. These kinds of claims are part of a broader history of what Charles Tilly calls "spaces of contention" or "spatial claims making," linking geographic and symbolic space to political claims. Tilly, "Spaces of Contention."

57. White supremacists and white separatists have long sought to create separate white enclaves in the United States, as detailed in Perry and Blazak, "Places for Races." Also see Casey Michel, "White Supremacists Look to Remake the Map of America," ThinkProgress, August 12, 2019, https://thinkprogress.org/are-far-right-extremists-turning-more-toward-breaking-up-the-us-outright-a1af53156968/.

58. Blee, "Geography of Racial Activism," 50.

59. As reported in Tenold, *Everything You Love*, 66.

60. Stern, *Proud Boys*, 51. For a discussion about far right groups' claims to be nonracist, see the analysis in Pilkington, *Loud and Proud*.

61. Stern, 69.

62. Macklin, "Greg Johnson," 210.

63. Macklin, 212, quoting Johnson's Counter-Currents publication "The Slow Cleanse."

64. Stern, *Proud Boys*, 67.

65. Perry and Blazak, "Places for Races."

66. Stabile, "Pursuit of an Ethnostate," 24.

67. Perry and Blazak, "Places for Races," 43.

68. Döring, *Angstzonen*, 82.

69. Döring, 39.

70. Döring, esp. 51–53. Also see Land Brandenburg, "'National befreite Zonen.'"

71. Land Brandenburg, "'National befreite Zonen.'"

72. Land Brandenburg. On the interaction between extremist groups and the mainstream's infrastructure, see Koehler, "Contrast Societies."

73. Döring, *Angstzonen*. Also see Land Brandenburg.

74. Döring, *Angstzonen*, 53.

75. Land Brandenburg, "'National befreite Zonen.'"

76. See Döring, *Angstzonen*, 62.

77. Land Brandenburg, "'National befreite Zonen.'"

78. Döring, "'Befreite Zonen,'" 41.

79. See Döring, *Angstzonen*, 62.

80. For a comprehensive discussion of "zones of fear" and no-go zones, especially as the latter terms emerged related to travel warnings around the 2006 World Cup in Germany, which suggested foreign visitors were at risk in specific geographic territories and regions, see Schultz and Weber, *Kämpfe um Raumhoheit*. No-go zones or no-go areas were terms later used by the far right to refer to the idea that Islamist extremists had taken over particular neighborhoods or regions in Europe. See David A. Graham, "Why the Muslim 'No-Go-Zone' Myth Won't Die," *Atlantic*, January 20, 2015, https://www.theatlantic.com/international/archive/2015/01/paris-mayor-to-sue-fox-over-no-go-zone-comments/384656/.

81. Döring, *Angstzonen*, 264–66.

82. For more on far-right summer camps in Germany, see "German Government Bans Neo-Nazi Youth Group," *Spiegel International*, March 31, 2009, https://www.spiegel.de/international/germany/far-right-summer-camps-german-government-bans-neo-nazi-youth-group-a-616499.html; "German Police Raids Nazi Youth Camp," *DW*, August 11, 2008, https://www.dw.com/en/german-police-raids-nazi-youth-camp/a-3555325; also see the documentary from the *Guardian's* YouTube channel covering a similar summer camp in Ukraine: "Ukraine's Far-Right Children's Camp: 'I Want to Bring Up a Warrior,'" YouTube, September 5, 2017, https://www.youtube.com/watch?v=jiBXmbkwiSw. These are also reminiscent of Nazi summer camps in the United States in the 1930s, in California, as described in Peter Dreier, "A California Suburb Reckons with Its Nazi Past—and Present-Day Controversy Follows," *Salon*, August 19, 2017, https://www.salon.com/2017/08/19/a-california-suburb-reckons-with-its-nazi-past-and-present-day-controversy-follows/; and in New York, as described in Nicholas Casey, "Nazi Past of Long Island Hamlet Persists in a Rule for Home Buyers," *New York Times*, October 19, 2015, https://www.nytimes.com/2015/10/20/nyregion/query-for-home-buyers-in-a-long-island-hamlet-are-you-german.html.

83. Alexander Durie, "At the Heart of Hate: Inside France's Identitarian Movement," *Are We Europe* 3 [January 2019], "Uprooted," https://magazine.areweeurope.com/stories/uprooted/generation-identitaire.

84. Simi and Futrell, *American Swastika*.

85. Flint, introduction to *Spaces of Hate*, 2.

Chapter 2

1. For a higher-tech version of the Overton window, see the Mackinac Center for Public Policy's sliding-feature infographic, which illustrates the window of politically acceptable policy solutions on school attendance, ranging from no government policy on school attendance to a mandate that all students attend federally controlled schools. Available at: https://www .mackinac.org/OvertonWindow.

2. Nathan Russell, "An Introduction to the Overton Window of Political Possibilities," Mackinac Center for Public Policy, January 4, 2006, https://www.mackinac.org/7504.

3. Maggie Astor, "How the Politically Unthinkable Can Become Mainstream," *New York Times*, February 26, 2019, https://www.nytimes.com/2019/02/26/us/politics/overton-window -democrats.html.

4. Portions of this chapter draw on earlier writing, including the following essays and articles: Miller-Idriss, "Global Dimensions"; Cynthia Miller-Idriss, "Why Does the Far Right Love Fred Perry?: Mainstream Fashion Is Its New Camouflage," *Guardian*, August 29, 2019, https:// www.theguardian.com/commentisfree/2019/aug/29/far-right-fred-perry-mainstream-fashion -camouflage-brands; Cynthia Miller-Idriss, "Mainstreaming Extremism through Clothing," *Islamic Horizons Magazine*, July–August 2019, 34–35, https://issuu.com/isnacreative/docs/ih _july-august_19.

5. Flint, introduction to *Spaces of Hate*, 8–9, citing Berlet and Lyons, *Right-Wing Populism*.

6. For coverage of this see, for example, Katie Rogers and Nicholas Fandos, "Trump Tells Congresswomen to 'Go Back' to the Countries They Came From," *New York Times*, July 14, 2019, https://www.nytimes.com/2019/07/14/us/politics/trump-twitter-squad-congress.html; and Griff Witte, "After El Paso, the 'Send Her Back' Chant Echoes to Some as a Prelude to Murder," *Washington Post*, August 13, 2019, https://www.washingtonpost.com/national/after-el-paso-the -send-her-back-chant-echoes-to-some-as-a-prelude-to-murder/2019/08/13/6e6ed198-bd15 -11e9-a5c6-1e74f7ec4a93_story.html.

7. Mudde, "Populist Zeitgeist"; also see Miller-Idriss, "Global Dimensions."

8. Canovan, "Trust the People!"; Berezin, "Populism and Fascism"; Müller, *What Is Populism?*

9. Finchelstein, *From Fascism to Populism*, esp. 15.

10. Mudde and Kaltwasser, *Populism*.

11. As Kubik articulated in keynote remarks on November 12, 2018, at the London School of Economics workshop on the politics of emotions.

12. Brubaker, "Why Populism?"; also see Berezin, "Populism and Fascism," and the longer discussion in Miller-Idriss, *Global Dimensions*. For a discussion of the mainstreaming of far-right ideas in the UK, see Stocker, *English Uprising*.

13. Bonikowski, "Ethno-nationalist Populism," 201. Also see Bonikowski and Gidron, "Populist Style."

14. Of course, critiques of global capitalism exist across the political spectrum, and even within the far right, so this is not a new strategy. Far-right parties across Western Europe have used the tactic for at least a couple of decades to sway working-class voters—who face more job losses and declining wages than transnationally mobile, high-skilled white-collar workers—in

favor of more protectionist policies. The issue remains a strong motivator for voters who are eager to blame globalization for their economic stresses. See Steegenbergen and Siczek, "Better the Devil"; Swank and Betz, "Globalization," esp. 221–22.

15. Mudde and Kaltwasser, *Populism*, 35; also see Bonikowski, "Ethno-nationalist Populism," 204.

16. Tenold, *Everything You Love*, 3.

17. Tenold, 45.

18. For discussions of the left's support for multiculturalism and globalization, see Haidt, "Nationalism Beats Globalism."

19. Haidt.

20. Zaslove, "Exclusion," 173.

21. Zaslove, 169.

22. Zaslove, 179.

23. Zaslove, 173

24. Zaslove, 175.

25. See especially the discussion in Zaslove, 176.

26. For example, one clothing brand in the United States at one point directly contrasted the "mental and physical capacities" of far-right youth with the "left's onslaught of degeneracy and drug cultures." As described on the now-defunct "Ethical Supply Chain and Procurement" section of The Right Brand's website, https://rightbrandclothing.com/ethical-supply-chain -and-procurement/, accessed June 25, 2018.

27. Zeke Miller, "Trump Attacks Majority-Black District Represented by Critic," *Associated Press*, July 28, 2019, https://www.apnews.com/3d49bd171f9b4245b3d24e62a77ad35f; Madeline Holcolmbe, "Baltimore Stands Up for Its City after Trump Tweets 'No Human Being Would Want to Live There,'" CNN *Politics*, July 28, 2019, https://www.cnn.com/2019/07/28/politics /baltimore-response-trump-tweets/index.html.

28. See these and other examples documented in the Media Matters report by Courtney Hagle, "How Fox News Pushed the White Supremacist 'Great Replacement' Theory," Media Matters, August 5, 2019, https://www.mediamatters.org/tucker-carlson/how-fox-news-pushed -white-supremacist-great-replacement-theory.

29. See Bayrakli and Hafez, *European Islamophobia Report*; Wodak, " Semiotics of Racism."

30. See Wodak, " Semiotics of Racism"; Korolczuk and Graff, "'Ebola from Brussels,'" 811.

31. For an overview of Pizzagate and its related conspiracy theory, see Amanda Robb, "Anatomy of a Fake News Scandal," *Rolling Stone Magazine*, November 16, 2017, https://www .rollingstone.com/politics/politics-news/anatomy-of-a-fake-news-scandal-125877/.

32. Tenold, *Everything You Love*, 168–69.

33. Tenold, 168–69.

34. Scholars refer to these groups as sexually modern nativists. See, for example, Lancaster, "Not So Radical"; Spierings, Lubbers, and Zaslove, "Sexually Modern Nativist Voters."

35. Neiwert, *Alt-America*, 41.

36. For a thoughtful discussion, see Merlan, *Republic of Lies*.

37. For a discussion of the conspiracy theory that led to the Comet Ping Pong pizza restaurant incident, see Wendling, *Alt Right*, especially chapter 9, "Conspiracy Theorists."

38. Merlan, *Republic of Lies*, 243–45.

39. Muirhead and Rosenblum, *People Are Saying*, 48.

40. Neiwert, *Alt-America*, 35.

41. Other examples include the Q-Anon conspiracy, which suggests there is a "deep state" plot against Trump, and the "cultural Marxism" conspiracy theory. See, for example, the discussion in Ari Paul, "Cultural Marxism: The Mainstreaming of a Nazi Trope," Fairness and Accuracy in Reporting (FAIR), June 4, 2019, https://fair.org/home/cultural-marxism-the-mainstreaming-of-a-nazi-trope/.

42. Konda, *Conspiracy of Conspiracies*, 1–2; also see Uscinski and Parent, *American Conspiracy Theories*.

43. Merlan, *Republic of Lies*, 8.

44. Muirhead and Rosenblum, *People Are Saying*, 2.

45. Muirhead and Rosenblum, 3.

46. Konda, *Conspiracy of Conspiracies*, 309.

47. Kirby, " Extreme Political Ideas."

48. Muirhead and Rosenblum, *People Are Saying*, 9.

49. Muirhead and Rosenblum, 48.

50. Muirhead and Rosenblum, 28.

51. Muirhead and Rosenblum, 3–4; also see Farkas and Schou, *Post-Truth*.

52. Merlan, *Republic of Lies*, 174.

53. David Bauder, "Fox's Carlson Calls White Supremacy 'a Hoax,'" Associated Press, August 7, 2019, https://apnews.com/e0f9f2ea88dc435db914c8e53dcaf59e; also see Emily Rueb and Derrick Bryson Taylor, "Tucker Carlson of Fox Falsely Calls White Supremacy a 'Hoax,'" *New York Times*, August 8, 2019, https://www.nytimes.com/2019/08/08/business/media/tucker-carlson-white-supremacy.html.

54. Jennifer Rubin, "A Guide to the Ugly Ideology We're Up Against, and How Politicians Like Trump Spread It," *Washington Post*, August 12, 2019, https://www.washingtonpost.com/opinions/2019/08/12/guide-ugly-ideology-were-up-against-how-politicians-like-trump-spread-it/.

55. Marantz, *Anti-Social*, 18.

56. FBI Phoenix Field Office, "Anti-Government." Also see Melissa Chan, "Conspiracy Theories Might Sound Crazy, but Here's Why Experts Say We Can No Longer Ignore Them," *Time*, August 15, 2019, https://time.com/5541411/conspiracy-theories-domestic-terrorism/.

57. FBI Phoenix Field Office, "Anti-Government." Also see Melissa Chan, "Conspiracy Theories Might Sound Crazy, but Here's Why Experts Say We Can No Longer Ignore Them," *Time*, August 15, 2019, https://time.com/5541411/conspiracy-theories-domestic-terrorism/.

58. K. Vogel, S. Shane, and P. Kinsley, "How Vilification of George Soros Moved from the Fringes to the Mainstream," *New York Times*, October 31, 2018; L. Beckett, "Pittsburgh Shooting: Suspect Railed against Jews and Muslims on Site Used by 'Alt-Right,'" *Guardian*, October 27, 2018.

59. Westervelt, "Synagogue Shooting." Anti-Semitic incidents continue to rise and overall are at near-historic highs in the United States. See ADL, *Audit of Anti-Semitic Incidents*.

60. Linda Qui, "Did Democrats, or George Soros, Fund Migrant Caravan?: Despite Republican Claims, No," *New York Times*, October 20, 2018; Brett Samuels, "Trump: 'I Wouldn't Be Surprised' if Soros Were Paying for Migrant Caravan," *The Hill*, October 31, 2018.

61. N. Chavez, E. Grinberg, and E. McLaughlin, "Pittsburgh Synagogue Gunman Said He Wanted All Jews to Die, Criminal Complaint Says," CNN, October 31, 2018, https://www.cnn .com/2018/10/28/us/pittsburgh-synagogue-shooting/index.html.

62. Finchelstein, *From Fascism to Populism*, 159; also see Haidt, "Nationalism Beats Globalism."

63. See, for example, J. Holmes, "The President Is Pushing the Exact Conspiracies Cited by the Pittsburgh Shooter 5 Days after the Attack," *Esquire*, November 1, 2018.

64. Bess Levin, "Trump: 'A Lot of People Say' George Soros Is Funding the Migrant Caravan," *Vanity Fair*, October 31, 2018, https://www.vanityfair.com/news/2018/10/donald-trump -george-soros-caravan?verso=true.

65. Merlan, *Republic of Lies*, 244.

66. See Robin Givhan, "Neo-Nazis Are Using Fashion in an Attempt to Normalize: The Fashion Industry Needs to Speak Up," *Washington Post*, August 22, 2017, https://www .washingtonpost.com/news/arts-and-entertainment/wp/2017/08/22/neo-nazis-are-using -fashion-in-an-attempt-to-normalize-the-fashion-industry-needs-to-speak-up/?noredirect=on; also see Donovan Myrie, "Hidden Hate in Clothing: Decoding the Symbols and the Brands," *WKMG ClickOrlando*, May 16, 2018, https://www.clickorlando.com/news/investigators /hidden-hate-in-clothing-decoding-the-symbols-and-the-brands.

67. Miller-Idriss and Johnson, "Free Advertising"; Ruth Perl Baharir, "From Hipster Fad to Neo-Nazi Tag: How America's Alt-Right Got Its Signature Hairstyle," *Haaretz*, February 8, 2017, https://www.haaretz.com/us-news/.premium.MAGAZINE-how-america-s-alt-right-got-its -signature-hairstyle-1.5495494.

68. "Hugo Boss Apology for Nazi Past as Book Is Published," *BBC News*, September 21, 2011, https://www.bbc.com/news/world-europe-15008682.

69. Dean Stephens, "10 Fascinating Ways the Nazis Influenced Fashion," Listverse, June 23, 2017, https://listverse.com/2017/06/23/10-fascinating-ways-the-nazis-influenced-fashion/.

70. See Jennifer Abbots, "True 'Skinheads' Are Not the Racist Thugs of Media Fame," letter to the editor, *New York Times*, April 8, 1994, https://www.nytimes.com/1994/04/19/opinion /l-true-skinheads-are-not-the-racist-thugs-of-media-fame-829412.html.

71. Allie Conti, "Neo-Nazi to Troll Army: 'We Have to Be Sexy' at the Big Alt-Right Rally," VICE, August 9, 2017, https://www.vice.com/en_us/article/599zmx/neo-nazi-to-troll-army -we-have-to-be-sexy-at-the-big-alt-right-rally.

72. Gaugele, "New Obscurity in Style."

73. For a discussion of how humor, satire, and irony have been weaponized by the US "alt right," see Greene, "'Deplorable.'"

74. See the definition and discussion of memes in Marwick and Lewis, *Media Manipulation and Disinformation*, 36.

75. Greene, "'Deplorable,'" 36.

76. Greene and Day, "Asking for It,", cited in Greene, "'Deplorable,'" 35.

77. Greene, "'Deplorable,'" 35. I am indebted to an anonymous reviewer for the point about the shift from defense to offense in the far right.

Chapter 3

1. Portions of this chapter are adapted from Cynthia Miller-Idriss, "The Rise of Fascist Fashion: How Clothing Helps the Far Right Sell Their Violent Message," *Salon*, April 21, 2018, https://www.salon.com/2018/04/21/the-rise-of-fascist-fashion-clothing-helps-the-far-right -sell-their-violent-message/; Miller-Idriss and Johnson, "Free Advertising"; Cynthia Miller-Idriss, "Selling Extremism: Nationalist Streetwear and the Rise of the Far Right," CNN *Style*, January 10, 2019, https://www.cnn.com/style/article/right-wing-fashion-streetwear/index .html; Cynthia Miller-Idriss, "Why Does the Far Right Love Fred Perry?: Mainstream Fashion Is Its New Camouflage," *Guardian*, August 29, 2019, https://www.theguardian.com /commentisfree/2019/aug/29/far-right-fred-perry-mainstream-fashion-camouflage-brands; and Cynthia Miller-Idriss, "Mainstreaming Extremism through Clothing," *Islamic Horizons Magazine*, July–August 2019, 34–35, https://issuu.com/isnacreative/docs/ih_july-august_19.

2. Martin Patriquin, Mack Lamoureux, Alheli Picazo, and Evan Balgord, "The Racist Podcaster Who Started a Neo-Nazi Coffee Company to Fund White Nationalism," VICE, May 16, 2018, https://www.vice.com/en_us/article/59qb93/the-racist-podcaster-who-started-a-neo -nazi-coffee-company-to-fund-white-nationalism. Also see Brett Barrouquere, "How about Some White Nationalism with Your Morning Jolt of Coffee?" SPLC, December 28, 2017, https://www.splcenter.org/hatewatch/2017/12/28/how-about-some-white-nationalism-your -morning-jolt-coffee. The coffee company, Rising Sun Coffee Company, shares a name with at least two other coffee companies, based in Pennsylvania and North Carolina, which do not appear to be connected to the white-supremacist company.

3. Forchtner and Tominc, "Kalashnikov and Cooking-Spoon."

4. Alexandra Minna Stern, "Alt-Right Women and the 'White Baby Challenge,'" *Salon*, July 14, 2019, https://www.salon.com/2019/07/14/alt-right-handmaidens-and-the-white-baby -challenge/; and the longer discussion in Stern, *Proud Boys*; also see Annie Kelly, "The Housewives of White Supremacy," *New York Times*, June 1, 2018, https://www.nytimes.com/2018/06 /01/opinion/sunday/tradwives-women-alt-right.html?login=email&auth=login-email.

5. See, for example, Caroline Sinders, "There's an Alt Right Version of Everything," *Quartz*, September 27, 2017, https://qz.com/1086797/theres-an-alt-right-version-of-everything/. For an overview of traditional white power music, see Corte and Edwards, "White Power Music."

6. See Surak, *Making Tea, Making Japan*; DeSoucey, *Contested Tastes*; Rabikowska, "Ritualization of Food"; Petrou and Connell, "Food, Morality and Identity."

7. Original full German phrase: "dann würde der Nazi, glaub ich eher sagen, 'ne Döner ist Scheiße, ist von den Türken, will ick nicht, brauch ich nicht. . . . Dass die echt ganz Deutschlastig sind, sag ich mal, dass die wirklich nur Deutsch sehn, in dem Sinne, dass die deutsche Sachen essen und ja." The interview with Jan is cited in Miller-Idriss, *Blood and Culture*, 150.

8. Shoshan, *Management of Hate*, 64–84, quote 82.

9. Forchtner and Tominc, "Kalashnikov and Cooking-Spoon," 416, 423.

10. Forchtner and Tominc, 425

11. Gerda Matthies, "Wenn Nazis vegan kochen—und Kidneybohnen essen," *Die Welt*, July 31, 2015, https://www.welt.de/vermischtes/article144670643/Wenn-Nazis-vegan-kochen -und-Kidneybohnen-essen.html. Also see Forchtner and Tominc, "Kalashnikov and Cooking-Spoon," 418–19.

12. For more on Jordan Peterson, see Dorian Lynskey, "How Dangerous Is Jordan B. Peterson, the Rightwing Professor Who 'Hit a Hornets' Nest'?" *Guardian*, February 7, 2018, https://www.theguardian.com/science/2018/feb/07/how-dangerous-is-jordan-b-peterson-the-rightwing-professor-who-hit-a-hornets-nest.

13. Evans, *Skin Deep*, 300; Kelly Weill, "Why Right Wingers Are Going Crazy about Meat," *Daily Beast*, August 25, 2018, https://www.thedailybeast.com/why-right-wingers-are-going-crazy-about-meat. Also see "The Bizarre Fad Diet Taking the Far Right by Storm," *Mother Jones*, September 7, 2018, https://www.motherjones.com/food/2018/09/carnivorism-zero-carb-jordan-peterson-mikhaila-shawn-baker-andrew-torba-alt-right/.

14. Weill, "Crazy about Meat."

15. Brenna Houck, "Why Conservatives Won't Stop Talking about Burgers," Eater, March 1, 2019, https://www.eater.com/2019/3/1/18246220/aoc-green-deal-burgers-backlash-creepshot.

16. See Samuel Moyn, "The Price of Meat," *New Republic*, May 7, 2019, https://newrepublic.com/article/153792/red-meat-republic-book-review-joshua-specht. On Sebastian Gorka's politics see Daniel Nexon, "Sebastian Gorka May Be a Far-Right Nativist, but for Sure He's a Terrible Scholar," *Foreign Policy*, March 17, 2017, https://foreignpolicy.com/2017/03/17/dr-sebastian-gorka-may-be-a-far-right-nativist-but-for-sure-hes-a-terrible-scholar-trump-radical-islam/.

17. Eyes on the Right, "Neo-Nazi Podcasters: 'Impossible Burger' a Jewish Plot to Turn U.S. into 'Third World' Country," Angry White Men, October 2, 2019, https://angrywhitemen.org/2019/10/02/neo-nazi-podcasters-impossible-burger-a-jewish-plot-to-turn-u-s-into-third-world-country/.

18. Sam Kestenbaum, "Did Wendy's Become the Accidental Neo-Nazi Happy Meal?" *Forward*, January 4, 2017, https://forward.com/news/359129/did-wendys-become-the-accidental-neo-nazi-happy-meal/; Kate Taylor, "I Ate Only Foods that Have Been Boycotted by the Alt-Right and Liberals—and It Revealed an Absurd Truth about Trump's America," *Business Insider*, December 1, 2017, https://www.businessinsider.com/alt-right-versus-left-boycotted-foods-diet-2017-12; Cristina Maza, "Alt-Right White Supremacists Claim Papa John's as Official Pizza," *Newsweek*, November 3, 2017, https://www.newsweek.com/papa-john-alt-right-nazis-white-supremacists-nfl-pizza-701648.

19. See the guide to off-the-grid living on the Conservation Institute's website, https://www.conservationinstitute.org/off-the-grid-food-guide/.

20. Davey, "'Conservative' Ideology." The recent case of antifascist protests against a Bloomington, Indiana, farmers' market stall run by a woman who refers to herself as an "identitarian" is also relevant in this regard. See Jack Healy, "Amid the Kale and Corn, Fears of White Supremacy at the Farmers' Market," *New York Times*, August 18, 2019, https://www.nytimes.com/2019/08/18/us/indiana-farmers-market-white-supremacy.html. I am indebted to Jeremy Price for discussions about the Bloomington farmers' market situation.

21. Tay Wiles, "Meet Your Local Anti-Government Extremist Groups," *High Country News*, September 27, 2017, https://www.hcn.org/articles/politics-anti-government-groups-in-the-west-right-now; also see Ryan Lenz, "Pondering a Coming Civil War, Oath Keepers Call for Armed Guards to Patrol Schools Nationwide," SPLC, February 27, 2018, https://www.splcenter.org/hatewatch/2018/02/27/pondering-coming-civil-war-oath-keepers-call-armed-guards-patrol-schools-nationwide.

22. See, for example, Koronowski, "Radical Right."

23. See the international sites listed on the Anastasia movement's US website at https://anastasiausa.land/new-international-kins-domain-listings-10-10-19/.

24. Davidov, "Beyond Formal Environmentalism"; Peter Paul Catterall, "Green Nationalism? How the Far Right Could Learn to Love the Environment," *Ecologist*, 12 April 2017, https://theecologist.org/2017/apr/12/green-nationalism-how-far-right-could-learn-love-environment. I am indebted to Kat Williams for discussions about the Anastasia movement.

25. Timothy Egan, "How the Far Right Came to Love Hippie Food," *New York Times*, September 8, 2017, https://www.nytimes.com/2017/09/08/opinion/gop-hippie-food-health.html.

26. As sold on the Infowars online store, at https://www.infowarsstore.com/patriot-blend -100-organic-coffee.html.

27. See the variety of products at the Infowars Store, www.infowarsstore.com.

28. Mattheis, "'Shieldmaidens of Whiteness.'" Also see Rogers and Litt, "Normalizing Racism."

29. Rogers and Litt, "Normalizing Racism," 108–9.

30. The Blonde Butter Maker's YouTube channel is available at https://www.youtube.com /channel/UCW9mamBv3maRhnCOFXf9d4A/about, accessed November 1, 2019. Also see analysis of her channel in Stern, *Proud Boys*, 101–9.

31. Stern, *Proud Boys*, 109.

32. See TheBlondeButterMaker, "Who Is the Blonde Butter Maker?" YouTube, September 8, 2019, https://www.youtube.com/watch?v=YHcgnvT_1ZY.

33. Nick Squires, "Golden Dawn's 'Greeks Only' Soup Kitchen Ends in Chaos," *Telegraph*, May 2, 2013, https://www.telegraph.co.uk/news/worldnews/europe/greece/10034010/Golden -Dawns-Greeks-only-soup-kitchen-ends-in-chaos.html.

34. I am indebted to Daniel Koehler for sharing the example of Der Dritte Weg. See the party's website description of the "winter help" initiative at https://der-dritte-weg.info/2018 /01/winterhilfe-mit-feldkueche-in-zwickau/.

35. See, for example, Tess Sheets and J. D. Gallop, "Bacon Used in Hate Crime: Titusville Man Gets 15 Years in Mosque Vandalism," *Florida Today*, December 5, 2017, https://www .floridatoday.com/story/news/crime/2017/12/05/titusville-man-sentenced-15-years-prison -after-mosque-vandalism/924987001/; also see "Pair Jailed for Edinburgh's Central Mosque Bacon Attack," *BBC News*, June 20, 2014, https://www.bbc.com/news/uk-scotland-edinburgh -east-fife-27941589.

36. Craig Smith, "Poor and Muslim? Jewish? Soup Kitchen Is Not for You," *New York Times*, February 26, 2008, https://www.nytimes.com/2006/02/28/world/europe/poor-and-muslim -jewish-soup-kitchen-is-not-for-you.html.

37. Time Hume, "Far-Right Extremists Are Threatening to Burn Down German Kindergartens for Taking Pork Off Their Menus," *VICE News*, August 2, 2019, https://www.vice.com/en _us/article/qvgdkq/far-right-extremists-are-threatening-to-burn-down-german-kindergartens -for-taking-pork-off-their-menus.

38. On the quote from neo-Nazi blogger Andrew Anglin see Allie Conti, "Neo-Nazi to Troll Army: 'We Have to Be Sexy' at the Big Alt-Right Rally," *VICE*, August 9, 2017, https://www.vice .com/en_us/article/599zmx/neo-nazi-to-troll-army-we-have-to-be-sexy-at-the-big-alt-right -rally.

39. Wolf, "Uniform of White Supremacy."

40. "Women Indicted after Hate-Filled Video Recorded at Mosque," *U.S. News & World Report*, March 26, 2018, https://www.usnews.com/news/best-states/arizona/articles/2018-03-26/women-indicted-after-hate-filled-video-recorded-at-mosque; Nick Martin, "Two Women Tied to Patriot Movement AZ Arrested after Incident at Arizona Mosque," *SPLC Hatewatch*, March 16, 2018, https://www.splcenter.org/hatewatch/2018/03/16/two-women-tied-patriot-movement-az-arrested-after-incident-arizona-mosque.

41. News Agencies, "Fashion Brand's Logo Likened to Nazi Eagle Symbol," *Telegraph*, May 5, 2014, https://www.telegraph.co.uk/finance/newsbysector/retailandconsumer/10809250/Fashion-brands-logo-likened-to-Nazi-eagle-symbol.html.

42. Tasneem Raja, "Decoding the Language of Extremist Clothing," *Topic Magazine*, October 2017, https://www.topic.com/decoding-the-language-of-extremist-clothing.

43. Miller-Idriss, *Extreme Gone Mainstream*. For other coverage of the phenomenon see, for example, Adam Sherwin, "Outrage as Far-Right's Favourite Outfitter 'Thor Steinar' Opens Shop in Heart of London's Jewish Community," *Independent*, April 16, 2014; Wolf, "Uniform of White Supremacy."

44. Together with a research assistant, I captured over a thousand screenshots of eleven brands of clothing in six countries during the 2018–19 academic year in order to see whether the same kinds of messages I analyzed in the German brands were consistent across other brands.

45. See Nick Robins-Early, "Instagram Let a Violent White Supremacist Group Promote Their Clothing Brand," *Huffington Post*, August 14, 2018, https://www.huffpost.com/entry/instagram-white-supremacy-clothing_n_5b730a38e4b03d52e490ecf8. According to the ADL, RAM launched The Right Brand Clothing company in January 2018 in what the ADL describes as "an effort to mainstream and monetize their ideology." See "Rise Above Movement (R.A.M.)," ADL, accessed March 12, 2020, https://www.adl.org/resources/backgrounders/rise-above-movement-ram.

46. See, e.g., the analysis of white-supremacist clothing in the MMA community in Zidan, "Fascism in MMA."

47. As displayed on the Certified White Boy brand website, www.certifiedwhiteboy.com.

48. See the OK-symbol hat for sale on the Infowars Store: https://www.infowarsstore.com/gear/apparel/ok-sign-hat.

49. See the "Walk Toward the Fire" T-shirt and marketing text at the Breitbart Store: https://store.breitbart.com/collections/men/products/walk-toward-the-fire-t-shirt-navy-1.

50. See the marketing text selling the "Second Amendment T-shirt" on the Infowars Store: https://www.infowarsstore.com/gear/apparel/second-amendment-t-shirt.html.

51. See the selection of shirts and stickers at www.gruntstyle.com.

52. Tess Owens, "How Telegram Became White Nationalists' Go-To Messaging Platform," *VICE News*, October 7, 2019, https://www.vice.com/en_us/article/59nk3a/how-telegram-became-white-nationalists-go-to-messaging-platform.

53. See the special issue on hate music "Hate Rock," ed. Arthur Jipson, *Popular Music and Society* 30, no. 4 (2007), https://www.tandfonline.com/toc/rpms20/30/4, in which several authors trace hate music across a variety of genres. For example, see B. Messner et al., "Hardest Hate." For an analysis of traditional far-right hate music, see Brown, "Subcultures."

54. "Hate Music," SPLC, n.d., accessed February 25, 2020, https://www.splcenter.org/fighting-hate/extremist-files/ideology/hate-music.

55. I am indebted to Elizabeth Knauer for her work on the mainstreaming of far-right music scenes as part of a coauthored book chapter in development, "Buying into the Far Right: Material Culture and Right-Wing Consumption."

56. See Pisoiu, "Subcultural Theory."

57. See Project Schoolyard information at the Tightrope Records website: http://www.tightrope.cc/sampler/about.shtml. It was modeled after a similar project in Germany—see the discussion in "Die Schulhof-CD," Mitteldeutscher Rundfunk's website, January 4, 2016, https://www.mdr.de/zeitreise/stoebern/damals/rechtsextremismus186.html.

58. Miller-Idriss, *Extreme Gone Mainstream.*

59. From Miranda Christou's talk "The Benign Feminism of an Extreme Right-Wing Party," at the Center for Analysis of the Radical Right (CARR) 2019 conference in Richmond, London, on May 16, 2019. A recording of the talk is available: "Miranda Christou—The Benign Feminism of an Extreme Right-Wing Party," Backdoor Broadcasting Company, Academic Podcasts, June 5, 2019, https://backdoorbroadcasting.net/2019/06/miranda-christou-the-benign-feminism-of-an-extreme-right-wing-party/.

60. See a longer discussion of this in Miller-Idriss and Johnson, "Free Advertising."

61. I am indebted to La'Nita Johnson for research assistance on these "brand fan" communities.

62. Keatinge, Keen, and Izenman, "Fundraising."

63. Keatinge, Keen, and Izenman, 17.

64. Keatinge, Keen, and Izenman, 18.

65. See article on White Rex on the Czech antifascist group's website: "What Is White Rex?" antifa.cz, August 3, 2015, http://www.antifa.cz/content/what-white-rex.

66. As described in the now-defunct website sections "Ethical Supply Chain and Procurement" and "Where the Money Goes," Right Brand Clothing, n.d., accessed June 22, 2018, https://rightbrandclothing.com/ethical-supply-chain-and-procurement/.

67. Keatinge, Keen, and Izenman, "Fundraising," 21–22.

68. "Glenn Beck," Right Wing Watch, n.d., accessed February 20, 2020, https://www.rightwingwatch.org/people/glenn-beck/.

69. See TheBlaze's shop and this particular T-shirt at https://shop.theblaze.com/products/stop-turning-the-friggin-frogs-gay-t-shirt?pr_prod_strat=copurchase&pr_rec_pid=1822787829827&pr_ref_pid=1822831575107&pr_seq=uniform.

70. Tucker Higgins, "Alex Jones' 5 Most Disturbing and Ridiculous Conspiracy Theories," CNBC, September 14, 2018, https://www.cnbc.com/2018/09/14/alex-jones-5-most-disturbing-ridiculous-conspiracy-theories.html.

71. For example, see the ADL's analysis in *Sounds of Hate.* Also see SPLC's "Hate Music" and Brown, "Subcultures."

72. See Samuel Gibbs, "Apple Denounces Neo-Nazis as Spotify Bans 'White Power' Tracks," *Guardian,* August 17, 2017, https://www.theguardian.com/technology/2017/aug/17/apple-denounces-neo-nazis-as-spotify-bans-white-power-tracks; Julia Carrie Wong, "Tech Companies Turn on Daily Stormer and the 'Alt Right' after Charlottesville," *Guardian,* August 14, 2017,

https://www.theguardian.com/technology/2017/aug/14/daily-stormer-alt-right-google-go-daddy-charlottesville; and Elizabeth Flock, "Spotify Has Removed White Power Music from Its Platform. But It's Still Available on Dozens of Other Sites," *PBS News Hour.* August 18, 2017, https://www.pbs.org/newshour/arts/spotify-removed-white-power-music-platform-still-available-dozens-sites. For a discussion of repercussions from banning policies, such as far-right individuals migrating to encrypted messaging apps, see Brian Hughes, "Thriving from Exile: Toward a Materialist Analysis of the Alt-Right," b2o, the online community of the *boundary 2* editorial collective, September 24, 2019, https://www.boundary2.org/2019/09/brian-hughes-thriving-from-exile-toward-a-materialist-analysis-of-the-alt-right/.

73. Anonymous, "What Happened after My 13-Year-Old Son Joined the Alt-Right: A Washington Family's Nightmare Year," *Washingtonian*, May 5, 2019, https://www.washingtonian.com/2019/05/05/what-happened-after-my-13-year-old-son-joined-the-alt-right/.

74. See the special issue "Hate Rock," ed. Arthur Jipson, *Popular Music and Society* 30, no. 4 (2007), https://www.tandfonline.com/toc/rpms20/30/4.

Chapter 4

1. Colborne, "Friday Night Fights."

2. Zidan, "Fascist Fight Clubs."

3. Karim Zidan, "La Phalange: The Rise of a Fascist Fight Club in Canada," SBNation, Bloody Elbow, March 15, 2018, https://www.bloodyelbow.com/2018/3/15/17120190/fascist-fight-club-canada-france-mma-boxing-politics-karim-zidan-feature. On the phrase "La Phalange" and its connection to the notion of Western civilization, see Louie Dean Valencia-Garcia, "The Ups and Downs and Clashes of Western Civilization," OpenDemocracy, July 23, 2019, https://www.opendemocracy.net/en/countering-radical-right/ups-and-downs-and-clashes-western-civilization/.

4. Tim Adams, "Ultimate Fighting Championship: The Fight of Our Lives?" *Guardian*, March 26, 2017, https://www.theguardian.com/sport/2017/mar/26/ultimate-fighting-championship-fight-of-our-lives-mma-donald-trump-vladimir-putin-conor-mcregor.

5. Andreasson and Johansson, "Negotiating Violence"; Buse, "No Holds Barred."

6. Vaccaro and Swauger, *Unleashing Manhood*, 20, citing John McCain as quoted in Greg Beato, "Bleeding into the Mainstream: How John McCain Popularized Human Cockfighting," *Reason*, October 2007, https://reason.com/2007/09/20/bleeding-into-the-mainstream.

7. Tim Adams, "Ultimate Fighting Championship: The Fight of Our Lives?" *Guardian*, March 26, 2017, https://www.theguardian.com/sport/2017/mar/26/ultimate-fighting-championship-fight-of-our-lives-mma-donald-trump-vladimir-putin-conor-mcregor.

8. Adams.

9. Andreasson and Johansson, "Negotiating Violence," 1184.

10. Adams, "Ultimate Fighting Championship."

11. The competitions on this illustrative list all had tickets for sale in August 2019 at vividseats.com. See https://www.vividseats.com/sports/bellator-fighting-championships-tickets.html.

12. Vaccaro and Swauger, *Unleashing Manhood*, 12.

13. Andreasson and Johansson, "Negotiating Violence," 1195.

14. I am indebted to Daniel Koehler for this insight. Also see brief discussion of the Sturmabteilung's focus on training its force in boxing and jujitsu in D. King, *Trial of Adolf Hitler*, 7.

15. I am indebted to Daniel Koehler for pointing out the role of Hak Pao in the Solingen bombers' backgrounds. Also see the discussion in Lee, *Beast Reawakens*, 333; "Das Wäre eine Bombe," *Der Spiegel*, May 30, 1994, https://www.spiegel.de/spiegel/print/d-13684942.html; Anton Maegerle, "Vor 25 Jahren: Der Brandanschlag in Solingen," *Disskursiv* (blog), Duisburg Institute for Language and Social Research, May 2, 2018, http://www.disskursiv.de/2018/05/02/vor-25-jahren-der-brandanschlag-in-solingen/; Mary Williams Walsh, "4 Guilty in Fatal Arson Attack on Turks in Germany," *Los Angeles Times*, October 14, 1995, https://www.latimes.com/archives/la-xpm-1995-10-14-mn-56738-story.html.

16. Tumblety, *Remaking the Male Body*; Linke, *German Bodies*.

17. Tumblety, *Remaking the Male Body*, 4; Anand, "Anxious Sexualities."

18. See the analysis of the National Socialists' racial hygiene and eugenics policies described by the Holocaust Education and Archive Research Team (HEART), in "The T-4 Program: Origins, Planning & Staff," HEART, 2007, http://www.holocaustresearchproject.org/euthan/t4.html, and the extensive discussion of race and representation in post–World War II Germany in Linke, *German Bodies*. Also see Wolf, "Uniform of White Supremacy."

19. Colborne, "Friday Night Fights."

20. Hume, "Russian Neo-Nazi"; also see Hume, "Europe's Far Right."

21. See Zidan, "Fascism in MMA."

22. As documented in the 2018 annual report from the German intelligence service (Verfassungsschutzbericht): "Das größte und wichtigste Kampfsportturnier der Szene ist der seit 2013 jährlich stattfindende 'Kampf der Nibelungen' (KdN), der am 13. Oktober 2018 in Ostritz (Sachsen) stattfand und circa 850 Besucher aus dem Bundesgebiet und dem europäischen Ausland hatte." Bundesministerium des Innern, *Verfassungsschutzbericht 2018*.

23. See McConnell and Wunderlich, *Nibelungen Tradition*.

24. "Während bei den meisten 'Fight Nights' im bundesweiten Raum die Teilnahme des jeweiligen Sportlers allzu oft mit dem abverlangten Bekenntnis zur freien demokratischen Grundordnung steht oder fällt, will der Kampf der Nibelungen den Sport nicht als Teil eines faulenden politischen Systems verstehen, sondern diesen als fundamentales Element einer Alternative zu eben jenem etablieren und in die Breite tragen. . . . Beteiligt euch, besucht unsere Veranstaltungen oder tretet selber aktiv an, kommt mit anderen Sportlern in Kontakt und animiert über euer Vorbild andere dazu, dem System der Versager, der Heuchler und der Schwächlinge den Rücken zu kehren." From the "About Us" section of Kampf der Nibelungen's website, https://www.kampf-der-nibelungen.com/ueber-uns/.

25. Quote in Zidan, "Fascist Fight Clubs"; see also Karim Zidan, "Kampf der Nibelungen: German neo-Nazis Are Combining Far Right Politics with MMA," SBNation, Bloody Elbow, June 14, 2018, https://www.bloodyelbow.com/2018/6/14/17464004/german-neo-nazis-combining-far-right-politics-mma-kairm-zidan-feature-news.

26. See the interview with Robert Claus by Josef Wirnshofer: "Der 'Kampf der Nibelungen' dient der Vernetzung und Finanzierung der Neonazi-Szene," *Jetzt*, April 20, 2018, https://www.jetzt.de/politik/robert-claus-ueber-hooligans-neonazis-und-den-kampf-der-nibelungen.

27. See, for example, Colborne, "Friday Night Fights"; Hume, "Russian Neo-Nazi"; Bryan Schatz, "The Terrifying Rise of Alt-Right Fight Clubs," *Mother Jones*, February 1, 2018, https://www.motherjones.com/politics/2018/02/the-terrifying-rise-of-alt-right-fight-clubs/; Karim Zidan, "La Phalange: The Rise of a Fascist Fight Club in Canada," SBNation, Bloody Elbow, March 15, 2018, https://www.bloodyelbow.com/2018/3/15/17120190/fascist-fight-club-canada-france-mma-boxing-politics-karim-zidan-feature; Zidan, "Kampf der Nibelungen." Also see Holthouse, "Racists Active"; the resource and background information on the Rise Above Movement available at the ADL's website, www.adl.org; and Claus and Gabler, "Kampf auf der Straße"; Claus and Brunßen, "Rechtsextremismus und Fanszenen." Also see Claus's essay for the German Federal Agency for Civic Education, "Der extrem rechte Kampfsportboom," Bundeszentrale für politische Bildung, November 5, 2018, https://www.bpb.de/politik/extremismus/rechtsextremismus/279552/der-extrem-rechte-kampfsportboom.

28. Karim Zidan, "Pride France: The French Martial Arts Brand Connected to the Neo-Nazi Fight Scene," SBNation, Bloody Elbow, October 23, 2019, https://www.bloodyelbow.com/2019/10/23/20926685/pride-france-french-martial-arts-brand-neo-nazi-fight-scene-mma-crime-politics-feature.

29. Lana Andelane, "Soldier Believed to Have Ties to Far-Right 'Christian Brotherhood' Arrested at Linton Military Camp," Newshub, December 18, 2019, https://www.newshub.co.nz/home/new-zealand/2019/12/soldier-believed-to-have-ties-to-far-right-christian-brotherhood-arrested-at-linton-military-camp.html.

30. Mikayla Lewis, "Group Plans to Protest New East Nashville Gym over Perceived Alt-Right Ties," *Fox 17 Nashville*, July 21, 2017, https://fox17.com/news/local/group-plans-to-protest-new-east-nashville-gym-over-perceived-alt-right-ties.

31. See Operation Werewolf's website at https://www.operationwerewolf.com/. Operation Werewolf was founded by Paul Waggener, who, along with his brother Matthias, was also a founder of the Wolves of Vinland, a group that is listed as a neo-Volkisch hate group by the SPLC. See "Neo-Volkisch," SPLC, n.d., accessed February 25, 2020, https://www.splcenter.org/fighting-hate/extremist-files/ideology/neo-volkisch. For more on the Vengeance Strength Kvlt gym and its founders, see Cari Wade Gervin, "Vengeance Strength Kvlt Gym in East Nashville Has Links to Alt-Right," *Nashville Scene*, July 20, 2017, https://www.nashvillescene.com/news/pith-in-the-wind/article/20868176/strength-cult-gym-in-east-nashville-has-ties-to-altright.

32. Vengeance Strength Kvlt gym's website, https://www.vengeance.me/about, "About" section, n.d., accessed February 25, 2020; this section also discusses the gym's ideology.

33. Bundesministerium des Innern, *Verfassungsschutzbericht 2018*. Original quote: "Eine Entwicklung, die die Gewaltorientierung eines Großteiles der rechtsextremistischen Szene plastisch untermauert, ist das im Berichtszeitraum gestiegene Interesse von Rechtsextremisten an Kampfsport. Entsprechende Veranstaltungen waren gekennzeichnet von einer zunehmend professionellen Organisation und konstant dreistelligen Besucherzahlen, die die gestiegene Bedeutung von Kampfsport für Rechtsextremisten dokumentieren."

34. "Der III. Weg" (Der Dritte Weg), Bundesamt für Verfassungsschutz, n.d., accessed February 25, 2020, https://www.verfassungsschutz.de/de/arbeitsfelder/af-rechtsextremismus/zahlen-und-fakten-rechtsextremismus/rechtsextremistische-parteien-2018/der-dritte-weg-2018. The page gives a descriptive analysis of "The Third Way" (Der Dritte Weg) by the German intelligence services.

35. See the analysis in Martin Kaul and Georg Mascolo, "Europol warnt vor rechten Gewalt-taten," *Süddeutsche Zeitung*, September 23, 2019, https://www.sueddeutsche.de/politik/europol -sicherheit-rechtsextremismus-1.4613424.

36. Hume, "Europe's Far Right."

37. One of the few academic mentions of the relationship between the MMA world and the far right I have found is in a research article by Barbara Perry and Ryan Scrivens, who suggest in passing that MMA is becoming a "rallying point" for Canadian right-wing extremists, who are attracted to the shared "love of violence" between the extreme-right-wing and MMA com-munities. Although similar trends are visible in the United States, at the time of this writing there are no published academic works documenting the phenomenon. See Perry and Scrivens, "Uneasy Alliances," 829. Others have interrogated a variety of aspects of MMA related to mas-culinity and the body, for example, but not with a specific focus on extremism or the far right. See, for example, Abramson and Modzelwski, "Caged Morality," and Vaccaro and Swauger, *Unleashing Manhood*.

38. One set of charges against three of the men was dismissed by a federal judge in California in June 2019, while three other RAM members and a RAM associate pled guilty in a separate case in a federal court in Virginia. See discussion in A. C. Thompson, "Federal Judge Dismisses Charges against 3 White Supremacists," ProPublica, June 4, 2019, https://www.propublica.org /article/federal-judge-dismisses-charges-against-3-white-supremacists. For more on RAM, see the description on the ADL's website, "Rise Above Movement (R.A.M.)," https://www.adl.org /resources/backgrounders/rise-above-movement-ram; also quoted in Zidan, "Fascist Fight Clubs."

39. Karim Zidan, "'Keep the Flame Alive': The Revival of a US Based Neo-Nazi Fight Club," SBNation, Bloody Elbow, November 6, 2019, https://www.bloodyelbow.com/2019/11/6 /20950190/alt-right-neo-nazi-fight-club-ram-rise-above-movement-charlottesville-mma -politics-feature.

40. According to Zidan, "Fascist Fight Clubs." For more on far-right festivals, see the recent analysis by Julia Ebner in her new book, *Going Dark*.

41. Soufan Center, *White Supremacist Extremism*, 33.

42. Soufan Center, 33.

43. Schatz, " Terrifying Rise."

44. See "Far Right Group Intimidates VICE Journalists in Their Montreal Office," *CBC News*, May 23, 2018, https://www.cbc.ca/news/canada/montreal/atalante-far-right-vice-1.4675660.

45. Bill Morlin, "New 'Fight Club' Ready for Street Violence," *Hate Watch*, April 25, 2017, https://www.splcenter.org/hatewatch/2017/04/25/new-fight-club-ready-street-violence. The confederation of volkish fight clubs is mentioned in Sarah Viets, "Tennessee White Supremacist Group Confederate Blood and Honour Returns," *Hate Watch*, August 2, 2017, https://www .splcenter.org/hatewatch/2017/08/02/tennessee-white-supremacist-group-confederate-blood -and-honour-returns. Also see Schatz, "Terrifying Rise."

46. For more on *The Matrix* see Yeffeth, *Taking the Red Pill*, along with C. King and Leonard, "Is Neo White?" Also see Swain, "MMAsculinities."

47. Vaccaro and Swauger, *Unleashing Manhood*.

48. Hume, "Russian Neo-Nazi."

49. Lenos and Jansen, "Role of Sports."

50. As in the "Ethical Supply Chain and Procurement" section of The Right Brand's now-defunct website, https://rightbrandclothing.com/ethical-supply-chain-and-procurement/, n.d., accessed June 25, 2018.

51. As in the "FAQ" section of Identity Evropa's now-defunct website, www.identityevropa.com/faq, n.d., accessed June 25, 2018.

52. Allie Conti, "Neo-Nazi to Troll Army: 'We Have to Be Sexy' at the Big Alt-Right Rally," VICE, August 9, 2017, https://www.vice.com/en_us/article/599zmx/neo-nazi-to-troll-army-we-have-to-be-sexy-at-the-big-alt-right-rally. For a longer discussion of Anglin and his neo-Nazi site Daily Stormer, see the discussion in D. Johnson, Hateland, esp. pp. 93–97.

53. As described on the now-defunct site, www.rightbrandclothing.com.

54. See the discussion in Stern, Proud Boys, 115.

55. See The Golden One, "Why I Don't Endorse Political Violence or Hateful Rhetoric. It Is Ineffective and I Want to Win," YouTube, June 17, 2019, https://www.youtube.com/watch?v=4EA9p9K1siA&list=PL7Q2Wk9q9OZLH3Fb22a9J1W3CZE9ZsHs8&index=2&t=0s.

56. Hume, "Russian Neo-Nazi."

57. Vaccaro and Swauger, Unleashing Manhood, 24.

58. Vaccaro and Swauger, 86.

59. Zidan, "Kampf der Nibelungen."

60. Hume, "Russian Neo-Nazi."

61. Karim Zidan, "Battle of the Nibelungen: The Dangerous Evolution of Neo-Nazi Fight Clubs in Germany," SBNation, Bloody Elbow, October 1, 2019, https://www.bloodyelbow.com/2019/10/1/20891729/dangerous-evolution-neo-nazi-fight-club-germany-far-right-mma-politics-feature.

62. Matt Miller, "Sorry Chuck Palahniuk, Fight Club Did Not Invent the Alt-Right's Favorite Insult," Esquire, January 30, 2017, https://www.esquire.com/entertainment/books/news/a52667/chuck-palahniuk-snowflake-alt-right-origin/.

63. See, e.g., Anand, "Anxious Sexualities"; Linke, "Gendered Difference," and German Bodies; Omel'chenko, "In Search of Intimacy"; Tumblety, Remaking the Male Body.

64. Surak, Making Tea, Making Japan, 5.

65. M. Messner, "Boyhood," 439.

66. See especially Vaccaro, Schrock, and McCabe, "Managing Emotional Manhood"; Vaccaro and Swauger, Unleashing Manhood.

67. Vaccaro and Swauger, Unleashing Manhood, 16–17.

68. Connell, Masculinities.

69. Meuser, Geschlect und Männlichkeit; Virchow, "Tapfer, stolz, opferbereit."

70. Green, "Tales from the Mat," esp. 421.

71. Channon and Matthews, "'It Is What It Is.'"

72. This doctrine was quoted in a 2014 essay by Anton Shekhovtsov, "Russian Extreme-Right White Rex Organisation Engaged in Training British Neo-Nazi Thugs," Interpreter, November 10, 2014, http://www.interpretermag.com/russian-extreme-right-white-rex-organisation-engaged-in-training-british-neo-nazi-thugs/. The link to the original doctrine is no longer functional, and neither is the "about us" section of White Rex's website, which used similar language in describing itself as advocating "pan-European pride and traditional values" and "encourag[ing] all Europeans to embrace the warrior spirit of their ancestors, and fight

back against the modern world." White Rex Store website, accessed February 27, 2020, www
.whiterexstore.com/about_us.

73. Colborne, "Friday Night Fights."

74. See Zidan, "Fascism in MMA."

75. White Rex's now-defunct Tumblr page, http://white-rex.tumblr.com/, accessed
June 22, 2018.

76. Aaron Winter, "Island Retreat: On Hate, Violence, and the Murder of Jo Cox," Open
Democracy, June 20, 2016, https://www.opendemocracy.net/en/opendemocracyuk/island
-retreat-on-hate-violence-and-murder-of-jo-cox/. Also see Philip Dewey, "Britain First Have Been
Holding an 'Activist Training Camp' in the Welsh Mountains," Wales Online, June 15, 2016, https://
www.walesonline.co.uk/news/wales-news/britain-first-been-holding-activist-11474970.

77. Belew, Bring the War Home, 193.

78. Belew, 40.

79. Belew, 34–39.

80. Belew, 33.

81. VICE News first broke the story of The Base in November 2018; a follow-up story in
summer 2019 reported on The Base's planning for a paramilitary-style "hate camp" in Washington State. See Mack Lamoureux and Ben Makuch, "Militant Neo-Nazo Group Actively Recruiting
Ahead of Alleged Training Camp," VICE News, August 16, 2019, https://www.vice.com/en_ca
/article/bjwx55/militant-neo-nazi-group-actively-recruiting-ahead-of-alleged-training-camp.

82. "The German Association of Martial Arts Schools against Violent Extremism," German
Institute on Radicalization and De-radicalization Studies, n.d., accessed February 27, 2020,
http://girds.org/projects.

83. As reported by Anne Armbrecht and Alexander Fröhlich, "Neonazis rüsten sich mit
Kampfsport für den 'Tag X,'" Der Tagesspiegel, September 9, 2019, https://www.tagesspiegel.de
/politik/erstarken-der-rechtsextremen-szene-neonazis-ruesten-sich-mit-kampfsport-fuer-den
-tag-x/25047084.html.

84. "Round 1 Awarded Projects," Institute for Strategic Dialogue, n.d., accessed February 27,
2020, https://www.isdglobal.org/innovation-fund/innovation-fund-round-1/.

85. Hume, "Russian Neo-Nazi."

Chapter 5

1. For more on the incident see, for example, "Nationalists Disrupt D.C. Bookstore Chanting 'This Land Is Our Land,'" CBS News, April 27, 2019, https://www.cbsnews.com/news
/politics-and-prose-nationalists-disrupt-dc-bookstore-chanting-this-land-is-our-land/.

2. Hayes Hickman, "Fire Destroys a Building at the Highlander Center, Burning 'Decades
of Archives,'" Knox News, April 3, 2019.

3. Dorman, "White Power Symbol."

4. Elizabeth King, "Why Fascists Storm Bookstores," Nation, May 20, 2019.

5. King.

6. Rietzschel, "Rechtsextreme machen Krawall."

7. For more coverage of the Syracuse incidents, see Mirna Alsharif, Rob Frehse, and Eric
Levenson, "Syracuse University Student Arrested after Graffiti Appears Supporting Protests

against Racism on Campus," CNN, November 21, 2019, https://www.cnn.com/2019/11/21/us
/syracuse-university-students-suspended/index.html; Teri Weaver, "#NotAgainSU: A Timeline of Racist Incidents at Syracuse University," Syracuse.com, November 22, 2019, https://www
.syracuse.com/syracuse-university/2019/11/notagainsu-a-timeline-of-racist-incidents-at
-syracuse-university.html.

8. Initial reports, from a variety of national media outlets, claimed the manifesto had been
shared online and AirDropped over Apple's platform to students' phones in the university li-
brary. After an investigation, however, the university chancellor noted that there was no evidence that any students had received the manifesto on their phones, describing this particular
detail as a likely hoax. However, the document was shared with a link on a Greekrank.com
discussion board as well as on a university discussion page, and was then deleted several hours
after it was posted. See Catherine Leffert, "Syracuse Police Find No Devices that Received
White Supremacist Manifesto So Far," *Daily Orange*, November 21, 2019, http://dailyorange
.com/2019/11/syracuse-police-department-finds-no-devices-received-white-manifesto
-investigation-continues/. Also see "Reports of Racist Manifesto at Syracuse University Likely
a Hoax, Chancellor Says," *CBS News*, November 21, 2019, https://www.cbsnews.com/news
/syracuse-university-kent-syverud-reports-of-racist-manifesto-likely-hoax-chancellor-says/.

9. Tyler Blint-Welsh, "Cuomo Calls for Monitor to Probe Racist Incidents at Syracuse
University," *Wall Street Journal*, November 19, 2019, https://www.wsj.com/articles/cuomo-calls
-for-monitor-to-probe-racist-incidents-at-syracuse-university-11574207264.

10. Greta Anderson, "White Supremacy in the Classroom," *Inside Higher Ed.*, December 11,
2019, https://www.insidehighered.com/news/2019/12/11/georgia-southern-student-promotes
-white-supremacist-theory-class.

11. Charles Huckabee, "Berkeley Cancels a Talk by Milo Yiannopoulos as Violent Protests
Break Out," *Chronicle of Higher Education*, February 2, 2017.

12. Gavriel Rosenfeld, "When an Actual Nazi Spoke on an American College Campus,"
Forward, November 28, 2016, https://forward.com/culture/355112/when-an-actual-nazi-spoke
-on-an-american-college-campus/.

13. I am indebted to Jon Friedman for discussions on this point. The 1978 US Supreme
Court Case, *Village of Skokie v. National Socialist Party of America* (432 U.S. 43), is perhaps the
best example of how the United States protects hateful speech, including the display of swastikas, under free-speech laws. See Chris Demaske, "*Village of Skokie v. National Socialist Part of
America (Ill) (1978)*," *The First Amendment Encyclopedia*, n.d., accessed February 27, 2020,
https://www.mtsu.edu/first-amendment/article/728/village-of-skokie-v-national-socialist
-party-of-america-ill. For an academic analysis and comparison of the United States and other
European countries see Bleich, *Freedom to be Racist*.

14. Huckabee, "Berkeley Cancels a Talk." On Yiannopoulos's ban from entering Australia,
see the discussion in Australia's public broadcasting service: Tyron Butson, "Milo Yiannopoulos
Banned from Australia over Christchurch Comment," *SBS News*, March 16, 2019, https://www
.sbs.com.au/news/milo-yiannopoulos-banned-from-australia-over-christchurch-comment. On
the shooting at the University of Washington, see "Couple Charged in Shooting of Protester at
Milo Yiannopoulos Event in Seattle," *Guardian*, April 25, 2017, https://www.theguardian.com
/us-news/2017/apr/25/milo-yiannopoulos-event-shooting-couple-charged-seattle.

15. See Katherine Mangan, "Richard Spencer, White Supremacist, Describes Goals of His 'Danger Tour' to College Campuses," *Chronicle of Higher Education*, November 28, 2016; and Katherine Mangan, "A White Supremacist Comes to Auburn," *Chronicle of Higher Education*, April 19, 2017. On Spencer's entry ban to twenty-six EU countries, see Maya Oppenheimer, "White Supremacist Richard Spencer 'Banned from 26 European Countries,'" *Independent*, November 23, 2017, https://www.independent.co.uk/news/world/americas /richard-spencer-ban-european-countries-alt-right-white-supremacist-neo-nazi-eu -a8071971.html. Also see Chris Graham, "Nazi Salutes and White Supremacism: Who Is Richard Spencer, the 'Racist Academic' behind the 'Alt Right' Movement?" *The Telegraph*, November 22, 2016, https://www.telegraph.co.uk/news/0/richard-spencer-white-nationalist -leading-alt-right-movement/.

16. "Richard Spencer: Five Things to Know," ADL, n.d., accessed February 27, 2020, https:// www.adl.org/news/article/richard-spencer-five-things-to-know.

17. The issue of free speech on US university campuses is extraordinarily complicated in ways that deserve more analysis than this chapter can provide. I am indebted to Jon Friedman, PEN America's Campus Free Speech Project director, for helpful discussions that informed my thinking. For a good analysis, see PEN America's reports: *Chasm in the Classroom* and *And Campus For All*. Also see Binder and Wood, *Becoming Right*, for a discussion of the broader landscape and tensions on college campuses around politics and provocation, and Martin and Tecklenburg, "White Nationalist on Campus," for an overview of current campus dilemmas around free speech and far-right speakers.

18. For media coverage see, for example, James Doubert, "Breitbart Editor's Event Canceled as Protests Turn Violent at UC Berkeley," *Two Way*, February 2, 2017, https://www.npr.org /sections/thetwo-way/2017/02/02/512992000/breitbart-editors-event-canceled-as-protests -turn-violent-at-uc-berkeley.

19. Samantha Raphelson, "Milo Yiannopoulos' 'Free Speech Week' at Berkeley Falls Apart, Organizers Say," NPR, September 17, 2017, https://www.npr.org/2017/09/22/552427627/why -a-potential-free-speech-week-at-berkeley-is-causing-a-stir.

20. Doubert, "Breitbart Editor's Event Canceled."

21. Heer, "Like Dr. Frankenstein."

22. TPUSA has been repeatedly embroiled in controversies related to its hosting of the blacklisting website "Professor Watchlist," racist statements from various TPUSA employees, and the appearance of white-supremacist groups at Turning Point events, although the group has repeatedly officially distanced itself from the "alt-right" and white-supremacist groups. See Turning Point USA's description of its mission and its campus reach at its website, https://www .tpusa.com/ourmission. Also see Heer, "Like Dr. Frankenstein."

23. As detailed in Jane Coaston, "Why Alt-Right Trolls Shouted Down Donald Trump, Jr.," *Vox*, November 11, 2019, https://www.vox.com/policy-and-politics/2019/11/11/20948317/alt -right-donald-trump-jr-conservative-tpusa-yaf-racism-antisemitism; see also Heer, "Like Dr. Frankenstein."

24. Heer, "Like Dr. Frankenstein."

25. See Martin and Tecklenberg, "White Nationalist on Campus."

26. I am indebted to Kai Drekheimer for discussions about this point.

27. Earl Rinehart, "Ohio State Could Learn from Florida's Security for Richard Spencer's Speech," *MyTownNEO*, October 24, 2017, https://www.mytownneo.com/news/20171024/ohio -state-could-learn-from-floridas-security-for-richard-spencers-speech?template=ampart.

28. Jeremy Bauer-Wolf, "Reclaiming their Campuses," *Inside Higher Ed.*, March 21, 2018, https://www.insidehighered.com/news/2018/03/21/colleges-changing-their-policies-after -visits-controversial-speakers.

29. Scott Jaschik, "Confronting 'It's OK to Be White' Posters," *Inside Higher Ed.*, November 5, 2018, https://www.insidehighered.com/news/2018/11/05/campuses-confront-spread-its -ok-be-white-posters.

30. For an analysis of the renewed use of paper propaganda by the far right, see Castle, Kristiansen, and Shifflett, "White Racial Activism."

31. The 2019 figures come from ADL's report, "ADL: White Supremacist Propaganda Distribution Hit All-Time High in 2019," ADL, February 12, 2020, https://www.adl.org/news/press -releases/adl-white-supremacist-propaganda-distribution-hit-all-time-high-in-2019. Also see ADL, "White Supremacists Continue to Spread Hate on American Campuses," *ADL Blog*, June 27, 2019, https://www.adl.org/blog/white-supremacists-continue-to-spread-hate-on -american-campuses. Also see Cynthia Miller-Idriss and Jonathan Friedman, "When Hate Speech and Free Speech Collide," *Diverse Issues in Higher Education*, December 5, 2018, https:// diverseeducation.com/article/133611/.

32. See "White Supremacist Propaganda on U.S. College Campuses Rises 77 Percent over Past Nine Months: ADL Report," ADL, June 28, 2018, https://www.adl.org/news/press -releases/white-supremacist-propaganda-on-us-college-campuses-rises-77-percent-over-past. Also see Jennifer Calfas, "White Supremacist Propaganda Swells to Record Levels on Campuses," *Wall Street Journal*, June 27, 2019, https://www.wsj.com/articles/white-supremacist -propaganda-swells-to-record-levels-on-campuses-11561654393.

33. NBC news reporting described in Anna Schechter, "White Nationalist Leader is Plotting to 'Take Over the GOP,'" *NBC News*, October 17, 2018, https://www.nbcnews.com/politics /immigration/white-nationalist-leader-plotting-take-over-gop-n920826. On entryism, see Burley and Reid Ross, "All You Have to Do."

34. Burley and Reid Ross.

35. Burley and Reid Ross.

36. Burley and Reid Ross.

37. Josh Harkinson, "The Push to Enlist 'Alt Right' Recruits on College Campuses," *Mother Jones*, December 6, 2016, as cited in Burley and Reid Ross.

38. See NBC News's *Today Show* clip, "How White Nationalists Are Trying to Infiltrate Campuses," *Today*, October 17, 2018, https://www.today.com/video/how-white-nationalists -are-trying-to-infiltrate-campuses-1346218563687.

39. Schechter.

40. Quoted in "James Orien Allsup," SPLC, n.d., accessed February 27, 2020, https://www .splcenter.org/fighting-hate/extremist-files/individual/james-orien-allsup, and cited in Burley and Reid Ross, "All You Have to Do."

41. See interview of Syracuse student by Anderson Cooper: "Syracuse Student after Racist Incidents: 'I Don't Feel Safe,'" *Full Circle*, CNN, November 18, 2019, https://www.cnn.com/videos /us/2019/11/18/syracuse-university-student-racist-incidents-protests-acfc-full-episode-vpx.cnn.

42. In August 2019, Dumpson won a lawsuit against Anglin and was awarded $725,000. For media coverage see, for example, "AU's First Black Woman Student President Awarded $725,000 in Case against Neo-Nazi Website Founder," *NBC Washington*, August 9, 2019, https://www.nbcwashington.com/news/local/AUs-First-Black-Woman-Student-President-Awarded-725000-in-Case-Against-Neo-Nazi-Website-Founder-531392681.html. Also see the New York Times' coverage of the harassment against Dumpson in Zraick, Karen. "Student Targeted by 'Troll Storm' Hopes Settlement Will Send Message to White Supremacists." *The New York Times*, December 21, 2018, https://www.nytimes.com/2018/12/21/us/american-university-racist-hate-training.html.

43. For media coverage of some of the incidents see, for example, Alejandra Matos, "'Racism at AU Is Bananas': Hundreds Protest Incidents on American U. Campus," *Washington Post*, September 19, 2016, https://www.washingtonpost.com/local/education/racism-at-au-is-bananas-hundreds-protest-incidents-on-american-u-campus/2016/09/19/4526a4ba-7e97-11e6-9070-5c4905bf40dc_story.html.

44. In mid-December 2019, hate crime charges were dropped because the judge ruled that the prosecution had failed to meet the burden of proof that the murder was motivated solely by race. One day later, the perpetrator was found guilty in the fatal stabbing death, and sentencing as of the time of this writing is delayed due to COVID-19. See Mike Hellgren, "Sean Urbanski Found Guilty in Richard Collins III's Fatal Stabbing," *CBS Baltimore*, December 18, 2019, https://baltimore.cbslocal.com/2019/12/18/sean-urbanski-case-jury-verdict-richard-collins-latest/. Also see "Hearing Delayed for Sean Urbanki Facing Hate-Crime Charge in Fatal Stabbing of Richard Collins III," *CBS Baltimore*, May 30, 2019, https://baltimore.cbslocal.com/2019/05/30/sean-urbanski-facing-hate-crime-charge-in-stabbing/.

45. Jake Sheridan, "Incidents on Campus Part of National Trend, Says Southern Poverty Law Center," *Chronicle*, November 26, 2018, https://www.dukechronicle.com/article/2018/11/hate-on-campus-part-of-national-trend-says-southern-poverty-law-center; also see Miller-Idriss and Friedman, "Hate Speech and Free Speech Collide."

46. Bauman, "Hate Crimes on Campuses."

47. Coleen Flaherty, "Belly of the Beast," *Inside Higher Ed.*, August 14, 2017, https://www.insidehighered.com/news/2017/08/14/sociologists-seek-systematic-response-online-targeting-and-threats-against-public.

48. See "Faculty under Attack," a website set up by Sociologists for Women in Society with resources and recommendations for scholars and institutions facing attacks: https://socwomen.org/public-targeted-online-harassment/. For additional examples, see Ferber, " Willing to Die," and "New Methods and Consequences."

49. Daniels, "Far-Right Attacks Faculty Online."

50. This isn't limited to the extreme right, of course; there have also long been conservative attacks on the purported liberal bias of universities. For discussion see, for example, Gross, *Why Are Professors Liberal*; Graham Vyse, "Liberals Can't Ignore the Right's Hatred for Academia," *New Republic*, July 13, 2017, https://newrepublic.com/article/143844/liberals-cant-ignore-rights-hatred-academia; Neil Gross, "The Indoctrination Myth," *New York Times*, March 3, 2012, https://www.nytimes.com/2012/03/04/opinion/sunday/college-doesnt-make-you-liberal.html?mtrref=undefined&gwh=F2D45B90FA4005BEF82B9FCA70A3EDFB&gwt=pay&assetType=REGIWALL; Lichtenstein, "US Sociology in Decline?"; Nicole Hemmer,

"Eternally Frustrated by "Liberal" Universities, Conservatives Now Want to Tear Them Down," *Vox*, March 8, 2017, https://www.vox.com/the-big-idea/2017/3/7/14841292/liberal-universities -conservative-faculty-sizzler-pc.

51. See, e.g., Tait, "Mencius Moldbug and Neoreaction."

52. Ari Paul, "Cultural Marxism: The Mainstreaming of a Nazi Trope," Fairness and Accuracy in Reporting, June 4, 2019, https://fair.org/home/cultural-marxism-the-mainstreaming -of-a-nazi-trope/.

53. Phillips-Fein, "Learned to Loathe."

54. The Anti-Defamation League reported that, in March 2018, Yiannopoulos announced that the charity administering the grant had closed. "Milo Yiannopoulos: Five Things to Know," ADL, n.d., accessed February 27, 2020, https://www.adl.org/resources/backgrounders/milo -yiannopoulos-five-things-to-know.

55. Nichols, *Death of Expertise*. Also see the discussion in Adam Frank, "Why Expertise Matters," NPR, April 7, 2017, https://www.npr.org/sections/13.7/2017/04/07/522992390/why -expertise-matters.

56. Muirhead and Rosenblum, *People Are Saying*, 5–6.

57. Muirhead and Rosenblum, 6–7.

58. Phillips-Fein, "Learned to Loathe."

59. See Social Science Research Council, *To Secure Knowledge*.

60. Stanley, *How Fascism Works*.

61. Parker, " Growing Partisan Divide."

62. Some of the arguments in this section were first developed in Cynthia Miller-Idriss, "The Far Right's Love/Hate Relationship with Social Science," *Times Higher Education*, September 18, 2018, https://www.timeshighereducation.com/blog/far-rights-lovehate-relationship-social -science; Putnam, *Bowling Alone*.

63. See, for example, the National Policy Institute's essay "'2050' Is Coming Sooner Than We Thought," NPI, August 17, 2018, https://nationalpolicy.institute/2018/08/17/2050-is -coming-sooner-than-we-thought/.

64. Catherine Hickley, "US Museum Criticises Use of Gérôme's Slave Market in German Right-Wing Campaign," *Art Newspaper*, April 30, 2019, https://www.theartnewspaper.com /news/us-museum-protests-use-of-gerome-s-slave-market-in-german-right-wing-campaign.

65. Valencia-Garcia, "Far Right Revisionism."

66. Silva, "*Reconquista* Revisited," 65, 59. As in the now-defunct Generation Identity UK website, "What Does the Term 'Reconquista' Mean?" "FAQ" section, n.d., accessed November 8, 2019, https://www.generation-identity.org.uk/faqs/; Valencia-Garcia, " Rise and Fall." For a deeper discussion of the Crusades and how they have been used over the past two centuries in a variety of modern political contexts, see Horswell and Awan, *Engaging the Crusades*.

67. Emma Yeomans, "The Far Right Is Using Antiquity to Re-brand Itself—but Classicists Are Fighting Back," *New Statesman America*, July 4, 2018, https://www.newstatesman.com /politics/media/2018/07/far-right-using-antiquity-re-brand-itself-classicists-are-fighting-back.

68. Margaret Talbot, "The Myth of Whiteness in Classical Sculpture," *New Yorker*, October 22, 2018, https://www.newyorker.com/magazine/2018/10/29/the-myth-of-whiteness-in -classical-sculpture.

69. As cited in the Pharos essay, "A New Roman Empire for White People," Pharos, July 26, 2019, http://pages.vassar.edu/pharos/2019/07/26/a-new-roman-empire-for-white-people/#more-3117. The essay links to an archived version of a transcript of Spencer's speech in order to "avoid generating traffic to his blog."

70. Bond, "Classical World in Color." On the harassment campaign, see Chris Quintana, "For One Scholar, an Online Stoning Tests the Limits of Public Scholarship," *Chronicle of Higher Education*, June 16, 2017, https://www.chronicle.com/article/For-One-Scholar-an-Online/240384.

71. Bond, "Classical World in Color."

72. Bond.

73. See, for example, McCoskey, "Greeks Bearing Gifts."

74. See the Pharos website at http://pages.vassar.edu/pharos/.

75. Saini, *Superior*, 86.

76. Mark Sedgwick makes this point in the comprehensive introduction to his edited volume on radical right intellectuals: Sedgwick, introduction to *Key Thinkers*, xiii.

77. Griffin, "Between Metapolitics and *Apoliteia*."

78. For a readable overview of the *Nouvelle Droit*, see Mudde, *Far Right Today*.

79. Valencia-Garcia, "Rise and Fall."

80. See Conor Friedersdorf, "How *Breitbart* Destroyed Andrew Breitbart's Legacy," *Atlantic*, November 14, 2017, https://www.theatlantic.com/politics/archive/2017/11/how-breitbart-destroyed-andrew-breitbarts-legacy/545807/.

81. Stern, *Proud Boys*, 22–23.

82. Mark Townsend, "Infiltrator Exposes Generation Identity UK's March Towards Extreme Far Right," *Guardian*, August 24, 2019, https://www.theguardian.com/world/2019/aug/24/generation-identity-uk-far-right-extremists.

83. Macklin, "Greg Johnson," 204.

84. Far-right intellectuals were not the only ones vying for alternative places and spaces for expertise and knowledge. American conservative activists had also pursued a strategy of creating what Kimberly Phillips-Fein described as "conservative intellectual networks" and "versions of higher education in keeping with their values." Their rationale was that the modern university's culture was so antithetical to conservative Christian values and capitalist norms that the only option was to build "alternative institutions. Mainstream higher education was beyond saving." Far-right efforts to build dedicated expertise take the same approach, but promote knowledge and views far outside the boundaries of even the most conservative intellectuals, including racist, white-supremacist, antidemocratic, and antiegalitarian views. See Phillips-Fein, "Learned to Loathe."

85. Stern, *Proud Boys*, p. 27.

86. Original quote from Greg Johnson's Counter-Currents publication "Metapolitics and Occult Warfare, Part 4," cited in Macklin, "Greg Johnson," 207.

87. Macklin, "Greg Johnson," 209–10.

88. Joel Rose, "Calls Grow for Stephen Miller to Leave White House after Leaked Emails," *All Things Considered*, NPR, November 25, 2019, https://www.npr.org/2019/11/25/782732922/calls-grow-for-stephen-miller-to-leave-white-house-after-leaked-emails.

89. Tait, "Mencius Moldbug and Neoreaction," 194–95, 187.

90. Simon Parkin, "The Rise of Russia's Neo-Nazi Soccer Hooligans," *Guardian*, April 24, 2018, https://www.theguardian.com/news/2018/apr/24/russia-neo-nazi-football-hooligans-world-cup. Also quoted in Karim Zidan's 2018 essay for the *Guardian*, "Fascist Fight Clubs."

91. Nellie Bowles, "Right-Wing Views for Generation Z, Five Minutes at a Time," *New York Times*, January 4, 2020, https://www.nytimes.com/2020/01/04/us/politics/dennis-prager-university.html; Marc Oppenheimer, "Inside the Right-Wing YouTube Empire that's Quietly Turning Millennials into Conservatives," *Mother Jones*, March/April 2018, https://www.motherjones.com/politics/2018/03/inside-right-wing-youtube-turning-millennials-conservative-prageru-video-dennis-prager/.

92. Bar-On, "Richard B. Spencer."

93. Teitelbaum, "Daniel Friberg and Metapolitics," 269; also see Valencia-Garcia, "Rise and Fall."

94. For a detailed discussion, see Valencia-Garcia, "Rise and Fall."

95. Elizabeth Zerofsky, "Steve Bannon's Roman Holiday," *New Yorker*, April 11, 2019, https://www.newyorker.com/news/dispatch/steve-bannons-roman-holiday.

96. See Maïa de La Baume, "France's Far Right Finishing School," *Politico*, September 14, 2018, https://www.politico.eu/article/france-far-right-finishing-school-lyon-issep-marion-marechal/.

97. As detailed in Mudde, *Far Right Today*.

98. As detailed in Bellingcat Anti-Equality Monitoring, "How to Mainstream Neo-Nazis: A Lesson from Ukraine's C14 and an Estonian Think Tank," Bellingcat, August 8, 2019, https://www.bellingcat.com/news/uk-and-europe/2019/08/08/how-to-mainstream-neo-nazis-a-lesson-from-ukraines-c14-and-an-estonian-think-tank/. Also see Zerofsky, "Steve Bannon's Roman Holiday." On the Lyon training academy, see Elaine Ganley, "Rising French Far-Right Star Resurfaces and Flirts with Fire," *Associated Press*, July 7, 2019, https://www.apnews.com/c cb8813cc9dc47e8b6b332994da6d282.

99. See Göpffarth, "Rethinking the German Nation."

100. Valencia-Garcia, "Rise and Fall."

101. For an overview, see Pascoe, "Miscegenation Law."

102. Saini, *Superior*, 74.

103. Evans, *Skin Deep*, 217.

104. Evans, 217.

105. Evans, 217–18; "Pioneer Fund," SPLC, n.d., accessed March 12, 2020, https://www.splcenter.org/fighting-hate/extremist-files/group/pioneer-fund.

106. Saini *Superior*, 68–69.

107. Stern, *Proud Boys*, 90.

108. Saini, *Superior*, 75.

109. Evans, *Skin Deep*, 225.

110. Saini, *Superior*, 81; Evans, *Skin Deep*, 228.

111. Evans, *Skin Deep*, 219–21.

112. See discussion of Rushton and his relationship to the Pioneer Fund in the SPLC's page "Pioneer Fund."

113. Peter Beinart, "A Violent Attack on Free Speech at Middlebury," *Atlantic*, March 6, 2017, https://www.theatlantic.com/politics/archive/2017/03/middlebury-free-speech-violence/518667/.

114. Evans, *Skin Deep*, 214.

115. Beinart, "Violent Attack"; Allison Stanger, "Understanding the Angry Mob at Middlebury that Gave Me a Concussion," *New York Times*, March 13, 2017, https://www.nytimes.com /2017/03/13/opinion/understanding-the-angry-mob-that-gave-me-a-concussion.html.

116. Evans, Skin Deep, 215. Also see Burley and Reid Ross. "All You Have to Do."

117. Evans, *Skin Deep*, 215.

118. Evans, 215.

119. Ezra Klein, "Sam Harris, Charles Murray, and the Allure of Race Science," *Vox*, March 27, 2019, https://www.vox.com/policy-and-politics/2018/3/27/15695060/sam-harris-charles -murray-race-iq-forbidden-knowledge-podcast-bell-curve.

120. Klein.

121. Morning, *Nature of Race*.

122. Evans, *Skin Deep*, 296.

123. Khalil Gibran Muhammed, "How the Alt-Right Uses Social Science to Make Racism Respectable," *Nation*, January 15, 2018.

124. Evans, *Skin Deep*, 298–99.

125. Saini, *Superior*, 68–69.

126. Tucker, *Racial Research*, 251; also see p. 252 for discussion of how FHU and TRF helped promote research and publications on "heredity, intelligence, and race."

127. See discussion of the Ulster Institute for Social Research in Saini, *Superior*, 68–71. For more on the Pioneer Fund, see the discussion in Saini and the overview by the SPLC, "Pioneer Fund."

128. Evans, *Skin Deep*, 235; also see Kevin Rawlinson and Richard Adams, "UCL to Investigate Eugenics Conference Secretly Held on Campus," *Guardian*, January 11, 2018, https://www .theguardian.com/education/2018/jan/10/ucl-to-investigate-secret-eugenics-conference-held -on-campus.

129. "UCL Statement on the London Conference on Intelligence," UCL, January 18, 2018, https://www.ucl.ac.uk/news/2018/jan/ucl-statement-london-conference-intelligence-0; also see Ben Van der Merwe, "It Might Be a Pseudo Science, but Students Take the Threat of Eugenics Seriously," *New Statesman America*, February 19, 2018, https://www.newstatesman.com /politics/education/2018/02/it-might-be-pseudo-science-students-take-threat-eugenics -seriously.

130. Evans, *Skin Deep*, 4–5.

131. Saini, *Superior*, 92.

132. Stern, *Proud Boys*, 92.

133. Cloud, "Right-Wing Attacks."

Chapter 6

1. Baldauf, Ebner, and Guhl, *Hate Speech and Radicalisation*, 12. Also see Koehler, " Radical Online."

2. Davey and Ebner, *Fringe Insurgency*, 8.

3. For a rich discussion of the global ecology of hate and how these clusters adapt and move between platforms see N. Johnson et al., "Hidden Resilience." Also see the discussion in

Noemi Derzsy, "Strategies for Combating Online Hate," *Nature*, News and Views, 21 August 2019, https://www.nature.com/articles/d41586-019-02447-1. For an overview of the range of issues related to online spaces and radicalization, see Fielitz and Thurston, *Post-Digital Cultures*. My arguments about bans were partially developed in Cynthia Miller-Idriss, "Why Banning Hate Groups Won't End Them," *Huffington Post*, August 24, 2017, https://www.huffpost.com/entry/hate-groups-ban_b_599ca5a5e4b0d8dde999a009.

4. Janko Roettgers, "How YouTube's Far Right Is Using Classic Influencer Tactics to Promote Its Views," *Variety*, September 18, 2018, https://variety.com/2018/digital/news/youtube-far-right-influencers-1202946918/.

5. Cynthia Miller-Idriss and Daniel Köhler, "The United German Right," Open Democracy, September 10, 2018, https://www.opendemocracy.net/en/can-europe-make-it/united-german-extreme-right/ (originally published in French as "En Allemagne, 'un niveau de coopération inédit entre les groupes d'extrême droite,'" *Le Monde*, 8 September 2018, https://www.lemonde.fr/idees/article/2018/09/06/chemnitz-un-niveau-de-cooperation-inedit-entre-les-groupes-d-extreme-droite_5350930_3232.html).

6. Elizabeth Flock, "Spotify Has Removed White Power Music from Its Platform. But It's Still Available on Dozens of Other Sites," *PBS Newshour*, August 18, 2017, https://www.pbs.org/newshour/arts/spotify-removed-white-power-music-platform-still-available-dozens-sites.

7. See Samuel Gibbs, "Apple Denounces Neo-Nazis as Spotify Bans 'White Power' Tracks," *Guardian*, August 17, 2017, https://www.theguardian.com/technology/2017/aug/17/apple-denounces-neo-nazis-as-spotify-bans-white-power-tracks; also see Julia Carrie Wong, "Tech Companies Turn on Daily Stormer and the 'Alt-Right' after Charlottesville," *Guardian*, August 14, 2017, https://www.theguardian.com/technology/2017/aug/14/daily-stormer-alt-right-google-go-daddy-charlottesville.

8. See Neumann, foreword to Baldauf, Ebner, and Guhl, *Hate Speech and Radicalisation*.

9. Sunstein, *Going to Extremes*.

10. See Zannettou et al., "Understanding Online Antisemitism." Also see the discussion in the ADL's report "Gab and 8chan."

11. See the report from the ADL's Center on Extremism in partnership with the Network Contagion Research Institute, which analyzed social-media data: "When Twitter Bans Extremists, Gab Puts out the Welcome Mat," ADL, March 11, 2019, https://www.adl.org/blog/when-twitter-bans-extremists-gab-puts-out-the-welcome-mat.

12. For more on VKontake see Masood Farivar, "US White Nationalists Barred by Facebook Find Haven on Russia Site," *Voice of America News*, April 10, 2019, https://www.voanews.com/usa/us-white-nationalists-barred-facebook-find-haven-russia-site.

13. N. Johnson et al., "Hidden Resilience," 2.

14. See discussion of alternative platforms in Keatinge, Keen, and Izenman, "Fundraising," 18–19.

15. Michelle Castillo, "The Far Right Uses This Site to Fund Its Favorite Causes—and Its Founder Hopes to Build a 'Very Profitable Business,'" CNBC, June 24, 2017, https://www.cnbc.com/2017/06/24/wesearchr-charles-johnson-alt-right-causes.html.

16. Keatinge, Keen, and Izenman, "Fundraising," 19.

17. Keatinge, Keen, and Izenman, 19.

18. Keatinge, Keen, and Izenman, 19.

19. David Heath and Kevin Crowe, "Sites Like Facebook, Google and Twitter Allowed White Supremacists to Flourish. Now What?" *USA Today*, August 21, 2019, https://www.usatoday.com/story/news/investigations/2019/08/21/4-chan-el-paso-new-zealand-shooter-white-supremacy/2054378001/; Lizzie Deardon, "Man Who Stormed Mosque 'Armed with Shotguns' Was Inspired by Christchurch and El Paso Attackers, Messaging Board Post Suggests," *Independent*, August 11, 2019, https://www.independent.co.uk/news/world/europe/norway-mosque-shooting-attack-suspect-philip-manshaus-christchurch-el-paso-4chan-a9052106.html.

20. April Glaser, "Telegram Was Built for Democracy Activists. White Nationalists Love It," *Slate*, August 8, 2019, https://slate.com/technology/2019/08/telegram-white-nationalists-el-paso-shooting-facebook.html.

21. Tess Owens, "How Telegram Became White Nationalists' Go-To Messaging Platform," *VICE News*, October 7, 2019, https://www.vice.com/en_us/article/59nk3a/how-telegram-became-white-nationalists-go-to-messaging-platform.

22. Johnson et al., "Hidden Resilience," 2.

23. Isaac Saul, "This Twitter Alternative Was Supposed to Be Nicer, but Bigots Love It Already," *Forward*, July 18, 2019, https://forward.com/news/national/427705/parler-news-white-supremacist-islamophobia-laura-loomer/.

24. Keatinge, Keen, and Izenman, "Fundraising," 20.

25. Ryan Broderick, "iFunny Has Become a Hub for White Nationalism," *Buzzfeed*, August 14, 2019, https://www.buzzfeednews.com/article/ryanhatesthis/the-meme-app-ifunny-is-a-huge-hub-for-white-nationalists.

26. Cyrus Farivar, "Extremists Creep into Roblox, an Online Game Popular with Children," *NBC News*, August 21, 2019, https://www.cnbc.com/2019/08/22/extremists-creep-into-roblox-an-online-game-popular-with-children.html.

27. "Free to Play? Hate, Harassment, and Positive Social Experiences in Online Games," ADL, July 2019, https://www.adl.org/free-to-play.

28. Laurence Dodds, "Why Parents Should Worry Less about Violent Video Games—and More about the Extremist 'Groomers' Who Target Them," *Telegraph*, 9 August 2019, https://www.telegraph.co.uk/technology/2019/08/09/parents-should-worry-less-violent-video-games-extremists-play/; Farivar, "Extremists Creep into Roblox."

29. Nagle, *Kill All Normies*.

30. Salter, "Geek Masculinity to Gamergate," 255.

31. Billy Perrigo, "'A Game of Whack-a-Mole': Why Facebook and Others Are Struggling to Delete Footage of the New Zealand Shooting," *Time*, March 15, 2019, https://time.com/5552367/new-zealand-shooting-video-facebook-youtube-twitter/.

32. Baldauf, Ebner, and Guhl, *Hate Speech and Radicalisation*, citing A. Ritzmann, *Vom Selbst- zum Massenmord: Terroristische Propaganda und die Verantwortung der Media* [From suicide to mass murder: terrorist propaganda and the responsibility of the media], *TV Diskurs*, April 20, 2016 [July 18, 2018], https://tvdiskurs.de/beitrag/vom-selbst-zum-massenmord/.

33. Amy Gunia, "Facebook Tightens Live-Stream Rules in Response to the Christchurch Massacre," *Time*, May 15, 2019, https://time.com/5589478/facebook-livestream-rules-new-zealand-christchurch-attack/.

34. Berger, "Violent White Supremacy."

35. Berger.

36. Berger.

37. Forchtner and Tominc, "Kalashnikov and Cooking-Spoon," 425.

38. Forchtner and Tominc, 425.

39. Holt, "White Supremacy."

40. See especially Nagle, *Kill All Normies*.

41. Neumann, foreword to Baldauf, Ebner, and Guhl, *Hate Speech and Radicalisation*, 5; also see recent data from the California State University San Bernardino Center for the Study of Hate & Extremism's *Report to the Nation*.

42. "White Supremacists Use Black-on-White Crime as Propaganda Tool," ADL, September 7, 2012, https://www.adl.org/news/article/white-supremacists-use-black-on-white-crime -as-propaganda-tool?referrer=https%3A//www.google.com/#.WG53H1MrLcs.

43. Rebecca Hersher, "What Happened When Dylann Roof Asked Google for Information about Race?" *Two-Way*, NPR, January 10, 2017, https://www.npr.org/sections/thetwo-way /2017/01/10/508363607/what-happened-when-dylann-roof-asked-google-for-information -about-race; also see Cory Collins, "The Miseducation of Dylann Roof," *Teaching Tolerance Magazine*, fall 2017, https://www.tolerance.org/magazine/fall-2017/the-miseducation-of -dylann-roof, and Noble, *Algorithms of Oppression*.

44. Noble, *Algorithms of Oppression*.

45. Reed et al., "Radical Filter Bubbles," 5.

46. Reed et al., 4, citing O'Callaghan et al., "(White) Rabbit Hole."

47. Roose, "Caleb Cain."

48. Reed et al., "Radical Filter Bubbles," 4–5, 10; Berger, "Zero Degrees,"; Waters and Postings, *Spiders of the Caliphate*.

49. Roose, "Caleb Cain."

50. See Eli Pariser, "Beware Online Filter Bubbles," TED Talks, March 2011, https://www .ted.com/talks/eli_pariser_beware_online_filter_bubbles?language=en.

51. See Reed et al., "Radical Filter Bubbles," 4.

52. Reed et al., 18.

53. I am indebted to Oren Segal for this point.

54. See Miller-Idriss and Johnson, "Free Advertising."

55. See discussion in Davey and Ebner, *Fringe Insurgency*, 28.

56. Jackson Rawlings, "What Does the X Emoji on Twitter Mean?" *Medium*, August 2, 2018, https://medium.com/the-politicalists/what-does-the-emoji-on-twitter-mean-498ebc861638; also see Amy Harmon, "Why White Supremacists Are Chugging Milk (and Why Geneticists Are Alarmed)," *New York Times*, October 17, 2018, https://www.nytimes.com/2018/10/17/us /white-supremacists-science-dna.html; Iselin Gambert and Tobias Linne, "How the Alt-Right Uses Milk to Promote White Supremacy," *Conversation*, April 26, 2018, http://theconversation .com/how-the-alt-right-uses-milk-to-promote-white-supremacy-94854.

57. For more on the varied meanings of these and other emoji, see Sasha Lekach, "The Real Meaning of All Those Emoji in Twitter Handles," *Mashable*, June 3, 2017, https://mashable.com /2017/06/03/emoji-twitter-handles-meanings/; Jared Holt, "White Nationalists Adopt Clowns as Their Next Racist Symbol (Yes, Seriously)," Right Wing Watch, April 4, 2019, http://www

.rightwingwatch.org/post/white-nationalists-adopt-clowns-as-their-next-racist-symbol-yes
-seriously/.

58. Adam Serwer, "It's Not Easy Being Meme," *Atlantic*, September 13, 2016.

59. Daniels, "Algorithmic Rise," 64.

60. Jessica Roy, "How 'Pepe the Frog' Went from Harmless to Hate Symbol," *Los Angeles Times*, October 11, 2016.

61. Daniels, "Algorithmic Rise."

62. I am indebted to a Nick Thurston and Maik Fielitz for this point and for their insightful editorial review of an earlier version of portions of this chapter more generally.

63. Önnerfors, "'Finspång.'"

64. Sam Sanders, "What Pepe the Frog's Death Can Teach Us about the Internet," *All Things Considered*, NPR, May 11, 2017, https://www.npr.org/sections/alltechconsidered/2017/05/11/527590762/what-pepe-the-frogs-death-can-teach-us-about-the-internet?t=1582035380655.

65. "ADL Adds 'Pepe the Frog' Meme, Used by Anti-Semites and Racists, to Online Hate Symbols Database," ADL, September 27, 2016, https://www.adl.org/news/press-releases/adl-adds-pepe-the-frog-meme-used-by-anti-semites-and-racists-to-online-hate.

66. Baynard Woods, "Where the Hell Is Kekistan?: How Pepe-Posting Meme Warriors Responded to Real Violence of the Alt-Right," *Washington City Paper*, September 27, 2017.

67. Jessica Chasmer, "U.S. Military Contractor Fired over Alt-Right 'Kekistan' Flag Patch," *Washington Times*, September 25, 2018, https://www.washingtontimes.com/news/2018/sep/25/us-military-contractor-fired-after-sporting-alt-ri/; David Neiwert, "What the Kek: Explaining the Alt-Right 'Deity' behind Their 'Meme Magic,'" SPLC, May 9, 2017, https://www.splcenter.org/hatewatch/2017/05/08/what-kek-explaining-alt-right-deity-behind-their-meme-magic. In 2018, cartoonist Matt Furie, Pepe's creator, filed a lawsuit against the media platform Infowars, charging copyright infringement. Joe Sommerlad, "Pepe the Frog Creator Sues Infowars for Breach of Copyright," *Independent*, March 7, 2018.

68. Önnerfors, "'Finspång.'"

69. Önnerfors.

70. See for example Emma Green, "The Tide of Hate Directed against Jewish Journalists," *Atlantic*, October 19, 2016, https://www.theatlantic.com/politics/archive/2016/10/what-its-like-to-be-a-jewish-journalist-in-the-age-of-trump/504635/.

71. Neiwert, *Alt-America*, 256.

72. Marwick and Lewis, *Media Manipulation and Disinformation*, 47. Also see Daniels, *Cyber-Racism*.

73. Marwick and Lewis, *Media Manipulation and Disinformation*, 47. Also see Daniels, *Cyber-Racism*.

74. See, for example, the discussion of shame and online narratives about oversensitivity in Scott Simon and Emma Bowman, "How One Mom Talks to Her Sons about Hate on the Internet," NPR, August 17, 2019, https://www.npr.org/2019/08/17/751986787/writer-joanna-schroeder-on-preventing-teenage-boys-from-turning-to-hate.

75. See California State University San Bernardino Center for the Study of Hate & Extremism, *Report to the Nation*.

76. Davey and Ebner, *Fringe Insurgency*, 7.

77. Davey and Ebner, 26.

78. From Brooks, "Testimony."

79. See Berger "Violent White Supremacy"; quote in Davey and Ebner, *Fringe Insurgency*, 26.

80. Davey and Ebner, *Fringe Insurgency*, 28.

81. See, for example, the discussion of Generation Identity's project of "metapolitics" in Mark Townsend, "Infiltrator Exposes Generation Identity UK's March Towards Extreme Far Right," *Guardian*, August 24, 2019, https://www.theguardian.com/world/2019/aug/24/generation-identity-uk-far-right-extremists.

82. Davey and Ebner, *Fringe Insurgency*, 19.

83. See, for example, Oliver Darcy, "Fox News Stands by Laura Ingraham after She Defends White Supremacist, Other Extremists on Her Prime Time Show," CNN *Business*, May 31, 2019, https://www.cnn.com/2019/05/31/media/laura-ingraham-paul-nehlen-extremists/index.html/; see examples documented in the Media Matters report by Courtney Hagle: "How Fox News Pushed the White Supremacist 'Great Replacement' Theory," *Media Matters*, August 5, 2019, https://www.mediamatters.org/tucker-carlson/how-fox-news-pushed-white-supremacist-great-replacement-theory.

84. Davey and Ebner, *Fringe Insurgency*, 11.

85. Stav Ziv, "Hate Pays: Alt-Right Raises $150,000 to Save Neo-Nazi Website the Daily Stormer," *Newsweek*, June 8, 2017, https://www.newsweek.com/hate-pays-alt-right-raises-150000-save-neo-nazi-website-daily-stormer-623336.

86. Nagle, *Kill All Normies*, 45–46.

87. As reported in Soufan Center, *White Supremacist Extremism*. The Soufan Center report cites the source on Southern's income as Alex Newhouse, "From Classifieds to Crypto: How White Supremacist Groups Have Embraced Crowdfunding," Center on Terrorism, Extremism, and Counterterrorism Publications at the Middlebury Institute of International Studies 72 (June 2019), 9, https://www.middlebury.edu/institute/sites/www.middlebury.edu.institute/files/2019-06/Alex%20Newhouse%20CTEC%20Paper.pdf?fv=9T_mzirH.

88. See, e.g., Salter, "Geek Masculinity to Gamergate," 255.

89. Gabriel Pogrund, Matthew Mulligan, and Keven Donnellan, "YouTube Cashes in on Neo-Nazi's Hate Videos," *The Times*, August 11, 2019, https://www.thetimes.co.uk/article/youtube-cashes-in-on-neo-nazis-hate-videos-9ggonbvd6; also see Alexandra Wells, "YouTube Paid Neo-Nazi Thousands of Dollars for Hate Videos," *Forward*, August 14, 2019, https://forward.com/fast-forward/429555/youtube-neo-nazi-mark-collett-anti-semitism/.

90. Sarah Perez, "YouTube Is Giving Creators More Ways to Make Money," TechCrunch, July 11, 2019, https://techcrunch.com/2019/07/11/youtube-is-giving-creators-more-ways-to-make-money/.

91. Roose, "Caleb Cain."

92. Pogrund, Mulligan, and Donnellan, "YouTube Cashes In." Michael Salter points out that because crowdfunding, social-media, and video-hosting sites earn income from user activity, they profit from controversial or salacious content, including online abuse, in ways that need more attention. See Salter, "Geek Masculinity to Gamergate," 255.

93. For a discussion of the Chemnitz protests, see Cynthia Miller-Idriss and Daniel Köhler, "En Allemagne, 'un niveau de coopération inédit entre les groupes d'extrême droite,'" *Le Monde*, September 8, 2018, https://www.lemonde.fr/idees/article/2018/09/06/chemnitz-un-niveau-de-cooperation-inedit-entre-les-groupes-d-extreme-droite_5350930_3232.html (published in

English as "The United German Right," Open Democracy, September 10, 2018, https://www
.opendemocracy.net/en/can-europe-make-it/united-german-extreme-right/).

94. Tim Hume, "German Neo-Nazis Are Doxxing Journalists on 'Enemy' Lists: 'We Will
Get You All,'" VICE News, August 30, 2019, https://www.vice.com/en_us/article/7x5bga
/german-neo-nazis-are-doxxing-journalists-on-enemy-lists-we-will-get-you-all.

95. Wendy's was celebrated by the "alt right" after a company representative tweeted a meme
of Pepe-as-Wendy on the company's social-media account; the company's official response was
to plead ignorance, noting that the employee who had sent the tweet was "unaware of the recent
evolution of the Pepe meme's meaning." As described in Cristina Maza, "Why Neo-Nazis Love
Papa John's Pizza—and Other 'Official' Alt-Right Companies," Newsweek, November 10, 2017.
In 2017, Zara pulled a denim skirt with a patch depicting a Pepe-like cartoon from both its "real
and virtual shelves" after a customer tweeted an image of the skirt. See discussion in Jessica Roy,
"Zara Pulls Denim Skirt after 'Pepe the Frog' Accusations," Los Angeles Times, April 19, 2017,
https://www.latimes.com/business/la-fi-zara-skirt-pepe-frog-20170419-story.html. Also see
Serwer, "It's Not Easy." For more on Zara's previous controversies, see Lauren Raab, "Zara
Apologizes, Stops Selling Shirt Likened to Holocaust Uniform," Los Angeles Times, August 27,
2014; also see Roy, "Pepe the Frog."

96. Alex Hern, "Antisemitism Watchdog Adds ((((Echo))) Symbol to Hate List after Jews
Targeted," Guardian, June 7, 2016.

97. Bhareth Ganash, "Radical Right Digital Communications: Webforums, Political Blogs,
and the Swarm," Centre for Analysis of the Radical Right, Insight (blog), February 20, 2019,
https://www.radicalrightanalysis.com/2019/02/20/radical-right-digital-communications
-webforums-political-blogs-and-the-swarm/.

Conclusion

1. As explained in Annett Graefe-Geusch's dissertation, "Teaching Ethics for Peace and
Integration: Ethics Teachers and the Question of Diversity in Berlin's Secondary Schools," 2020.
New York University, Ph.D. Dissertation. Graefe-Geusch's research analyzed the need for
inclusive education in the context of Berlin's ethics curriculum.

2. As argued by Mark Potok in his May 15, 2019, keynote, "Two Americas: The Radical
Right, Then and Now," at the Centre for Analysis of the Radical Right's 2019 annual conference
in Richmond, London, and available as a podcast at https://backdoorbroadcasting.net/2019
/06/a-century-of-radical-right-extremism-new-approaches/.

3. See Clayton, "Psychological Approach"; Zoë Henry, "Why Kind Founder Daniel Lu-
betzky Invested $20 Million to Connect Kids around the World," Inc., October 17, 2017, https://
www.inc.com/zoe-henry/kind-founder-empatico.html. The arguments in this section were first
developed in "The Moral World of the Radical Right," Fair Observer, August 7, 2018, https://
www.fairobserver.com/politics/radical-right-ideology-psychology-culture-news-62719/. For
research on mental health problems and violent white-supremacist extremism, see Simi and
Bubolz, "Problem of Overgeneralization."

4. Blazak, "'Getting It.'" Also see Jane Hu, "To Deradicalize Extremists, Former Neo-Nazis
Use a Radical Method: Empathy," Quartz, November 9, 2018, https://qz.com/1457014/to
-deradicalize-extremists-former-neo-nazis-use-a-radical-method-empathy/. For more on

empathy as it relates to the rise of the US far right, see the discussion in Hochschild, *Strangers*. Also see Michaelis and Kaleka, *Gift of Our Wounds*.

5. David Barnes, "The Fascist in the Classroom: Teaching Pound, Race and Radical Right Politics," Centre for Analysis of the Radical Right, April 17, 2018, https://www.radicalrightanalysis .com/2018/04/17/the-fascist-in-the-classroom-teaching-pound-race-and-radical-right-politics/.

6. See especially Kendi, *Antiracist*.

7. Carla Bleiker, "Lonsdale Shows Love for the Left," *Deutsche Welle*, June 3, 2014, https:// www.dw.com/en/lonsdale-shows-love-for-the-left/a-17476089.

8. Futrell and Simi, "Free Spaces." Also see the extensive work by Kathleen Blee on women in the KKK, including *Inside Organized Racism* and *Women of the Klan*.

9. See the English-language website of the Bundesamt für Verfassungsschutz at https:// www.verfassungsschutz.de/en/index-en.html.

10. This section is adapted from Cynthia Miller-Idriss, "How to Counter Far-Right Extremism? Germany Shows the Way," *Guardian*, May 18, 2019, https://www.theguardian.com /commentisfree/2019/may/17/counter-far-right-extremism-germany-uk-teachers, and "L'Allemagne a développé l'approche la plus complète de la lutte contre l'extrême droite," *Le Monde*, April 4, 2019 (published in English as "How to Prevent Hate," Centre for Analysis of the Radical Right, *Insight* [blog], April 9, 2019).

11. See the German-language discussion of the pilot project: "Starke Lehrer gegen Rechtsextremismus," Robert Bosch Foundation, press release, November 2018, https://www.bosch -stiftung.de/en/node/3057.

12. For examples, see the German Federal Agency for Civic Education's description of projects aiming to counter right-wing-extremist attitudes with youth in a variety of school-based and everyday life settings: http://www.bpb.de/lernen/grafstat/rechtsextremismus/172907 /umgang-mit-rechtsextremismus-in-der-schule, and DEVI's (Association for Democracy and Diversity in Schools and Vocational Education) description of its work to counter right-wing extremism, xenophobia, discrimination, and religious-based extremism by strengthening democracy in vocational schools, teacher training, and direct engagement with students: http:// demokratieundvielfalt.de/.

13. For examples, see the website of the Wuppertaler Initiative for Democracy and Tolerance, which includes a link to "Mobile Advice against Right-Wing Extremism" in the Düsseldorf region at https://www.wuppertaler-initiative.de/mobile-beratung-nrw.

14. See the website of Mobile Advice against Right-Wing Extremism in the Detmold region at http://mobile-beratung-owl.de/angebote.html.

15. See the website of the Bundesarbeitsgemeinschaft Kirche & Rechtsextremismus at https://bagkr.de/ueber-uns/organisation/.

16. See, for example, the website for the Soccer Association against the Right Wing, and the part of its page describing the action "We don't rent to Nazis," at: https://www.fussballvereine -gegen-rechts.de/unsere-aktionen/aktion-wir-vermieten-nicht-an-nazis/.

17. For example, see the *Initiative* blog at the Federal Center for Civic Education at http:// www.bpb.de/politik/extremismus/rechtsextremismus/165168/initiativenblog.

18. Austin Davis, "Right-Wing Extremists in Germany to Face Amped Up Intelligence," *Deutsche Welle*, December 17, 2019, https://p.dw.com/p/3Uxfx.

19. "European Intelligence Service See Far-Right Extremism as Growing Threat," France24, March 3, 2019, https://www.france24.com/en/20190319-europe-intelligence-far-right -extremism-growing-threat-christchurch.

20. CNN International, "Jacinda Ardern asks students to help stomp out racism and extremism in New Zealand." https://www.facebook.com/cnninternational/videos/21276603 83995344/

21. Flint, introduction to *Spaces of Hate*, 10.

22. The SPLC, for example, has tracked the rise in white-supremacist propaganda in public space, noting an expansion from the 2016–17 targeting of college campus spaces to more public spaces. See its online tool and a description in "SPLC Releases Online Tool that Tracks Rising Number of Hate Group Flyers and Banners," SPLC, January 11, 2019, https://www.splcenter.org /news/2019/01/11/splc-releases-online-tool-tracks-rising-number-hate-group-flyers-and -banners.

Bibliography

Abramson, Corey M., and Darren Modzelwski. "Caged Morality: Moral Worlds, Subculture, and Stratification among Middle-Class Cage Fighters." *Qualitative Sociology* 34 (2011): 143–75.

———. "Gab and 8chan: Home to Terrorist Plots Hiding in Plain Sight." ADL, n.d., accessed March 5, 2020. https://www.adl.org/resources/reports/gab-and-8chan-home-to-terrorist-plots-hiding-in-plain-sight.

———. "Murder and Extremism in the United States in 2018." ADL, n.d., accessed March 5, 2020. https://www.adl.org/murder-and-extremism-2018.

———. "Murder and Extremism in the United States in 2019." ADL, n.d., accessed February 28, 2020. https://www.adl.org/murder-and-extremism-2019.

———. *The Sounds of Hate: The White Power Movement in the United States.* New York: ADL, 2012. https://www.adl.org/sites/default/files/documents/assets/pdf/combating-hate/Sounds-of-Hate-White-Power-Music-Scene-2012.pdf.

———. "White Supremacists Embrace Acceleration." *ADL Blog*, April 19, 2019. https://www.adl.org/blog/white-supremacists-embrace-accelerationism.

Adams, Tim. "Ultimate Fighting Championship: The Fight of Our Lives?" *Guardian*, March 26, 2017. https://www.theguardian.com/sport/2017/mar/26/ultimate-fighting-championship-fight-of-our-lives-mma-donald-trump-vladimir-putin-conor-mcregor.

Agnew, John. "Space and Place." In *Handbook of Geographical Knowledge*, ed. J. Agnew and D. Livingstone, 316–30. London: SAGE, 2011.

Alba, Richard, and Guillermo Yrizar Barbosa. "Room at the Top?: Minority Mobility and the Transition to Demographic Diversity in the USA." *Ethnic and Racial Studies* 39, no. 6 (2016): 917–38.

Altier, Mary Beth, Emma Leonard Boyle, and John G. Horgan. "Returning to the Fight: An Empirical Analysis of Terrorist Reengagement and Recidivism." *Terrorism and Political Violence* (online), November 18, 2019. doi:10.1080/09546553.2019.1679781.

Anand, Dibyesh. "Anxious Sexualities: Masculinity, Nationalism, and Violence." *British Journal of Politics and International Relations* 9 (2007): 257–69.

Anderson, Benedict. *Imagined Communities: Reflections on the Origin and Spread of Nationalism.* New York: Verso, 1983.

Andreasson, Jesper, and Thomas Johansson. "Negotiating Violence: Mixed Martial Arts as a Spectacle and Sport." *Sport in Society* 22, no. 7 (2019): 1183–97.

Anti-Defamation League (ADL). *Audit of Anti-Semitic Incidents: Year in Review 2018.* New York: ADL, 2018.

Baier, Dirk, Christian Pfeiffer, and Susann Rabold. "Jugendgewalt in Deutschland: Befunde aus Hell- und Dunkelfelduntersuchungen unter besonderer Berücksichtigung von Geschlechterunterschieden." *Kriminalistik* 6 (2009): 323–33.

Baldauf, Johannes, Julia Ebner, and Jakob Guhl, eds. *Hate Speech and Radicalisation Online: The OCCI Research Report.* London: Institute for Strategic Dialogue, 2019. https://pdfs.semanticscholar.org/007d/def05d82f3551bb2fd5e58105b81cf5dce52.pdf.

Bar-On, Tamir. "Richard B. Spencer and the Alt Right." In *Key Thinkers of the Radical Right: Behind the New Threat to Liberal Democracy*, ed. Mark Sedgwick, 224–41. New York: Oxford University Press, 2019.

Bauman, Dan. "Hate Crimes on Campuses Are Rising, New FBI Data Show." *Chronicle of Higher Education*, November 14, 2018. https://www.chronicle.com/article/Hate-Crimes-on -Campuses-Are/245093.

Bayrakli, Enes, and Farid Hafez, eds. *European Islamophobia Report: 2017*. Ankara: SETA, 2018. http://www.islamophobiaeurope.com/wp-content/uploads/2018/04/EIR_2017.pdf.

Beirich, Heidi. "The Year in Hate: Rage against Change." *Intelligence Report*, February 20, 2019. https://www.splcenter.org/fighting-hate/intelligence-report/2019/year-hate-rage-against -change.

Belew, Kathleen. *Bring the War Home: The White Power Movement and Paramilitary America*. Cambridge, MA: Harvard University Press, 2018.

Berezin, Mabel. 2019. "Populism and Fascism: Are They Useful Categories for Comparative Sociological Analysis?" *Annual Review of Sociology* 45 (2019): 345–61.

Berger, J. M. *Extremism*. Cambridge, MA: MIT Press, 2018.

———. "The Strategy of Violent White Supremacy Is Evolving." *Atlantic*, August 7, 2019.

———. "Zero Degrees of Al Qaeda." *Foreign Policy*, August 14, 2013.

Berlet, Chip, and Matthew N. Lyons. *Right-Wing Populism in America: Too Close for Comfort*. New York: Guilford, 2000.

Billig, Michael. *Banal Nationalism*. London: SAGE, 1995.

Binder, Amy, and Kate Wood. *Becoming Right: How Campuses Shape Young Conservatives*. Princeton, NJ: Princeton University Press, 2013.

Blazak, Randy. "'Getting It': The Role of Women in Male Desistance from Hate Groups." In *Home-Grown Hate: Gender and Organized Racism*, ed. Abby Ferber, 161–80. New York: Routledge, 2004.

Blee, Kathleen. "The Geography of Racial Activism." In *Spaces of Hate: Geographies of Discrimination and Intolerance in the USA*, ed. Colin Flint, 49–68. New York: Routledge, 2004.

———. *Inside Organized Racism: Women in the Hate Movement*. Berkeley: University of California Press, 2003.

———. *Women of the Klan: Racism and Gender in the 1920s*. Berkeley: University of California Press, 1991.

Bleich, Erik. *The Freedom to Be Racist?: How the United States and Europe Struggle to Preserve Freedom and Combat Racism*. New York: Oxford University Press, 2011.

Bond, Sarah. "Why We Need to Start Seeing the Classical World in Color." *Hyperallergic*, June 7, 2017. https://hyperallergic.com/383776/why-we-need-to-start-seeing-the-classical-world -in-color/.

Bonds, Anne. "Race and Ethnicity II: White Women and the Possessive Geographies of White Supremacy." *Progress in Human Geography* (2019). doi:10.1177/0309132519863479.

Bonikowski, Bart. "Ethno-nationalist Populism and the Mobilization of Collective Resentment." *British Journal of Sociology* 68, suppl. 1 (2017): S181–S213.

Bonikowski, Bart, and Noam Gidron. "The Populist Style in American Politics: Presidential Campaign Rhetoric, 1952–1996." *Social Forces* 94, no. 4 (2016): 1593–621.

Brooks, Lecia. "Testimony of Lecia Brooks, Southern Poverty Law Center, Before the Subcommittee on Civil Rights and Civil Liberties Committee on Oversight and Reform, United States House of Representatives." Testimony at the hearing "Confronting White Supremacy (Part II): Adequacy of the Federal Response." June 4, 2019. https://docs.house.gov/meetings/GO/GO02/20190604/109579/HHRG-116-GO02-Wstate-BrooksL-20190604.pdf.

Brown, Timothy Scott. "Subcultures, Pop Music and Politics: Skinheads and 'Nazi Rock' in England and Germany." *Journal of Social History* 38, no. 1 (2004): 157–78.

Brubaker, R. "Why Populism?" *Theory and Society* 46 (2017): 357–85.

Bundesministerium des Innern, für Bau und Heimat (Federal Ministry of the Interior, Construction and Home). *Verfassungsschutzbericht 2018: Fakten und Tendenzen* (Office for the Protection of the Constitution Report 2018: Facts and Trends). Berlin: Bundesministerium des Innern, für Bau und Heimat, 2019. https://www.verfassungsschutz.de/de/oeffentlichkeitsarbeit/publikationen/verfassungsschutzberichte.

Burley, Shane, and Alexander Reid Ross. "'All You Have to Do Is Show Up': How White Nationalists Are Infiltrating the GOP." Political Research Associates, June 20, 2019. https://www.politicalresearch.org/2019/06/20/all-you-have-to-do-is-show-up-how-white-nationalists-are-infiltrating-the-gop.

Buse, G. J. "No Holds Barred Sport Fighting: A 10-Year Review of Mixed Martial Arts Competitions." *British Journal of Sports Medicine* 40, no. 2 (2006): 169–72.

Busher, Joel, and Graham Macklin. "Interpreting 'Cumulative Extremism': Six Proposals for Enhancing Conceptual Clarity." *Terrorism and Political Violence* 27, no. 5 (2015): 885–905.

California State University San Bernardino (CSUSB) Center for the Study of Hate & Extremism (CSHE). *Report to the Nation: 2019.* CSUSB and CSHE, 2019. https://csbs.csusb.edu/sites/csusb_csbs/files/CSHE%202019%20Report%20to%20the%20Nation%20FINAL%207.29.19%2011%20PM_0.pdf.

Canovan, M. "'Trust the People!': Populism and the Two Faces of Democracy." *Political Studies* 47, no. 1 (1999): 2–16.

Castells, Manuel. *The Informational City.* Oxford: Blackwell, 1989.

Castle, Tammy, Lars Kristiansen, and Lantz Shifflett. "White Racial Activism and Paper Terrorism: A Case Study in Far Right Propaganda." *Deviant Behavior* 41, no. 2 (2018): 252–67.

Channon, Alex, and Christopher Matthews. "'It Is What It Is': Masculinity, Homosexuality, and Inclusive Discourse in Mixed Martial Arts." *Journal of Homosexuality* 62, no. 7 (2015): 936–56.

Claus, Robert, and Pavel Brunßen. "Rechtsextremismus und Fanszenen: Ein analytischer Blick auf die gesellschaftlichen Strukturen." In *Zurück am Tatort Stadion,* ed. Gerd Dembowski Claus, Martin Endemann, and Jonas Gabler, 179–94. Göttingen: Die Werkstatt, 2015.

Claus, Robert, and Jonas Gabler. "Kampf auf der Straße und Kampf um die Kurve: Was HoGeSa für die Gesellschaft und die Fußballfankultur bedeutet." *Journal für politische Bildung* 1 (2016): 54–63.

Clayton, Victoria. "The Psychological Approach to Educating Kids." *Atlantic,* March 30, 2017. https://www.theatlantic.com/education/archive/2017/03/the-social-emotional-learning-effect/521220/.

Cloud, Dana. "Responding to Right-Wing Attacks." *Inside Higher Ed.*, November 7, 2017. http://www.insidehighered.com/advice/2017/11/07/tips-help-academics-respond-right-wing-attacks-essay.

Colborne, Michael. "Friday Night Fights with Ukraine's Far Right." *New Republic*, July 9, 2019. https://newrepublic.com/article/154434/friday-night-fights-ukraines-far-right.

Connell, Raewyn W. *Masculinities*. Berkeley: University of California Press, 1995.

Corte, Ugo, and Bob Edwards. "White Power Music and the Mobilization of Racist Social Movements." *Music and Arts in Action* 1, no. 1 (2008): 4–20.

Cresswell, Tim. *Place: An Introduction*. 2nd ed. Chichester: Wiley-Blackwell, 2015.

Daniels, Jessie. "The Algorithmic Rise of the 'Alt Right.'" *Contexts* 17, no. 3 (2018): 60–65.

———. *Cyber-Racism: White Supremacy Online and the New Attack on Civil Rights*. Lanham, MD: Rowman and Littlefield, 2009.

———. "When the Far-Right Attacks Faculty Online, They Are Attacking Public Higher Education." *CUNY Academic Works*, winter 2018. https://academicworks.cuny.edu/hc_pubs/345.

Davey, Andrew. "'Conservative' Ideology and the Politics of Local Food." *Agriculture and Human Values* 35, no. 4 (2018): 853–65.

Davey, Jacob, and Julia Ebner. *The Fringe Insurgency: Connectivity, Convergence and Mainstreaming of the Extreme Right*. London: Institute for Strategic Dialogue. 2017. https://www.isdglobal.org/wp-content/uploads/2017/10/The-Fringe-Insurgency-221017.pdf.

———. *"The Great Replacement": The Violent Consequences of Mainstreamed Extremism*. London: Institute for Strategic Dialogue, 2019. https://www.isdglobal.org/wp-content/uploads/2019/07/The-Great-Replacement-The-Violent-Consequences-of-Mainstreamed-Extremism-by-ISD.pdf.

Davidov, Veronica. "Beyond Formal Environmentalism: Eco-nationalism and the 'Ringing Cedars' of Russia." *Culture, Agriculture, Food and Environment* 37, no. 1 (2015): 2–13.

Department of Homeland Security (DHS). *Strategic Framework for Countering Terrorism and Targeted Violence*. DHS, September 2019. https://www.dhs.gov/sites/default/files/publications/19_0920_plcy_strategic-framework-countering-terrorism-targeted-violence.pdf.

DeSoucey, Michaela. *Contested Tastes: Foie Gras and the Politics of Food*. Princeton, NJ: Princeton University Press, 2016.

Dinas, Elias. "Opening 'Openness to Change': Political Events and the Increased Sensitivity of Young Adults." *Political Research Quarterly* 66, no. 4 (2013): 868–82.

Döring, Uta. *Angstzonen: Rechtsdominierte Orte aus medialer und lokaler Perspektive*. Wiesbaden: VS Verlag für Sozialwissenschaften, 2017.

———. "'Befreite Zonen': Konzept für eine Gegenmacht von Rechts." In Schultz and Weber, *Kämpfe um Raumhoheit*, 37–51.

Dorman, Travis. "White Power Symbol Found at Highlander Center Fire Used by Christchurch Shooter," *Knox News*, April 3, 2019.

Duyvendak, Jan Willem. *The Politics of Home: Belonging and Nostalgia in Western Europe and the United States*. New York: Palgrave Macmillan, 2011.

Duyvendak, Jan Willem, and Loes Verplanke. "Struggling to Belong: Social Movements and the Fight to Feel at Home." In *Spaces of Contention: Spatialities and Social Movements*, ed. Walter Nicholls, Byron Miller, and Justin Beaumont, 69–84. New York: Routledge, 2013.

Ebner, Julia. *Going Dark: The Secret Social Lives of Extremists*. London: Bloomsbury, 2020.

——. *The Rage: The Vicious Circle of Islamist and Far-Right Extremism*. New York: I. B. Taurus, 2017.

Eller, Cynthia. "Matriarchy and the Volk." *Journal of the American Academy of Religion* 81, no. 1 (2013): 188–221.

Entrikin, Nick. Introduction to *The Betweenness of Place: Critical Human Geography*, 1–5. London: Palgrave, 1991.

Evans, Gavin. *Skin Deep: Journeys in the Divisive Science of Race*. London: One World, 2019.

Farkas, Johan, and Jannick Schou. *Post-Truth, Fake News and Democracy: Mapping the Politics of Falsehood*. New York: Routledge, 2019.

FBI Phoenix Field Office. "Anti-Government, Identity Based, and Fringe Political Conspiracy Theories Very Likely Motivate Some Domestic Extremists to Commit Criminal, Sometimes Violent Activity." FBI Intelligence Bulletin, May 30, 2019. https://info.publicintelligence.net/FBI-ConspiracyTheoryDomesticExtremism.pdf.

Fekete, Liz. "The Muslim Conspiracy Theory and the Oslo Massacre." *Race and Class* 53, no. 3 (2011): 30–47.

Ferber, Abby L. "'Are You Willing to Die for This Work?' Public Targeted Online Harassment in Higher Education: SWS Presidential Address." *Gender and Society* 32, no. 3 (2018): 301–20.

——. "New Methods and Consequences of Right-Wing Attacks on Professors." *Gender and Society*, June 21, 2018. https://gendersociety.wordpress.com/2018/06/21/new-methods-and-consequences-of-right-wing-attacks-on-professors/.

Fielitz, Maik, and Nick Thurston, eds. *Post-Digital Cultures of the Far Right: Online Actions and Offline Consequences in Europe and the US*. Bielefield, Germany: Transcript Verlag, 2019.

Finchelstein, Federico. *From Fascism to Populism in History*. Berkeley: University of California Press, 2017.

Flint, Colin. Introduction to *Spaces of Hate: Geographies of Discrimination and Intolerance in the USA*, ed. Flint, 1–20. New York: Routledge, 2014.

Forchtner, Bernhard, and Ana Tominc. "Kalashnikov and Cooking-Spoon: Neo-Nazism, Veganism and a Lifestyle Cooking Show on YouTube." *Food, Culture and Society* 20, no. 3 (2017): 415–41.

Futrell, Robert, and Pete Simi. "Free Spaces, Collective Identity, and the Persistence of U.S. White Power Activism." *Social Problems* 51, no. 1 (2004): 16–42.

Ganesh, Bharath. "Radical Right Digital Communications: Webforums, Political Blogs, and the Swarm." Centre for Analysis of the Radical Right, *Insight* (blog), February 20, 2019. https://www.radicalrightanalysis.com/2019/02/20/radical-right-digital-communications-webforums-political-blogs-and-the-swarm/.

Gaugele, Elke. 2019. "The New Obscurity in Style: Alt-right Faction, Populist Normalization, and the Cultural War on Fashion from the Far Right." *Fashion Theory* 23, no. 6 (2019): 711–31.

Gieryn, Thomas F. "A Space for Place in Sociology." *Annual Review of Sociology* 26 (2000): 463–96.

Goodhart, David. *The Road to Somewhere: The Populist Revolt and the Future of Politics*. London: Hurst, 2017.

Göpffarth, Julian. "Rethinking the German Nation as German *Dasein:* Intellectuals and Heiddiger's Philosophy in Contemporary German New Right Nationalism." *Journal of Political Ideologies* 25, 2020. doi.org/10.1080/13569317.2020.1773068.

Grandon, Greg. *The End of the Myth: From the Frontier to the Border Wall in the Mind of America.* New York: Metropolitan Books, 2019.

Green, Kyle. "Tales from the Mat: Narrating Men and Meaning Making in the Mixed Martial Arts Gym." *Journal of Contemporary Ethnography* 45, no. 4 (2016): 419–50.

Greene, Viveca. "'Deplorable' Satire: Alt-Right Memes, White Genocide Tweets, and Redpilling Normies." *Studies in American Humor* 5, no. 1 (2019): 31–69.

Greene, Vivica, and Amber Day. "Asking for It: Rape Myths, Satire, and Feminist Lacunae." *Signs: Journal of Women in Culture and Society* 45, no. 2 (2020): 449–72.

Griffin, Roger. "Between Metapolitics and *Apoliteia:* The Nouvelle Droite's Strategy for Conserving the Fascist Vision in the 'Interregnum.'" *Modern and Contemporary France* 8, no. 1 (2000): 35–53.

———. "Fixing Solutions: Fascist Temporalities as Remedies for Liquid Modernity." *European Journal of Modern History* 13, no. 1 (2015): 5–23

Gross, Neil. *Why Are Professors Liberal and Why Do Conservatives Care?* Cambridge, MA: Harvard University Press, 2013.

Haidt, Jonathan. "When and Why Nationalism Beats Globalism." *American Interest,* July 10, 2016.

Hall, Stuart, Dorothy Hobson, Andrew Lowe, and Paul Willis, eds. *Culture, Media, Language: Working Papers in Cultural Studies, 1972–1979.* London: Routledge, 1991.

Heer, Jeet. "Like Dr. Frankenstein, Republicans Now Face the Monster They Created." *Nation,* November 13, 2019. https://www.thenation.com/article/fuentes-alt-right-republican-trump/.

Hochschild, Arlie. *Strangers in Their Own Land: Anger and Mourning on the American Right.* New York: New Press, 2016.

Holt, Jared. "White Supremacy Figured Out How to Become YouTube Famous." Right Wing Watch: A Project of People for the American Way, October 2017. http://www.rightwingwatch.org/report/white-supremacy-figured-out-how-to-become-youtube-famous/.

Holthouse, David. "Racists Active in Mixed Martial Arts." *Intelligence Report,* Spring 2008. https://www.splcenter.org/fighting-hate/intelligence-report/2008/racists-active-mixed-martial-arts.

Horswell, Mike, and Akil Awan. *Engaging the Crusades.* Vol. 2, *The Crusades in the Modern World.* New York: Routledge, 2019.

Hubbard, Phil, and Rob Kitchin. "Introduction: Why Key Thinkers?" In *Key Thinkers on Space and Place,* 2nd ed., ed. Hubbard and Kitchin, 1–17. Los Angeles: SAGE, 2011.

Hughes, Brian. "'Pine Tree' Twitter and the Shifting Ideological Foundations of Eco-Extremism." *Journal of the Violence Prevention Network* 14 (2020): 18–25.

Hume, Tim. "Europe's Far Right Is Recruiting from the Military and Police to Get More Weapons." *VICE News,* September 25, 2019. https://www.vice.com/en_us/article/7x5wxb/europes-far-right-is-recruiting-from-the-military-and-police-to-get-more-weapons.

———. "A Russian Neo-Nazi Football Hooligan Is Trying to Build an MMA Empire across Europe." *VICE News,* July 26, 2018. https://news.vice.com/en_us/article/435mjw/a-russian-neo-nazi-football-hooligan-is-trying-to-build-an-mma-empire-across-europe.

Johnson, Daryl. *Hateland: A Long, Hard Look at America's Extremist Heart.* New York: Prometheus Books, 2019.

Johnson, N. F., R. Leahy, N. Johnson Restrepo, N. Velasquez, M. Zheng, P. Manrique, P. Devkota, and S. Wuchty. "Hidden Resilience and Adaptive Dynamics of the Global Online Hate Ecology." Letter to the editor, *Nature*, August 21, 2019.

Keatinge, Tom, Florence Keen, and Kayla Izenman. "Fundraising for Right-Wing Extremist Movements." *RUSI Journal* 164, no. 2 (2019): 10–23.

Kelshall, C. M., and S. Meyers. *Addressing the Normalization of Extremism: PREPARED. Manual for Youth Educators.* 2nd ed. Vancouver: Canada Association for Security and Intelligence Services, 2019.

Kendi, Ibram X. *How to Be an Antiracist.* New York: One World, 2019.

King, C. Richard, and David J. Leonard. "Is Neo White?: Reading Race, Watching the Trilogy." In *Jacking In to the Matrix Franchise: Cultural Reception and Interpretation*, ed. Matthew Kapell and William Doty, 32–47. New York: Continuum, 2004.

King, David. *The Trial of Adolf Hitler: The Bee Hall Putsch and the Rise of Nazi Germany.* New York: W.W. Norton, 2017.

Kirby, Andrew. "When Extreme Political Ideas Move into the Mainstream." In Flint, *Spaces of Hate*, 209–25.

Koehler, Daniel. "Contrast Societies. Radical Social Movements and Their Relationships with Their Target Societies: A Theoretical Model." *Behavioral Sciences of Terrorism and Political Aggression* 7, no. 1 (2014): 18–34.

———. "The Radical Online: Individual Radicalization Processes and the Role of the Internet." *Journal for Deradicalization* 1 (2014–15): 116–34.

Konda, Thomas Milan. *Conspiracy of Conspiracies: How Delusions Have Overrun America.* Chicago: University of Chicago Press, 2019.

Korolczuk, Elzbieta, and Agnieszka Graff. "Gender as 'Ebola from Brussels': The Anticolonial Frame and the Rise of Illiberal Populism." *Signs: Journal of Women in Culture and Society* 43, no. 4 (2018): 797–821.

Koronowski, Ryan. "The Radical Right Is Becoming an Unlikely Advocate for Solar Power." *Think Progress*, October 22, 2013, https://thinkprogress.org/the-radical-right-wing-is -becoming-an-unlikely-advocate-for-solar-power-350aa9abad11/.

Lancaster, Caroline M. "Not So Radical After All: Ideological Diversity among Radical Right Supporters and Its Implications." *Political Studies* (September 2, 2019). doi:10.1177/003232171 9870468.

Land Brandenburg. "'National befreite Zonen'—Kampfparole und Realität." Info-sheet. Verfassungsschutz des Landes Brandenburg, Ministerium des Innern, 2001. https://verfassungsschutz .brandenburg.de/media_fast/4055/national_befreite_zonen.pdf.

Lee, Martin. *The Beast Reawakens: Fascism's Resurgence from Hitler's Spymasters to Today's Neo-Nazi Groups and Right-Wing Extremists.* New York: Routledge, 1999.

Lefebre, Henri. *The Production of Space.* Oxford: Blackwell, 1991.

Lenos, Steven, and Annelies Jansen. "The Role of Sports and Leisure Activities in Preventing and Countering Violent Extremism." Sports, Extremism and P/CVE Ex Post Paper, RAN YF&C. Radicalisation Awareness Network (RAN) Centre of Excellence, March 6–7, 2019. https://ec.europa.eu/home-affairs/sites/homeaffairs/files/what-we-do/networks

/radicalisation_awareness_network/about-ran/ran-yf-and-c/docs/ran_yfc_sports_and
_leisure_06-07_03_2019_en.pdf.

Lichtenstein, Bronwen. "Is US Sociology in Decline?" *Global Dialogue* 3, no. 2 (2013). http://
globaldialogue.isa-sociology.org/is-us-sociology-in-decline/.

Linke, Uli. "Gendered Difference, Violent Imagination: Blood, Race, Nation." *American Anthropologist* 99, no. 3 (1997): 559–73.

———. *German Bodies: Race and Representation After Hitler*. New York: Routledge, 1999.

Liulevicius, Vejas Gabriel. *The German Myth of the East: 1800 to the Present*. New York: Oxford
University Press, 2009.

Macklin, Graham. "Greg Johnson and Counter-Currents." In Sedgwick, *Key Thinkers*, 204–23.

Main, Thomas. *The Rise of the Alt-Right*. Washington, DC: Brookings, 2018.

Malkki, L. "National Geographic: The Rooting of Peoples and the Territorialization of
National Identity among Scholars and Refugees." *Cultural Anthropology* 7, no. 1 (1992):
24–44.

Manne, Kate. *Down Girl: The Logic of Misogyny*. New York: Oxford University Press, 2018.

Marantz, Andrew. *Anti-Social: Online Extremists, Techo-Utopians, and the Hijacking of American
Conversation*. New York: Viking, 2019.

Martin, Kimberly, and H. Chris Tecklenburg. "The White Nationalist on Campus: Re-
examining University Free Speech and Leading through Crisis." *Journal of Cases in Educational Leadership* 23, no. 1 (2020): 111–23.

Marwick, Alice, and Rebecca Lewis. *Media Manipulation and Disinformation Online*. Data and
Society Research Institute, 2017. https://datasociety.net/pubs/oh/DataAndSociety_Med
iaManipulationAndDisinformationOnline.pdf.

Massey, Doreen. "Power-Geometry and a Progressive Sense of Place." In *Mapping the Futures:
Local Cultures, Global Change*, ed. J. Bird, B. Curtis, T. Putnam, G. Robertson, and L. Tickner,
59–69. London: Routledge, 1993.

Materna, Kryštof, Jiří Hasman, and David Hána. "Acquisition of Industrial Enterprises and Its
Relations with Regional Identity: The Case of the Beer Industry in Central Europe." *Norsk
Geografisk Tidsskrift—Norwegian Journal of Geography* 73, no. 4 (2019): 197–214.

Mattheis, Ashley. "'Shieldmaidens of Whiteness': (Alt) Maternalism and Women Recruiting
for the Far/Alt-Right." *Journal of Deradicalization* 19, no. 17 (2018): 128–61.

McAuliffe, Terry. *Beyond Charlottesville: Taking a Stand against White Nationalism*. New York:
St. Martin's, 2019.

McConnell, Winder, and Werner Wunderlich. *The Nibelungen Tradition: An Encyclopedia*. New
York: Routledge, 2015.

McCoskey, Denise. "Beware of Greeks Bearing Gifts: How Neo-Nazis and Ancient Greeks Met
in Charlottesville." *Origins* 11, no. 11 (2018). http://origins.osu.edu/article/beware-greeks
-bearing-gifts-how-neo-nazis-and-ancient-greeks-met-charlottesville.

McGarrity, Michael. "Statement of Michael McGarrity, Assistant Director, Counterterrorism
Director, Federal Bureau of Investigation." Statement to the Subcommittee on Civil Rights
and Civil Liberties, Committee on Oversight and Reform, US House of Representatives, at
the hearing "Confronting White Supremacy (Part II)." June 4, 2019. https://docs.house.gov
/meetings/GO/GO02/20190604/109579/HHRG-116-GO02-Wstate-McGarrityM
-20190604.pdf.

McVeigh, Rory, and Kevin Estep. *The Politics of Losing: Trump, the Klan, and the Mainstreaming of Resentment*. New York: Columbia University Press, 2019.

Merlan, Anna. *Republic of Lies: American Conspiracy Theorists and Their Surprising Rise to Power*. New York: Metropolitan Books, 2019.

Messner, Beth, Art Jipson, Paul Becker, and Bryan Byers. 2007. "The Hardest Hate: A Sociological Analysis of Country Hate Music." In "Hate Rock," ed. Art Jipson, special issue, *Popular Music and Society* 30, no. 4 (2007): 513–31.

Messner, Michael. "Boyhood, Organized Sports and the Construction of Masculinties." *Journal of Contemporary Ethnography* 18, no. 4 (1990): 416–44.

Metzl, Jonathan. *Dying of Whiteness: How the Politics of Racial Resentment Is Killing America's Heartland*. New York: Basic Books, 2019.

Meuser, Michael. *Geschlect und Männlichkeit: Soziologische Theorie und kulturelle Deutungsmuster*. Opladen, Germany: Leske und Budrich, 1998.

Michael, George. "David Lane and the Fourteen Words." *Totalitarian Movements and Political Religions* 10, no. 1 (2009). https://www.tandfonline.com/doi/full/10.1080/1469076090 3067986.

Michaelis, Arno, and Pardeep Singh Kaleka. *The Gift of Our Wounds: A Sikh and a Former White Supremacist Find Forgiveness after Hate*. New York: St. Martin's, 2018.

Miller-Idriss, Cynthia. *Blood and Culture: Youth, Right-Wing Extremism, and National Belonging in Contemporary Germany*. Durham, NC: Duke University Press, 2009.

———. *The Extreme Gone Mainstream: Commercialization and Far Right Youth Culture in Germany*. Princeton, NJ: Princeton University Press, 2018.

———. "The Global Dimensions of Nationalist Populism." *International Spectator* 54, no. 2 (2019): 17–34.

———. "Statement of Dr. Cynthia Miller-Idriss, Professor of Education and Sociology, American University, Washington, DC, Senior Fellow and Director of Outreach, Centre for Analysis of the Radical Right (U.K.)." Statement at hearing "Meeting the Challenge of White Nationalist Terrorism at Home and Abroad," held by the Committee on Foreign Affairs' Subcommittee on the Middle East, North Africa, and International Terrorism and the Committee on Homeland Security's Subcommittee on Intelligence and Counterterrorism. September 18, 2019. https://homeland.house.gov/imo/media/doc/Miller-Testimony.pdf.

———. "Youth and the Radical Right." In *The Oxford Handbook of the Radical Right*, ed. Jens Rydgren, 348–65. New York: Oxford University Press, 2018.

Miller-Idriss, Cynthia, and La'Nita Johnson. "The Far Right Is Really Good at Tricking You into Giving It Free Advertising." *Quartz*, July 30, 2019. https://qz.com/1677549/how-the-far-right-tricks-online-shoppers-into-spreading-its-message/.

Miller-Idriss, Cynthia, and Hilary Pilkington, eds. *Gender and the Radical and Extreme Right: Mechanisms of Transmission and the Role of Educational Interventions*. London: Routledge, 2018.

Morning, Ann. *The Nature of Race: How Scientists Think and Teach about Human Difference*. Berkeley, CA: University of California Press, 2011.

Mudde, Cas. *The Far Right Today*. Cambridge, UK: Polity, 2019.

———. "The Populist Zeitgeist." *Government and Opposition* 39, no. 4 (2004): 541–63.

———. *Youth and the Extreme Right*. New York: IDebate, 2014.

Mudde, Cas, and Cristobal Kaltwasser. *Populism: A Very Short Introduction.* Oxford: Oxford University Press, 2017.

Muggleton, David. *Inside Subculture: The Postmodern Meaning of Style.* New York: Berg, 2000.

Muirhead, Russell, and Nancy L. Rosenblum. *A Lot of People Are Saying: The New Conspiracism and the Assault on Democracy.* Princeton, NJ: Princeton University Press, 2019.

Müller, J.-W. *What Is Populism?* Philadelphia: University of Pennsylvania Press, 2016.

Nagle, Angela. *Kill All Normies: Online Culture Wars from 4chan and Tumblr to Trump and the Alt-Right.* Washington: Zero Books, 2016.

Nayak, Anoop. *Race, Place and Globalization: Youth Cultures in a Changing World.* New York: Berg, 2003.

Neiwert, David. *Alt-America: The Rise of the Radical Right in the Age of Trump.* New York: Verso, 2018.

Neumann, Peter. Foreword to Baldauf, Ebner, and Guhl, *Hate Speech and Radicalisation,* 5–6.

Nichols, Tom. *The Death of Expertise: The Campaign against Established Knowledge and Why It Matters.* New York: Oxford University Press, 2017.

Noble, Safiya Umoja. *Algorithms of Oppression: How Search Engines Reinforce Racism.* New York: New York University Press, 2018.

O'Callaghan, Derek, Derek Greene, Maura Conway, Joe Carthy, and Pádraig Cunningham. 2015. "Down the (White) Rabbit Hole: The Extreme Right and Online Recommender Systems." *Social Science Computer Review* 33, no. 4 (2015): 459–78.

Omel'chenko, Elena. "In Search of Intimacy: Homosociality, Masculinity and the Body." In *Russia's Skinheads: Exploring and Rethinking Subcultural Lives,* ed. Hilary Pilkington, Omel'chenko, and Al'bina Garifzianova, 166–86. London: Routledge, 2010.

Önnerfors, Andreas. "'Finspång': An Execution Meme of the Swedish Radical Right Ignites the Political Discourse." Centre for Analysis of the Radical Right, *Insight* (blog), July 6, 2018. https://www.radicalrightanalysis.com/2018/07/06/finspang-an-execution-meme-of-the -swedish-radical-right-ignites-the-political-discourse/.

Parker, Kim. "The Growing Partisan Divide in Views of Higher Education." Pew Research Center, August 19, 2019. https://www.pewsocialtrends.org/essay/the-growing-partisan-divide -in-views-of-higher-education/.

Pascoe, Peggy. "Miscegenation Law, Court Cases, and Ideologies of 'Race' in Twentieth-Century America." *Journal of American History* 83, no. 1 (1996): 44–69.

PEN America. *And Campus for All: Diversity, Inclusion, and Freedom of Speech at U.S. Universities.* PEN America, [2016]. https://pen.org/wp-content/uploads/2017/06/PEN_campus _report_06.15.2017.pdf.

———. *Chasm in the Classroom: Campus Free Speech in a Divided America.* PEN America, 2019. https://pen.org/wp-content/uploads/2019/04/2019-PEN-Chasm-in-the-Classroom-04.25 .pdf.

Perry, Barbara, and Randy Blazak. "Places for Races: The White Supremacist Movement Imagines U.S. Geography." *Journal of Hate Studies* 8, no. 1 (2009): 29–51.

Perry, Barbara, and Ryan Scrivens. "Uneasy Alliances: A Look at the Right-Wing Extremist Movement in Canada." *Studies in Conflict and Terrorism* 39, no. 9 (2016): 819–41.

Petrou, Kristie, and John Connell. "Food, Morality and Identity: Mobility, Remittances and the Translocal Community in Paama, Vanauatu." *Australian Geographer* 48, no. 2 (2017): 219–34.

Phillips-Fein, Kim. "How the Right Learned to Loathe Higher Education." *Chronicle of Higher Education*, January 31, 2019. https://www-chronicle-com.proxyau.wrlc.org/article/How-the-Right-Learned-to/245580.

Pilkington, Hilary. *Loud and Proud: Passion and Politics in the English Defence League*. Manchester: University of Manchester Press, 2016.

Pisoiu, Daniela. "Subcultural Theory Applied to Jihadi and Right-Wing Radicalization in Germany." *Terrorism and Political Violence* 27, no. 1 (2015): 9–28.

Pitcavage, Mark. *Surveying the Landscape of the American Far Right*. George Washington University Program on Extremism, August 2019. https://extremism.gwu.edu/sites/g/files/zaxdzs2191/f/Surveying%20The%20Landscape%20of%20the%20American%20Far%20Right_0.pdf.

Plattner, Marc F. "Illiberal Democracy and the Struggle on the Right." *Journal of Democracy* 30, no. 1 (2019): 5–19.

Putnam, Robert. *Bowling Alone: The Collapse and Revival of American Community*. New York: Simon and Schuster, 2000.

Rabikowska, Marta. "The Ritualization of Food, Home, and National Identity among Polish Migrants in London." *Social Identities* 16, no. 3 (2010): 377–98.

Reed, Alastair, Joe Whittaker, Fabio Votta, and Sean Looney. "Radical Filter Bubbles: Social Media Personalisation Algorithms and Extremist Content." Global Research Network on Terrorism and Technology Paper no. 8. Royal United Services Institute for Defense and Security Studies, 2019. https://rusi.org/sites/default/files/20190726_grntt_paper_08_0.pdf.

Rietzschel, Antonie. "Rechtsextreme machen Krawall in Neukölln." *Süddeutsche Zeitung*, February 22, 2017.

Rogers, Joann, and Jacquelyn S. Litt. "Normalizing Racism: A Case Study of Motherhood in White Supremacy." In *Home-Grown Hate: Gender and Organized Racism*, ed. Abby Ferber, 97–112. New York: Routledge, 2003.

Roose, Kevin. "Caleb Cain Was a College Dropout Looking for Direction. He Turned to YouTube." *New York Times*, June 8, 2019. https://www.nytimes.com/interactive/2019/06/08/technology/youtube-radical.html?mtrref=undefined&assetType=REGIWALL.

Rössler, Mechthild. "'Blut und Boden—Volk und Raum': Thesen zur Geographie im Nationalsozialismus." In *Deutscher Soziologentag 1986*, ed. Jürgen Friedrichs, 741–44. Wiesbaden: VS Verlag für Sozialwissenschaften, 1987.

Rubenstein, Richard. "Bat Ye'or and the Coming Universal Caliphate." *New English Review*, January 2013. https://www.newenglishreview.org/custpage.cfm/frm/130221/sec_id/130221.

Sack, Robert. "The Power of Place and Space." *Geographical Review* 83, no. 3 (1993): 326–29.

Saini, Angela. *Superior: The Return of Race Science*. Boston: Beacon, 2019.

Salter, Michael. "From Geek Masculinity to Gamergate: The Technological Rationality of Online Abuse." *Crime Media Culture* 14, no. 2 (2018): 247–64.

Schatz, Bryan. "The Terrifying Rise of Alt-Right Fight Clubs." *Mother Jones*, February 1, 2018. https://www.motherjones.com/politics/2018/02/the-terrifying-rise-of-alt-right-fight-clubs/.

Schultz, Christoph, and Ella Weber. *Kämpfe um Raumhoheit: Rechte Gewalt, "No Go Areas" and "National befreite Zonen."* Münster, Germany: UNRAST Verlag, 2011.

Sedgwick, Mark. Introduction to *Key Thinkers of the Radical Right: Behind the New Threat to Liberal Democracy*, ed. Sedgwick, xiii–xxvi. Cambridge: Oxford University Press, 2019.

Selim, George. "Congressional Testimony: Mr. George Selim, Senior Vice President, Programs, ADL." Testimony before the Civil Rights and Civil Liberties Subcommittee of the House Oversight and Government Reform Committee, at the hearing "Confronting White Supremacy (Part I): The Consequences of Inaction." May 15, 2019. https://docs.house.gov/meetings/GO/GO02/20190515/109478/HHRG-116-GO02-Wstate-SeliumG-20190515.pdf.

Shoshan, Nitzan. *The Management of Hate: Nation, Affect and the Governance of Right-Wing Extremism in Germany.* Princeton, NJ: Princeton University Press, 2016.

Siedler, T. "Parental Unemployment and Young People's Extreme Right-Wing Party Affinity: Evidence from Panel Data." *Journal of the Royal Statistical Society*, ser. A (Statistics in Society), 174 (2011): 737–58.

Silva, Tiago João Queimade e. "The *Reconquista* Revisited: Mobilising Medieval Iberian History in Spain, Portugal and Beyond." In *Engaging the Crusades*, vol. 2, *The Crusades in the Modern World*, ed. Mike Horswell and Akil Awan, 57–74. New York: Routledge, 2019.

Simi, Pete, and Bryan Bubolz. "The Problem of Overgeneralization: The Case of Mental Health Problems and U.S. Violent White Supremacists." *American Behavioral Scientist* (February 28, 2019). doi:10.1177/0002764219831746.

Simi, Pete, and Robert Futrell. *American Swastika: Inside the White Power Movement's Hidden Spaces of Hate.* New York: Rowman and Littlefield, 2010.

Smith, David Livingstone. *Less than Human: Why We Demean, Enslave, and Exterminate Others.* New York: St. Martin's, 2011.

Smith, Nicolas. "Blood and Soil: Nature, Native and Nation in the Australian Imaginary." *Journal of Australian Studies* 35, no. 1 (2011): 1–18.

Social Science Research Council (SSRC). *To Secure Knowledge: Social Science Partnerships for the Public Good.* Report of the To Secure Knowledge Task Force of the SSRC. New York: SSRC, 2018.

Soufan, Ali H. "Written Statement for House Committee on Homeland Security." Soufan Center, September 10, 2019. https://homeland.house.gov/imo/media/doc/Testimony-Soufan.pdf.

Soufan Center. *White Supremacist Extremism: The Transnational Rise of the Violent White Supremacist Movement.* 2019. https://thesoufancenter.org/research/white-supremacy-extremism-the-transnational-rise-of-the-violent-white-supremacist-movement/.

Spencer, Hawes. *Summer of Hate: Charlottesville, USA.* Charlottesville: University of Virginia Press, 2019.

Spierings, Niel, Andreas Lubbers, and Andrej Zaslove. "Sexually Modern Nativist Voters: Do They Exist and Do They Vote for the Populist Radical Right?" *Gender and Education* 29, no. 2 (2017): 216–37.

Stabile, Joseph. "Pursuit of an Ethnostate: Political Culture and Violence in the Pacific Northwest." *Georgetown Security Studies Review* 7, no. 2 (2019): 22–34.

Stanley, Jason. *How Fascism Works: The Politics of Us and Them*. New York: Random House, 2018.

Steegenbergen, M., and T. Siczek. "Better the Devil You Know?: Risk-Taking, Globalization and Populism in Great Britain. *European Union Politics* 18, no. 1 (2017): 119–36.

Steinberg, Laurence, and Jason M. Chein. "Multiple Accounts of Adolescent Impulsivity." *Proceedings of the National Academy of Sciences of the USA* 112, no. 29 (2015): 8807–8.

Stern, Alexander Minna. *Proud Boys and the White Ethnostate: How the Alt-Right Is Warping the American Imagination*. Boston: Beacon, 2019.

Stocker, Paul. *English Uprising: Brexit and the Mainstreaming of the Far Right*. London: Melville House, 2017.

Sunstein, Cas. *Going to Extremes: How Like Minds Unite and Divide*. New York: Oxford University Press, 2009.

Surak, Kristin. *Making Tea, Making Japan: Cultural Nationalism in Practice*. Stanford, CA: Stanford University Press, 2013.

Swain, Stephen. "MMAsculinities: Spectacular Narratives of Masculinity in Mixed Martial Arts." PhD dissertation, School of Graduate and Professional Studies, University of Western Ontario, 2011.

Swank, D., and H.-G. Betz. "Globalization, the Welfare State and Right-Wing Populism in Western Europe." *Socio-Economic Review* 1, no. 2 (2003): 215–46.

Tait, Joshua. "Mencius Moldbug and Neoreaction." In Sedgwick, *Key Thinkers*, 187–203.

Teitelbaum, Benjamin. "Daniel Friberg and Metapolitics in Action." In Sedgwick, *Key Thinkers*, 259–75.

Tenold, Vegas. *Everything You Love Will Burn: Inside the Rebirth of White Nationalism in America*. New York: Nation Books, 2018.

Throop, Susanna. "Engaging the Crusades in Context: Reflections on the Ethics of Historical Work." In *Engaging the Crusades*, vol. 2, *The Crusades in the Modern World*, ed. Mike Horswell and Akil Awan, 129–45. New York: Routledge, 2019.

Tilly, Charles. "Spaces of Contention." *Mobilization: An International Journal* 5, no. 2 (2000): 135–59.

Tuan, Yi-Fu. *Space and Place: The Perspective of Experience*. Minneapolis: University of Minnesota Press, 1977.

Tucker, William H. *The Science and Politics of Racial Research*. Chicago: University of Illinois Press, 1996.

Tumblety, Joan. *Remaking the Male Body: Masculinity and the Uses of Physical Culture in Interwar and Vichy France*. New York: Oxford University Press, 2012.

Uscinski, Joseph, and Joseph Parent. *American Conspiracy Theories*. Oxford: Oxford University Press, 2014.

Vaccaro, Christian A., Douglas P. Schrock, and Janice M. McCabe. "Managing Emotional Manhood: Fighting and Fostering Fear in Mixed Martial Arts." *Social Psychology Quarterly* 74, no. 4 (2011): 414–37.

Vaccaro, Christian A., and Melissa Swauger. *Unleashing Manhood in the Cage: Masculinity and Mixed Martial Arts*. New York: Lexington Books, 2016.

Valencia-García, Louie Dean. *Antiauthoritarian Youth Culture in Francoist Spain: Clashing with Fascism*. London: Bloomsbury Academic, 2018.

———. "Far Right Revisionism and the End of History." In *Far Right Revision and the End of History: Alt/Histories*, ed. Valencia-Garcia. London: Routledge, 2020.

———. "The Rise and Fall of the Far Right in the Digital Age." In *Far Right Revision and the End of History: Alt/Histories*, ed. Valencia-Garcia. London: Routledge, 2020.

Virchow, Fabian. "Tapfer, stolz, opferbereit—Überlegungen zum extrem rechten Verständnis 'idealer Männlichkeit.'" In *"Was ein rechter Mann ist" . . . Männlichkeit im Rechtsextremismus*, ed. Robert Claus, Esther Lehnert, and Yves Müller, 39–52. Berlin: Karl Dietz Verlag, 2010.

Von der Goltz, Anna. *Hindenburg: Power, Myth, and the Rise of the Nazis*. New York: Oxford University Press, 2009.

Ware, Jacob. *Siege: The Atomwaffen Division and Rising Far-Right Terrorism in the United States*. International Centre for Counter-Terrorism (ICCT) Policy Brief, July 2019. The Hague: ICCT, 2019.

Waters, Gregory, and Robert Postings. *Spiders of the Caliphate: Mapping the Islamic State's Global Support Network on Facebook*. Counter Extremism Project, May 2018. https://www.counterextremism.com/sites/default/files/Spiders%20of%20the%20Caliphate%20%28May%202018%29.pdf.

Wendling, Mike. *Alt Right: From 4Chan to the White House*. London: Pluto Books, 2018.

Westervelt, E. "Synagogue Shooting Follows Historic Rise in Anti-Semitic Incidents and Online Attacks." National Public Radio, October 29, 2018. https://www.npr.org/2018/10/29/661676117/synagogue-shooting-follows-rise-in-anti-semitic-incidents-adl-says.

Wicke, Christian, Stefan Berger, and Jana Golombeck, eds. *Industrial Heritage and Regional Identities*. New York: Routledge, 2018.

Wiegel, Gerd. "Rechte Erlebniswelten." In *Jahrbuch für Pädagogik*, ed. Martin Dust, Ingrid Lohmann, and Gerd Steffens, 95–106. Frankfurt am Main: Peter Lang, 2016.

Williamson, George S. *The Longing for Myth in Germany: Religion and Aesthetic Culture from Romanticism to Nietzsche*. Chicago: University of Chicago Press, 2004.

Wodak, R. "The Semiotics of Racism: A Critical Discourse-Historical Analysis." In *Discourse, of Course: An Overview of Research in Discourse Studies*, ed. J. Renkema, 311–26. Amsterdam: John Benjamins, 2009.

Wolf, Cam. "The New Uniform of White Supremacy." *GQ*, August 17, 2017. https://www.gq.com/story/uniform-of-white-supremacy.

Yeffeth, Glenn. *Taking the Red Pill: Science, Philosophy, and Religion in the Matrix*. Dallas: Ben-Bella Books, 2003.

Ye'Or, Bat. *EurAbia: The Euro-Arab Axis*. Madison, NJ: Fairleigh Dickenson, 2005.

Zannettou, Savvas, Joel Finkelstein, Barry Bradlyn, and Jeremy Blackburn. "A Quantitative Approach to Understanding Online Antisemitism." Paper to be presented at the 14th International AAAI Conference on Web and Social Media (ICWSM 2020). Posted on arXiv.org November 24, 2019. https://arxiv.org/pdf/1809.01644.pdf.

Zaslove, A. "Exclusion, Community and a Populist Political Economy: The Radical Right as an Anti-Globalization Movement." *Comparative European Politics* 6, no. 2 (2008): 169–89.

Zidan, Karim. "Fascism in MMA: How White Rex, with Ties to Neo-Nazi Ideologies, Thrived as an MMA Promotion and Clothing Brand." SBNation, Bloody Elbow, October 12, 2017. https://www.bloodyelbow.com/2017/10/12/16350612/white-rex-fascist-neo-nazi-groups-thrive-mma-promotions-clothing-brands-karim-zidan-mma-feature.

————. "Fascist Fight Clubs: How White Nationalists Use MMA as a Recruiting Tool." *Guardian*, September 22, 2018. https://www.theguardian.com/sport/2018/sep/11/far-right-fight-clubs-mma-white-nationalists.

————. "Kampf der Nibelungen: German neo-Nazis Are Combining Far Right Politics with MMA." SBNation, Bloody Elbow, June 14, 2018. https://www.bloodyelbow.com/2018/6/14/17464004/german-neo-nazis-combining-far-right-politics-mma-kairm-zidan-feature-news.

Index

A NOTE ON THE TYPE

This book has been composed in Arno, an Old-style serif typeface in the classic Venetian tradition, designed by Robert Slimbach at Adobe.